NO ONE CAN EXPLAIN THEM,

YET THESE AMAZING EVENTS REALLY HAPPENED!

*MEDICAL MIRACLES . . .*
A young housewife, in despair over the multiple sclerosis that had crippled her, began praying—and was cured. Her physician said, "When I saw Mrs. Nastasi walk into my office, I thought I was dreaming!"

*DIVINE MIRACLES . . .*
A grandmother whose body erupts with stigmata—the wounds of Jesus—discovers that her touch can help heal the sick and ailing.

*SKIN-OF-THE-TEETH MIRACLES . . .*
A family of five were in their car when it was sideswiped and pushed over a 100-foot parapet, landing on its roof in an asphalt parking lot . . . yet no one was injured.

*DISASTER MIRACLES . . .*
Two family heirloom Bibles miraculously did not burn when a fire swept through an Alabama farmhouse and consumed everything, even the table the Bibles sat upon . . . but left the precious books untouched.

*MIRACLES BIRTHS . . .*
After being told she could never have children, this loving foster mother of 269 children unexpectedly became pregnant, surprising her husband of 22 years with a bundle of joy. . . .

*FEEL DIVINE POWER IN YOUR LIFE WITH . . .*

# BLESSED BY MIRACLES

# BLESSED BY MIRACLES

*William A. Burt*

A SIGNET BOOK

SIGNET
Published by the Penguin Group
Penguin Putnam Inc., 375 Hudson Street,
New York, New York 10014, U.S.A.
Penguin Books Ltd, 27 Wrights Lane,
London W8 5TZ, England
Penguin Books Australia Ltd, Ringwood,
Victoria, Australia
Penguin Books Canada Ltd, 10 Alcorn Avenue,
Toronto, Ontario, Canada M4V 3B2
Penguin Books (N.Z.) Ltd, 182–190 Wairau Road,
Auckland 10, New Zealand

Penguin Books Ltd, Registered Offices:
Harmondsworth, Middlesex, England

First published by Signet, an imprint of Dutton NAL,
a member of Penguin Putnam Inc.

First Printing, September, 1998
10  9  8  7  6  5  4  3  2  1

*For Alexander—the sweetest and most generous little guy I ever met*

# ACKNOWLEDGMENTS

Everyone, it appears, has a miracle to share. And for that I am grateful.

Without the generous cooperation of friends old and new, colleagues, and an army of miracle believers willing to share their experiences, this book could never have been written.

First and foremost I am grateful to the efficient and very professional research staff at the *National Enquirer*—Martha Moffett and her assistants Sandy Belinsky and Nan Dubiel—for placing their precious library files at my disposal.

I'd like to thank Steve Coz, editor, and David Perel, executive editor, of the *Enquirer,* for their permission to peruse the tabloid's vast files.

Christopher Bowen, chief researcher at *Star* magazine, also merits my gratitude for his kind cooperation.

For their advice and assistance with research, I have to thank fellow authors Cliff Linedecker and Philip St. Vincent Brennan, editor Eddie Clontz of the *Weekly World News,* Tony Leggett, a spiritual soul if ever there was one, my son, Peter Burt, a rising star, and my colleague Elizabeth H. Dole.

And this book would not exist if it weren't for the support and encouragement of Danielle Perez, my editor at Signet, and my agent, the ebullient Arthur Pine—a big thank-you to both.

Then there's my loyal wife, Norma, who not only gave me the necessary moral support every step of the way, but was an invaluable right arm with her dedicated researching and transcribing. Norma, what can I say?

Lastly, as always, hugs and kisses for the kids, Nicholas and Victoria, for their patience.

# Contents

# An Introduction
# to Miracles

Miracles happen every day. And they come in all shapes and sizes.

They can happen when you want them to happen. They will happen if you pray for them to happen. And they can happen when you least expect it.

For years, as a newspaper reporter and editor, I have been fascinated by the miracles that take place all around us every hour of every day.

Too many people, unfortunately, take these wondrous happenings for granted—dismissing them with a shrug of the shoulders as either coincidence or luck.

I strongly disagree. Miracles occur on such a timely, regular basis that they defy all mathematical odds known to man or science.

"Miracles are happening all around us, but we don't notice them," says Rabbi Neil Gillman of the Jewish Theological Seminary. "We take the daily wonders of the world for granted. Yet there is a miraculous quality to the fact the laws of nature work, that the sun rises and sets, that there is food to eat, and that there is love and intimacy in the world."

The brilliant Albert Einstein held this much-quoted view on miracles: "There are only two ways to live your life: One is as though nothing is a miracle; the other is as though everything is a miracle."

Says the Reverend James J. Gill, S.S.J., M.D., a Hartford psychiatrist who is also one of the Catholic Church's chief investigators of reputed modern-day miracles: "Maybe there will be a breakthrough one of these days, and science will figure out how these things work. Or maybe we'll see that some of these sudden cures are true miracles."

Meantime, why are we seeing and acknowledging more and more miracles every day?

Adds Father Gill, "It's a response to anxiety. Life is so stressful; the future is so uncertain. People are hungry for a reassuring sign that God still cares for his children on earth."

Whatever the point of view, miracles are consummate proof that we are all—whether we like it or not—potential recipients of a greater power's love, compassion, mercy, and help.

The dictionary defines a miracle as "an extraordinary event manifesting divine intervention in human affairs."

But in my research I have found that a miracle is much more than that, as more and more former nonbelievers are finding out for themselves.

Since the early 1990s, there's been an astonishing boom in reports of miracles—and an overwhelming eagerness to believe in them. Whether we are religious or not, whether we are skeptics or believers, even if we are firm believers in controlling our own destinies, the evidence is clear—miracles are for real. And they manifest themselves in a myriad of ways, as you will find in this book, which covers everything from Blessed Virgin Mary manifestations to angel-sent miracles, rescue miracles, miracle births, saintly miracles, lifesaving miracles, miracle kids—even miraculous animals.

It's also encouraging to note that we can make miracles happen in our lives. Probably the most familiar way to make a miracle happen is to harness the tremendous, often underestimated power of prayer—particularly if you are one of those blessed with faith.

There's no doubt whatsoever, as you will find from the wonderful case histories included in this book, that prayers are answered. And, fortunately, we Americans are a praying people.

In a recent *Newsweek* magazine poll, a majority of American adults—fifty-four percent—reported praying on a daily basis. Twenty-nine percent said they prayed more than once a day. And—of all those who prayed—more than eighty-five percent said they believed that God answers their prayers at least some of the time. Only thirteen percent say they have lost faith, at any time, because their prayers went unanswered.

Statistics indicating the widespread belief in miracles is even more staggering. Indeed, a 1990 poll revealed that fifty-three percent of Americans report having felt " a presence or power" in their lives that is "different from their ordinary selves." And according to a 1988 poll published by the Princeton Religion Research Center, four out of five Americans are unshaken in their belief that "even today, miracles are performed by the power of God."

Isn't it wonderful that in this great land, where so much attention is paid to material gain and greed and where cynicism is rampant, so many of us retain such a profound trust in God—or at least loyalty to and acceptance of a greater spiritual power?

But we shouldn't be too surprised that the belief in miracles is so widespread. After all, all major religions are based on miracles—Christians celebrate the miracles of Christmas, Jews remember the wonders of Hanukkah, and Buddhists mark the mysteries of Tet.

Not only do true believers pray for miracles in their own lives, they pray for miracles to happen for others. Every day, somewhere, groups of devout Americans gather together to wish miracles into the lives of the less fortunate.

A typical group is the one organized by Dorothy Reece at her Roman Catholic parish in Newton, Massachusetts. Reece runs a prayer group of about fifty caring parishioners who get together on a weekly basis to pray for a long list of needy people. Included on the group's list of those needing a miracle are individuals suffering from a heart attack, splenectomy, stomach cancer, drug addition, infertility, and a husband's desertion.

"We really do believe that God can take care of more than one person at a time," says Reece.

Miracles, however, are not just the domain of Catholics. Pentecostals are also firm believers.

At Oral Roberts University in Tulsa, Oklahoma, students run a very efficient and organized round-the-clock prayer ministry, taking requests by phone, fax, and e-mail.

You can even turn to the Internet for miracles. The Web's Praise and Prayer Center is a popular site for those seeking solace, comfort, and help.

And if you're Jewish and can't make it to Jerusalem, an Israeli company offers an e-mail service that will deliver your prayer requests directly to the Wailing Wall.

At Foundary Memorial United Methodist Church in Washington, D.C., where the Clintons usually worship, there are Thursday evening healing services for the sick in body, mind, or soul. And although the President has never attended one of these sessions, congregants there even prayed for a quick healing of the chief executive's injured knee.

You needn't feel you are being pushy or presumptuous when you pray for something. After all, it was Jesus himself, according to the New Testament, who repeatedly urged his followers to lobby God for their needs. "Ask and you shall receive," Jesus said. "Seek and you shall find. Knock and the door will be opened to you."

Always one to practice what he preached, Jesus did not hesitate to perform his wondrous miracles on those who asked him for a miracle.

But how do we know God really answers prayers? That question can probably only be answered in the words of one now-forgotten theologian: "If you believe, no proof is necessary. If you don't, no proof is sufficient."

In short, there is no way to prove conclusively that any miraculous occurrence is an act of God—but if you are open to the reality of miracles, chances are you will be blessed with one at one time or another in your life.

There is even strong medical evidence that miracles are a fact of life. For example, many doctors are convinced that prayers can significantly improve a patient's health, and in many documented cases, have saved lives.

Since most miracles seem to begin with a prayer, medical researchers are as keenly interested in the power of prayer as religious leaders are. In fact, so far some 140 laboratory studies have been published that are devoted to either proving or disproving the incredible power of prayer as a healing tool.

Many in the conservative medical community have come to accept the idea that a nonphysical power—whether we call it mind-body healing or alternative medicine or a miracle or God—can have a restorative effect on our bodies.

A few years ago the National Institutes of Health created an Office of Alternative Medicine to support research into these mysterious powers—and one of the first grants went to researchers measuring "the impact of prayer on the recovery of drug abusers."

Leading researcher in this field Larry Dossey, M.D., an author based in Santa Fe, New Mexico, and co-chairman of the Panel on Mind-Body Interventions at the National Institutes for Health Office of Alternative Medicine, gives the subject in-depth coverage in his book *Healing Words*. He points out that most of the experiments to date have been conducted on simple organisms, such as bacteria and fungi, seeds and grains—the idea being to see whether bacteria flourish more and seeds sprout more when prayers are said for them.

While bacteria and seeds are obviously easier to control and monitor in the laboratory than are human beings, the results came down heavily in favor of the miraculous power of prayer. In about two-thirds of the studies, bacteria seem to thrive and seeds to sprout faster when prayers are said for them.

But what does all this mean? Dr. Dossey says he does not draw any sweeping conclusions from these unusual lab studies. "I'm just putting the evidence on the table," he says. "I'm saying that medical science should pay attention because the effects just knock your socks off."

In another interesting study conducted at San Francisco General Hospital, cardiologist Randolph Byrd, M.D., followed almost four hundred heart patients who were admitted to the coronary care unit. Half of the patients were chosen at random to be prayed for by strangers; half were not prayed for.

The strangers knew only the first names of the patients they were praying for. And the patients, nurses, and doctors were totally unaware of who was being prayed for and who was not.

Ten months into the experiment, the results were astonishing. The prayed-for group did "significantly better" than the other patients. Very few had succumbed to heart attacks. None of the prayed-for needed mechanical help to breathe, while twelve of the unremembered group had to be on ventilators.

"If it were a drug or a new surgical procedure that was being studied, instead of prayer," concludes Dr. Dossey, "it would have been heralded as a medical breakthrough."

The San Francisco experiment, in simple terms, means that even a total stranger can help you experience a miracle that could change your life forever!

"The implication of that ought to fill people with joy," observes Dr. Dossey. "It means," he continues, "that there is some part of the human mind that is nonlocal, some part that is omnipresent in space and infinite in time. Even Nobel Prize-winning physicists are looking at this. They're saying that if there are no boundaries around the individual mind, then at some point there cannot be several billion separate minds. At some level, in some sense, there is only one mind."

But could it be the mind of God? The religious among us certainly think so.

Dr. Joan Borysenko, Ph.D., a Boulder, Colorado, psychologist, cell biologist, and author of *Fire in the Soul,* and a pioneer in the mind-body sciences, chooses to describe it as "the part of each of us that is birthless and deathless."

"The greatest wonder," she says, "is to connect with that part of yourself and to be guided by it. If we all did this, we would live in a world of peace and plenty. And that, of course, would be the real miracle."

Whatever the powerful force within us is that drives us to give and receive miracles is fodder for complex and controversial philosophical, religious, even scientific debate.

For the people who receive miracles, how exactly their miracle came about is less important than the fact that it happened in the first place. Miracle recipients simply don't look a gift horse in the mouth.

Take, for example, the case of young widow and mother Christine B., who was dying of cancer. Despite a mastectomy and chemotherapy, the cancer had spread from her breasts to her lungs. Doctors gave her two months to live.

She had even arranged for her nine-year-old daughter, Rachel, to be adopted by her oncologist and his wife after she was gone. Nevertheless, Christine clung to the hope that a miracle would enter her life.

She was encouraged in this belief by family friends and her fellow parishioners at her local Baptist church in rural Georgia, who had participated in a special prayer service for her healing. Christine, even in her most weakened moments, was bolstered by the strength of her faith.

At her thirty-eighth birthday party, friends and supporters gathered round her. "Make a wish," they urged as she was presented with a cake ablaze with candles.

Christine closed her eyes. Silently, she wished for a miracle: *For my daughter's sake, let me be cancer-free.*

Weak and short of breath, but concentrating hard, she filled her lungs and, with a single breath, blew out every single candle.

"At that moment, I knew I was going to live," she says today. "Even before I went back to the doctor, I knew a miracle had happened."

A week later, her doctor's tests confirmed it. Although X rays taken just a month before had revealed lungs completely clouded with cancer cells, and though a second doctor had agreed that Christine was terminal, the new X rays showed an astonishing change: Christine's lungs were now clear. Her cancer had simply disappeared.

Did a miracle take place at that unforgettable birthday celebration? Even her oncologist believes that was the case. "I wouldn't argue against it," he says.

Doctors all over the country agree and can attest to similar cures and healings that can't be explained away by science or logic.

"Spontaneous remission" is how the more pragmatic members of the medical community explain it. Nevertheless, they still can't explain how it happens, or why it happens to one patient and not another.

Here are two classic examples of spontaneous remission from medical casebooks:

- Debby O., of Shokan, New York, was forty-two when her doctor gave her a grim diagnosis: She had an incurable form of lymphoma, a cancer of the lymph system, and had only a short time to live. She was devastated.

  Her physician recommended radiation and chemotherapy to slow the disease, but Debby refused the rigorous treatment. "I wasn't going to be cured anyway," she said.

  To the astonishment of her doctor, her cancer began to go into remission a few months later. Within a year, all apparent signs of the disease were gone.

  That was more than ten years ago. "I've been in perfect health since," says Debby. "Today, I feel wonderful."
- Marlene M., a financial consultant and mother of four from Providence, Rhode Island, was diagnosed with a malignant melanoma (an aggressive skin cancer) at age thirty-seven.

  After several operations, she was told her cancer was terminal. Like Debby, she refused chemotherapy and other, more experimental treatments. Her doctors gave her less than a year to live. But today, after ten years, she's healthier than ever.

"It's a true miracle," says the dermatologist who first diagnosed Marlene's "extremely bleak" case of melanoma.

Does this mean "medical miracles" and "spontaneous remissions" are one and the same thing? Whatever label the more conservative researchers care to put on it, it certainly looks like it.

One thing is certain—serious scientific researchers are beginning to pay closer attention to these cases, in which seemingly incurable diseases disappear without standard medical treatment or with alternative therapies that most doctors consider inadequate.

Spontaneous remissions like Debby's and Marlene's are extraordinarily rare events—occurring perhaps a handful of times each year in the United States, where there are more than 500,000 annual cancer deaths.

But, however rare, there's no question that they do happen. Remarkable recoveries have been documented in every type of cancer and nearly every disorder, from diabetes to warts.

Strangely enough, the word "miracle" is seldom used. You will hear doctors use the words "spontaneous remission" and "self-healing" over and over again. But it's difficult to concede a "miracle" has occurred.

"Instead of miracles, I like to think of these things as mysteries, because mysteries can sometimes be solved," says Bernie Siegel, M.D., author or *Love, Medicine & Miracles,* one of the first books to suggest that medical science does not have all the answers.

More and more researchers believe the mystery is beginning to unravel. "I think we have plenty of evidence to say that the body has a natural ability to heal itself," says Andrew Weil, M.D., professor of medicine at the University of Arizona College of Medicine in Tucson and author of *Spontaneous Healing,* a book that explores the phenomenon.

"The capacity for self-healing exists, to some extent,

in all of us," agrees Caryle Hirshberg, a medical researcher and coauthor—with Marc Ian Barasch—of *Remarkable Recovery*.

Ms. Hirshberg spent eight years scouring databases, medical journals, and libraries for mentions of miraculous recoveries, finding more than seven hundred documented cases and 3,500 references to the topic, some from as far back as 1846.

She also suggests that these remarkable healings are not as rare as medical statistics suggest, and raises the possibility that many doctors who witness miraculous recoveries tend to dismiss them as the result of laboratory error or an initial misdiagnosis. She suggests that there are probably many other recoveries in patients who have never seen doctors at all.

The possibility that patients might be able to heal themselves by utilizing the power of their minds is yet another theory winning acceptance in medical research circles. In fact, there's a whole new field, psychoneuroimmunology, or PNI, that is based on the theory that our attitudes and emotions are linked in critical ways to our bodies, specifically our brain, and nervous, endocrine, and immune systems.

Numerous brain chemicals—released in response to everything from sadness to euphoria—have been proved to affect the immune system.

"We used to think that things like hypnotic suggestion or visualizations (in which people imagine their illness disappearing) were just relaxing people," says Marc Schoen, Ph.D., PNI researcher and assistant clinical professor at the University of California at Los Angeles (UCLA) School of Medicine. "But what we've learned in the last five years in particular is that these kinds of interventions are having a cellular impact."

Exactly why the emotions affect the body is not fully understood. But evidence is mounting that certain psychological and spiritual states can change the course of disease.

To devout miracle believers, however, it is irrelevant how the medical establishment cares to categorize these amazing cures and healings. To them, a miracle is a miracle is a miracle.

From a more mystical-religious standpoint, the most common modern-day miracles involve apparitions, either of Jesus or his Blessed Mother. These apparitions are everywhere, and the multitudes have been flocking to behold them.

In recent years, the image of Jesus has reportedly been seen on a maple tree in Fairfield, Maine, and on a Pizza Hut billboard in Stone Mountain, Georgia.

Holy images have been sighted in the sky over Lubbock, Texas, on a soybean-oil storage tank in Fostoria, Ohio, and on a refrigerator in Estill Springs, Tennessee.

The Virgin Mary is said to appear on the first Sunday of every month in Marlboro, New Jersey, and the stigmata of her Son on the bleeding hands and feet of a priest in Lake Ridge, Virginia.

Then there's the more whimsical report of people seeing the Virgin Mary on the side of a bank building in Clearwater, Florida, and others seeing Mother Teresa on a cinnamon roll in Tennessee.

These incidents and many more will be discussed in further detail elsewhere in this book.

But are they true miracles? Whatever your religion or viewpoint, it would be unfair to dismiss these events as hysterical hokum. After all, many devout believers are claiming remarkable cures and other amazing happenings at apparition sites. The documented healings at the more famous shrines in Lourdes in France and, more recently, at Medjugorje in Europe are legend.

People are traveling to Lourdes and other holy sites in increasing numbers. In fact, religious shrines and pilgrimage sites have become the most popular tourist attractions worldwide—from Fatima in Portugal and the tomb of St. James in Santiago de Compostela, Spain, to Varanasi in India, the Hindu "city of Chiva" on the Ganges.

Lourdes is, of course, a very popular pilgrimage site—more frequented than Jerusalem, Mecca, or Rome. In 1994 it welcomed five and a half million visitors, a million and a half more than a decade earlier. On any given day, more than five thousand pilgrims from around the world show up in the small town of Lourdes in the French Pyrenees, where they gather for a candlelight ceremony.

All are there for one reason: They are hoping for a miracle. Their faith tells them that many of the afflicted among them will be healed by one of the miracles for which Lourdes is internationally famous.

Pilgrimages to Lourdes in search of healing miracles have been going on since the shrine's beginning in 1858, when the shepherd girl Bernadette Soubirous first saw a vision of a lady dressed in a white robe with a blue sash. The vision directed Bernadette to dig at the site. She uncovered a spring. She was told to drink and wash in the spring's water.

Word of Bernadette's visions spread like wildfire, and soon people from all over France were flocking to the site, where they set up a crude shrine.

Although local government officials first disparaged the visions and tried to close the shrine, the faithful still came. And soon the miracles began. A blind man who washed his eyes in the spring regained sight, and a neighbor of Bernadette's dipped her dying baby in the waters and the child lived.

A miraculous legend was born. . . .

In 1862, an investigating committee set up by a local bishop declared that some cures at Lourdes were "contrary to all known biological laws and medical science"—and thus genuine miracles.

Emperor Napoleon III's son was cured by the waters. That's when the emperor declared the shrine open to the general public. Lourdes became an international mecca for the sick and disabled. Hotels sprang up—Lourdes now has more than any city in France, after Paris. And souvenir shops soon followed.

Criticism of Lourdes as being a gigantic hoax continued from many quarters—in particular the mainstream medical establishment. So in 1885, the Church appointed a full-time doctor to the site to authenticate healings and to eliminate the possibility of fakery.

Today the on-site doctor is Roger Pilon, M.D., president of the Lourdes Medical Bureau. Here's what he has to say about the miraculous healings at the shrine:

"In every disease there is a psychological part. Any doctor will tell you that someone who wants to be cured is a better patient and has a better chance of recovery than one who gives up.

"Coming to Lourdes gives people hope. And while some may not be granted a physical cure, they are always granted hope—hope for a better life, no matter what their condition."

Dr. Pilon is quick to stress that his role at Lourdes is not to determine what is and what isn't a miracle. "For us—as doctors of the Medical Bureau of Lourdes—there are only 'cures' and 'unexplainable cures,'" he says. "Miracles are a spiritual matter."

Before the possibility of a miracle can even be considered, says Dr. Pilon, the unexplained cure must satisfy a number of rigorous medical criteria. "The cure must be from a serious disease, an organic disease. There must be laboratory proof, such as X rays and biopsies," says the doctor. "The patient cannot have received any medical treatment for the disease. The cure must be extremely quick, if not immediate, and come without convalescence. It must be a definite cure, followed by a waiting time—five years with no return of cancer, for example."

If, after all this, Dr. Pilon and the medical bureau

are convinced that they have found an unexplained cure, they pass the case and its paperwork on to the International Medical Commission of Lourdes. The commission is comprised of two dozen specialists from throughout Europe.

After the commission has reviewed the case and deemed it worthy, it goes to a canonical commission in the diocese of the claimant—the representative of the Church—to determine the theological basis for a miracle.

Then the bishop must wait another five years to see if the healed person has been a good Christian during that period. It is up to the bishop to decide if the cure happened through the intercession of God and is, therefore, a miracle.

Lourdes Medical Bureau receives hundreds of reports about healings every year. But only one or two cases satisfy their rigid criteria for warranting further investigation.

Nevertheless, Dr. Pilon's files carry two thousand reports accumulated over the years of cases that are classified as "unexplainable cures." Although they met all the medical criteria, only sixty-five of those two thousand have been declared miracles by the Church.

One of the most impressive healing stories to come out of Lourdes is that of a Christian Brother, Leo Schwage, who, in 1952, was part of a Swiss-German pilgrimage to the shrine.

Brother Leo was an invalid in the last stages of multiple sclerosis. He couldn't even swallow. But after his companions took him to the Procession of the Blessed Sacrament and helped him bathe in the shrine's healing waters, he was able to return home walking and talking.

Brother Leo Schwage described what happened to him after his immersion in the waters of the shrine: "All at once I felt something like an electric shock and immediately got out of my wheelchair without knowing what had happened to me."

His affliction of five years—along with the numbness, headaches, backaches, and paralysis—was totally gone. His "instant and extraordinary cure" without relapse was verified after six years, and proclaimed miraculous in 1960.

In his eighties today, Brother Leo still leads an annual pilgrimage to Lourdes.

But the facts show you don't have to go to Lourdes for a miracle. Research of U.S. medical journals published in the 1960s revealed 182 cases of cancer that had undergone spontaneous regression without any recognized treatment.

And as recently as 1993, the Institute of Noetic Sciences, a research and educational foundation, examined more than 830 medical journals, published in more than twenty languages, and came up with more than 1,385 case histories of spontaneous remission. Compared with these statistics, the sixty-five certified miracles among millions of pilgrims visiting Lourdes in its 136-year existence is far from staggering.

But Lourdes's believers argue that thousands upon thousands of on-site miracles go unreported.

Says Irish-born nun Sister Mary Patrick, who has worked at Lourdes for years, "Everyone who comes has his own miracle. They're transformed in some way, even if they're not physically healed. The emphasis here is now on spiritual and emotional healing."

For example, at one time, not too many years ago, one of the most dramatic tourist attractions at Lourdes was a mountain of crutches and other walking aids discarded by those healed at the shrine. These have since been removed. The crutches were "a distraction" to the "spiritual" healing that is emphasized now, Sister Mary Patrick explained.

We mustn't forget that the shrine at Lourdes started after an apparition. And apparitions, particularly those of the Virgin Mary, are the most commonly reported miracles in the United States and around the world in this day and age.

Of the hundreds of Marian apparitions that have been reported, only about ten have some degree of acceptance by the Roman Catholic Church. These include those at Lourdes and the shrines of Guadalupe in Mexico and Fatima in Portugal.

With even the Church so cautious to give its stamp of approval, why then are so many people conditioned to accept incidents that have occurred at locations such as these as true miracles?

According to Eileen Elias Freeman, author of *Touched by Angels,* there's a real hunger for accounts of miracles.

"Materialism hasn't made us happy," she explains. "Money and power haven't solved our problems. So now people are looking for spiritual answers."

And, says Dr. Joan Borysenko: "We are also a nation of closet mystics. We like to think of ourselves as rational beings, but we wear the idea of miracles like a seat belt. Just in case."

Lest you think the Roman Catholic Church endorses miraculous visions willy-nilly, it should be stressed here that, around the world, the Catholic Church has recognized only eight episodes of holy apparitions in the past two hundred years.

And when it comes to "miracle" cures, the Vatican is equally careful, insisting on a lengthy investigative process.

As we've seen from the strict rules and restrictions in force at Lourdes, a team of medical doctors must check on whether the pathology actually existed, how grave it really was, and whether it was truly and completely healed in a way that science can't explain.

One of the few modern American miracles to be authenticated by the Vatican is the amazing story of Ann Hooe, a wife, mother, and hairstylist in Catonsville, Maryland, who, in 1952 at the age of four and a half, was dying of leukemia.

Doctors could do nothing more for her. But her devoted sisters urged her parents to pray for her at the tomb of Mother Elizabeth Ann Seton, a pioneer of Catholic education in America (more about Mother Seton in the upcoming chapter of saintly miracles). Ann Hooe's sisters—hoping to have Mother Seton declared a saint—wanted a miracle to be credited to her intercession.

Three weeks after the prayers began, the young girl's blood count was normal!

Nine years later, when she was still cancer-free, the archdiocese of Baltimore conducted an extensive investigation and sent the results to the Vatican in Rome. In 1963 Pope John XXIII agreed that a miraculous event had taken place. His successor, Paul VI, agreed with the findings in 1975.

The case of Ann Hooe was recognized by the Church as a bona fide miracle—a leading factor in the subsequent canonization of Mother Seton.

The Roman Catholic Church does not have the monopoly on saintly miracles—after all, didn't Buddha walk on air, Moses draw water from a rock, Muhammad ascend to heaven on a winged horse, and Ramakrishma converse with a stone statue?

Miracles are common to every world religion and, for centuries, have been intriguing and perplexing not only to theologians but also scientists and philosophers from Einstein to Kierkegaard.

Hinduism, Sufism, Christianity, and other faiths have all had their share of miraculous characters who have shared such powers as levitation, bilocation, healing, mind reading, and walking on water.

Even stigmata, which in Christian cultures mirror the wounds of the crucified Christ, appear in Hindu and Muslim lore—to Muslims, they represent the battle wounds of Muhammad.

But miracles don't just happen to biblical saints and other exalted figures. They can happen to the most unlikely and humble people, as our upcoming chapter on saintly miracles will reveal.

One of the most unlikely miracle workers in modern times has got to be the Italian stigmatist and healer, Padre Pio of Pietrelcina, who died in 1968. A short-tempered man, Padre Pio was known to yell at his fellow priests in public. And when pilgrims traveled to see him to bow at his feet offering penance, he would yell at them, "Go away!"

As a closing thought to this introductory chapter, here are some age-old but uncomfortable questions about miracles that never go away:

Why do some people get a miracle and others don't?

Why wasn't there a miraculous invention to prevent the Holocaust?

Why was there not a miracle to avert wars and assassinations and other senseless killings?

Or to save innocent children dying from AIDS?

Those are questions without answers. The very nature of a miracle is that it cannot be explained.

## Chapter One

## Medical · Miracles

Although many medical miracles simply can't be explained by science, theologians and an increasing number of prestigious names in the medical and scientific communities are acknowledging more and more the power of prayer as the force behind many medical miracles.

Perhaps the most intriguing experiment involving the power of prayer as a healer is the one involving sixty patients at the Arthritis Treatment Center in Clearwater, Florida. Arthritic patients were specially chosen because rheumatoid arthritis has clear manifestations—including swollen joints and crippling pain. And relief of these symptoms can be easily measured.

The ongoing study is being carried out under the general direction of Dr. Dale Matthews, an associate professor of medicine at the Georgetown University School of Medicine in Washington, D.C. Dr. Matthews is also a religious man, a staunch Presbyterian who has been praying for and with patients for years. His mission these days is to find out if science can confirm that prayer really has healing effects. In an earlier study of 212 cases in which Dr. Matthews participated, researchers found a "positive linkage" between faith and health in seventy-five percent of the cases.

For his current experiment, Dr. Matthews has divided the participants into two general groups. All patients receive four days of healing prayer through the traditional Christian practice of laying on of hands by members of the Christian Healing Ministry. In addition, half of the patients receive six months of long-distance intercessory prayer. Then both groups are examined by the same clinician who saw them before the experiment. There are follow-ups at one, three, six, and twelve months. Throughout, Dr. Matthews uses strict scientific protocols and standards set by the American College of Rheumatology.

As the study is ongoing, the jury is still out. But so far a videotape of the early phase of the study shows that some individual patients have experienced "extraordinary short-term results from prayer."

"There's something weird going on here, and I love it," says one patient. At the beginning of the experiment he had forty-nine tender joints. After four sessions with a hands-on praying minister, he had only eight. Six months later, he says he has no pain at all and no need of medication.

Dr. Matthews doesn't expect that all the cases will turn out so well. He's mainly interested in discovering whether prayer has *any* kind of long-term benefits.

What exactly is being tested at Clearwater—the power of prayer or God's willingness to take part in scientific experiments?

"That's a fair question," Dr. Matthews acknowledges. "God can bless or not bless this study."

Some amazing results of the amazing power of prayer are given throughout this book. But what about medical miracles that occur without the power of prayer? What about the healings and cures that happen just because of the grit and determination of patients with enormous wills to live? And what takes place within the bodies of people who are near the brink of death—yet the next day are diagnosed as fit as a fiddle?

Some examples of these truly wondrous cases follow in this chapter.

## Loving Family Refused to Let Mom Go in Peace

"A living, walking miracle!"

That's how Big Bear, California, housewife Valerie Wolfe describes herself these days.

These days are changed days from a dark period in 1993 when Valerie, fifty-seven, had an aneurysm burst in her brain and lapsed into a deep coma. Doctors gave her little or no chance of recovery. She was hooked up to life support and feeding systems. As the days and weeks wore on, her doctors advised the Wolfe family to let her go.

"Unplug the tubes and let her go in peace," a doctor advised Valerie's loyal husband, John.

"Never!" was his answer.

It was that kind of faith and determination that prompted a miracle—a miracle that brought Valerie back to life and into the bosom of her loving family once again.

Thanks to her family's love and devotion, Valerie Wolfe is living proof that miracles can and do happen if you really want them to happen.

As she lay in her coma, husband John was at her bedside every day, reading to her from the Bible. One daughter played guitar to her, and another yelled at her at the top of her voice, urging her to come back from the brink of death—and she responded!

Valerie first lapsed into her coma on January 5, 1993, when her world went dark and she was admitted to St. Bernardine Medical Center in San Bernardino, California.

"Her family was told by the first doctors to examine her that there was virtually no hope for survival. And even if she did survive, she'd be a vegetable," said Dr. John Merritt, medical director of the Tustin Rehabilitation Hospital where Valerie still goes for therapy.

The family—instead of throwing in the towel—bonded together in a positive manner to make a miracle happen. Husband John, seventy-two, ruled out any question of "pulling the plug" on Valerie. Daughter Loretta, thirty-four, read up on how to treat a patient in a coma. All the books recommended that coma patients should be continually stimulated. And that's exactly what the Wolfe family did.

"We read to her, sang to her, played music to her. We held her hands, bathed her, massaged her. I played sergeant-major—tough love. I challenged her, 'Come on, Mom, talk to me. Come back.' I shouted at her. At night I slept with her in the hospital bed, cradling her in my arms and giving her my love," recalled Loretta.

Valerie was in her coma for only six days when she gave her first clue that there was still hope. An eyelid flickered. Overjoyed, Loretta ran screaming along the hospital corridors, saying, "Mom's alive!"

The Wolfe family maintained their vigil. It cost them $100,000 of their own money after medical insurance ran out. But it all proved to be worth it. By March 1993, Valerie was recognizing her loved ones and making an effort to talk again. By May, she was allowed to go home.

Progress from then on was slow, but remarkable. She learned to walk again, began eating normally, began watching television and reading books.

By October she was playing her piano again. "She'd always loved to play," remembered John. "And miracle of miracles, she just sat down at the piano and started playing 'Silent Night.' "

By Christmas she was singing and playing all the seasonal carols. Valerie Wolf had truly come home.

"My family is the reason I'm here today," says Valerie of her personal miracle. "They engulfed me in love."

## Hole in the Heart: Boy's Amazing Recovery

"Our son is living proof that miracles do happen," declared overjoyed parents Nick and Sue Feast, whose six-year-old son Jack's weakened heart began beating on its own again—just hours before he was to undergo a risky transplant operation.

The boy's recovery was hailed by British newspapers as a medical miracle after his doctors were unable to explain his spontaneous recovery. "Jack should not be here today," declared Dr. David Anderson. "We just didn't know why his heart suddenly improved. There is no doubt he defied all the odds."

The South London youngster was diagnosed with a hole in his heart shortly after his birth in May 1990. His parents were doubly worried, because mom Sue had earlier lost a daughter, who was stillborn.

"You couldn't tell Jack was ill just by looking at him," explains his father, Nick, a thirty-seven-year-old mail carrier. "But the hole was in a dangerous position in his heart, and we knew that sooner or later Jack would have to face surgery."

When doctors did get around to operating, they succeeded in closing the hole in his heart—but the boy still showed no signs of recovery. His family kept a bedside vigil while their little lad was hooked up to sophisticated life support machines.

A high-tech medical instrument called an Extra-Corporeal Membrane Oxygenator did the work of Jack's heart for him for eleven days as he teetered on the brink of death.

His doctors did not give the boy much of a chance. No other child had survived longer than seven days linked up to the Ecmo machine.

Meantime, the conscientious medical staff was scouring Europe for a matching heart. Their last hope was to give the boy a transplant. Even then, they weren't sure if his weakened body could stand up to the hazardous operation.

A matching heart was found in the Czech Republic and flown immediately to London. Jack was being prepped for the operation. His nurses took him off the Ecmo machine—and were astounded to find his heart was beginning to work on its own.

Mom Sue explained: "It was only a faint heartbeat at first, but we could all see a slow, gradual improvement. The nurses were dumbfounded. But we were all delighted!"

Added Dr. Anderson: "The decision was made then and there not to operate. We were wondering whether we were doing the right thing."

But the miracle has stayed a miracle. Today, Jack runs and jumps and plays with the other kids. He romps and frisks with the family dog.

Declares Sue: "If there's one thing I have learned from this experience, it is never, never give up hope!"

# Docs Baffled As Cancer Kid Makes Miracle Recovery

Just weeks away from death, brave teenager Shawn Clarke received the wondrous gift of life for Christmas in 1990 when a tennis-ball-size tumor inside his spine miraculously vanished!

"God granted me a miracle and made my malignant tumor disappear," the then fourteen-year-old from Mitchell, Ontario, told the *National Enquirer.* "I prayed for God to keep me alive so that I could spend Christmas with my family . . . and He did."

Shawn's amazing return from the brink of death left the ninth-grader's doctors completely baffled.

"The tumor has totally disappeared. I think it's as much of a miracle as I'll ever see," declared family physician Mark Diotallevi. "We're very happy for Shawn—yet we have no way to explain his recovery. The odds were one in a million—it was something we've never heard of or seen before."

But Shawn knows in his heart that he was cured by prayer. "I knew God could succeed where doctors could not—even though I was at death's door," he declared.

A large malignant tumor was growing inside his spinal column, around the nerves of his spinal cord. The tumor was spreading quickly right into his brain stem—and that's when doctors said his case was hopeless.

On November 9, 1990, the experts visited Shawn in the hospital and told him he wouldn't live to see Christmas. By this point, Shawn looked more like a shriveled skeleton than a teenage boy. His weight had dropped from 125 to sixty-five pounds. The only thing keeping him alive was an intravenous feeding tube. Despite all his suffering, Shawn prayed that God would keep him alive a little longer.

Doctors sent Shawn home to die in the company of his mother Joanne, dad Gary, sister Tracey, and brothers Michael and Justin. His family put on a happy face for Shawn as he struggled to hold on to life. The weeks passed and then it was . . . Christmas.

"Shawn was just so happy to be with us and watch

us bring in the Christmas tree and decorations," said Joanne. "We all helped him for a few minutes as he put the angel on the top of the tree, and we all shed tears knowing this would be our last Christmas together."

Yet, amazingly, Shawn lived.

In January 1991 he began to get stronger. "Soon he was eating full meals and demanding to be let out of bed," said Joanne. "We were so happy we cried tears of joy."

By the time August rolled around, Shawn had improved so much that doctors checked his tumor. Incredibly, it was completely gone!

The gutsy teen says today, "I know God granted me a miracle. All I can say is, 'Thank you, God.'"

## Psychic Heals Hundreds— with Her Palms and Paintings

Psychic healer Neli Dimitrova has cured thousands of ill people by the laying on of hands—and, incredibly, even by having them look at one of her paintings, say medical experts.

Hundreds of patients from all over Europe brave Bulgaria's bitter cold and line up outside the forty-five-year-old woman's home each day to be relieved of cysts, psoriasis, phlebitis, migraines, burns, ulcers, and other illnesses that have resisted medical treatments.

Incredibly, so many people have been correctly diagnosed and cured by Neli that even the most skeptical of doctors sing her praises.

"Neli is a miraculous healer," said Dr. Martha Handjieva, professor of medicine at the Medical Academy of Bulgaria, as reported in the *National Enquirer*. "I am a patient of Neli's as well. She's made a believer out of me."

Neli heals in two ways: by touching or placing her hands just above the affected areas of the body, and by having patients touch and look at some of the more than fifty beautiful paintings she has created. She paints pastoral scenes of flowers and trees or country monasteries near her home in Sofia. The serenity of the scenes sets off a healing process in the people who look at them, she claims.

This double-barreled treatment cured dermatologist Ani Mikhailova of a painful growth and has also healed patients the doctor referred to Neli.

"Cases that wouldn't respond to the best medical techniques were cured quickly by Neli," said the doctor.

One such case involved a forty-year-old man with a rash on his chest that would not heal.

"Neli held her hands over the area," said Dr. Mikhailova. "Then she had him look at one of her paintings and touch some of the affected areas of his body with the painting. I had treated him for weeks with no results, but in a matter of days his rash began to heal and in a week it was gone."

A myoma, a painful noncancerous growth in the groin, sent Dr. Mikhailova to Neli. After two visits, the growth vanished. "We've never heard of a spontaneous remission of this type. Neli is a miracle worker!"

Until recent years, Neli was just an ordinary woman, a divorced mom who worked in a factory. But on June 28, 1990, her brother died in a car accident and Neli was devastated. She missed her brother so much, she asked a female psychic to contact him in a séance. The psychic contacted her brother, and it changed Neli's life.

"My brother told me through the psychic that he

was giving me a gift from the other side—the blessed gift of healing," Neli said.

Soon after, Neli discovered her power to heal with her hands. Then the woman, who had never painted before, suddenly began creating works of art with healing powers, say her followers.

And she's been helping people ever since. She makes a humble living from the coin donations people give her.

"I believe God puts you to a test, and if you pass He gives you a special gift," Neli said. "My gift was healing. I never turn anyone away, because God did not turn me away in my hour of need."

# Blind Man Gets New Eye —from His Tooth!

In one of the more bizarre modern medical miracles, a blind man gave his eyetooth to see again— literally!

In an incredible operation, doctors removed one of the man's teeth, fitted it with a miniature lens, and bonded it to the eye to replace a damaged cornea.

"A tooth is a small price to pay for being able to see again!" says pioneering surgeon Dr. Christopher Liu.

And the lucky guy who'll escape his world of darkness after being completely blind for twelve months, sixty-one-year-old Bhimji Varsani, declared: "I'm looking forward to seeing all my grandchildren again!"

He lost his right eye through smallpox when he was eight and contracted an infection in his good eye two years later. Over the years his eyesight deteriorated badly, and three corneal transplants failed.

"Human corneal grafts work well for the majority of patients, but there is a small group for whom they will fail," said Dr. Liu of the Sussex Eye Hospital in England.

In the historic eight-hour operation, a single tooth and the surrounding jawbone were removed and ground down with incredible precision to form a tiny curved plate. A miniature round window was drilled into the plate to hold an acrylic lens. Then the plate was transplanted into the soft flesh under Varsani's eye, where it will remain while living tissue grows around the "eye tooth." After two months, the lens was to be stitched to the eye using the newly grown tissue.

Medical experts say the revolutionary procedure is a much-needed alternative to transplanting the cornea, a transparent membrane that often "frosts over" in old age or succumbs to disease. It has the potential to bring the miracle of sight back to patients whose corneas have been destroyed through accident or disease, and who aren't suitable for human corneal grafts.

"The magic of this operation is that the transplant will stay in place when it's surrounded by tooth and bone," said Dr. Liu.

## Image of Jesus Shows Up on X Ray!

Even hospital staffers were convinced they were witnessing a miracle when the image of Jesus mysteriously turned up on an accident victim's X-ray film.

"I believe this is the image of Christ!" a hospital spokesman declared to a *National Enquirer* reporter.

"I've never seen anything like it before," echoed a baffled doctor.

After the bizarre incident hit the headlines, hundreds of believers trekked to Walker Regional Medical Center in Jasper, Alabama, to see for themselves.

The image was first spotted by Dr. Michael Gibson when he was studying the X ray of a local man who suffered a broken neck in a car crash—yet made a miraculous recovery! It appeared to display the image of a bearded man with his hands clasped in prayer.

The miracle unfolded in December 1993 when a motorist's car careened into a telephone pole, totaling the car and critically injuring its driver. Paramedics took him to Walker Regional where he was X-rayed.

"The real surprise came four months later, on March 23, when he went to Carraway Methodist Center in Birmingham for nerve treatment," said a relative of the injured man. "Dr. Gibson at Carraway said when he saw an X ray taken the day of the accident, he wanted our family to see it."

Susan Darby, director of public relations at Walker Regional, added: "The X-ray view was taken through the man's open mouth, with the intent of examining his upper spine. In the center of the mouth, surrounded by normal exposures of the jaw, teeth, and spine, is the image of a man's face. He has shoulder-length hair and a short beard."

According to others who saw the X ray, the image of Christ also had a flowing robe and His hands are clasped in prayer.

Hospital officials were convinced the image was not a result of malfunctioning equipment or outdated film.

"This film was properly exposed at the proper settings, and there's nothing on it that makes me think it might have been tampered with," said a hospital radiologist.

Doctors and nurses who tended to the injured motorist when he was first brought in are convinced his survival without paralysis was "a miracle."

"Doctors told me he would've died if his neck had moved half a centimeter to one side, and he would have been paralyzed if it moved a half a centimeter to the other side!" said his brother.

The X ray was put on display in the hospital's foyer, where thousands have made a pilgrimage to view it.

Incredibly, the 1994 incident was the second time in a decade that the Walker Regional hospital was the scene of a miraculous recovery associated with the mysterious appearance of a Christ-like image.

In 1983 more than ten thousand believers from around the world descended on the medical center after an astonishing story broke. A dying boy, sixteen-year-old Ray Naramore, had made a miraculous recovery after his dad saw the image of a man resembling Jesus in the center.

"I feel like Walker Regional is a miracle medical center!" a hospital employee told the *Enquirer*.

Added the Reverend David Stookey, pastor of the Manchester Baptist Church in Jasper: "God creates miracles every day, and sometimes he leaves a visible mark, like the image on the X ray. This image of Christ should be taken as a sign that He still walks among us!"

## Former Cop Brings Family a Rip Van Winkle Miracle

One of the most incredible miracles in 1996, which made national headlines, was the bizarre case of Gary Dockery—the former cop who came back from the dead for one last cheery farewell to his family.

For seven years, forty-two-year-old Gary had lain in a nursing home in what doctors believed to be an irreversible coma. Sometimes he grunted or grimaced. Occasionally he would blink his eyes. But at no time did he show signs of waking up.

When fluid began filling his lungs, doctors told his kinfolk that if he didn't have surgery, he wouldn't survive much longer. Gary's relatives gathered at Parkridge Medical Center in Chattanooga, Tennessee, to consider the grim options: Was there any point in operating, when Gary was not expected to walk, talk, or regain full consciousness? On the other hand, was this the humane way to let him die (in a comatose state) after being shot in the head in the line of duty in 1988?

His sister, Lisa, sat by his bedside at one point during these deliberations to whisper reassurances to him. To her astonishment, Gary responded, "Uh-huh," he whispered back.

"You're talking!" exclaimed Lisa.

"I sure am," answered Gary.

Lisa quickly dialed their brother, Dennis, and put Gary on the phone. "Hey, buddy," said Gary.

"I couldn't believe it was him!" said Dennis. "I started screaming his name—'Gary! Gary!'"

And once he started talking, Dockery wouldn't stop. For the next eighteen hours, he joked, reminisced, and astonished friends and relatives with his recall of his former world.

He had no trouble recognizing his sons, Colt and Sean, though they were now teenagers. He thought Ronald Reagan was still President.

He could remember the names of his horses, the color of his Jeep—everything but the gunshot blast that sent him into oblivion when he responded to a 911 call.

He only calmed down and stopped talking when medical staffers finally sedated him in preparation for the lung surgery. His assembled relatives were apprehensive about the upcoming surgery, saddened at the thought of possibly losing Gary—again.

The country's top neurologists were baffled by the case of Gary Dockery. After all, Gary wasn't in a simple comatose state. A real "coma"—a state of sleeplike unconsciousness—almost never lasts more than a month or so. Then patients who don't die or recover slip into a "vegetative state," where they may wake, sleep, and move involuntarily but remain unconscious.

There are only a handful of documented cases of patients awakening from vegetative states after more than a year. So the experts could only conclude that Gary hadn't been in either a coma or a vegetative state but in a twilight zone with some awareness—a condition tentatively labeled "minimally responsive state."

After the surgical procedure on his lungs, Gary lapsed back into a comalike state, although he did have some function of his arms and legs. He died without regaining full consciousness.

Whatever condition he was in for the previous seven years is a question for medical debate. What cannot be argued is that miraculous afternoon when he returned to life to share a final farewell with his loved ones.

## Chapter Two

*❧*

# Divine Miracles

Divine intervention is much discussed, but seldom appreciated. How many among us may have experienced divine intervention and not realized it? More than you think.

There are many times when we shake our heads and say, "Gosh, that was a lucky break."

Or there are times when we are sick and fear the worst. Then we go for a medical checkup and get the all-clear signal. That's when we breathe a sigh of relief and say, "Gee, I'm one lucky son of a gun."

What we don't give credit to is the likely possibility of divine intervention. Regardless of the strength of your religious convictions, you are subject to the love and care of a higher authority who works in mysterious ways—as the following stories clearly show.

## Lourdes's Holy Water
## Cures Deadly Cancer

Ravaged by cancer, a respected member of the Canadian Parliament was given little hope for recovery—

but a week after he visited the Shrine of Lourdes, his astounded doctor discovered the cancer had totally vanished.

"God brought me back from the brink of death!" said Jean-Claude Malepart, fifty, who was in such agony during the latter days of his so-called terminal illness he even considered suicide. "At Lourdes I was saved from death from widespread cancer of the lungs, liver, and bone," he told the *National Enquirer.*

Dr. Joseph Ayoub, who treated Malepart, whole-heartedly agrees. "It was a miracle. I believe the Lord helped him—that there was divine intervention," said Dr. Ayoub, associate professor of medicine at the University of Montreal.

Specialists diagnosed Malepart's cancer just before Christmas of 1988. Even at that time it was entering a terminal stage. It had spread throughout his entire body. But after Mr. Malepart's visit to Lourdes at the end of June 1989, his doctors did a new series of tests on him, including a CAT scan. All the tests showed he'd gone into complete remission. The medical experts were absolutely amazed.

Malepart, who represents a section of Montreal in the Quebec Legislature, said he was devastated when he learned he was riddled with cancer.

"I knew the odds were I'd be dead soon," he said. He began chemotherapy and radiation treatments, but says they failed to appreciably shrink the tumors. Over the next six months he suffered increasing weakness and pain.

"Many days, it was a tremendous struggle just to get out of bed because of my weakness and pain. At one point, I considered suicide because I felt so terrible."

Finally he decided his only hope was to go to France and bathe in the holy waters in Lourdes—famed for its miraculous healings since a vision of the Virgin Mary was seen there in 1858.

"By then, walking was very difficult and I had pain all over my body—in my chest area, liver, joints, absolutely everywhere," he said. "But I was determined to make this pilgrimage, and I forced myself to get on the plane. While I was at Lourdes, I prayed and splashed holy water onto my chest, back, and stomach. I could feel a kind of healing power penetrating right through my skin and into my body."

After only three days in Lourdes, Malepart returned to Canada, bringing back thirty-six bottles of the shrine's holy water to use at home.

"And as I kept using the water, I felt better and better," he said. "My strength returned and my pain gradually vanished!"

Seven days after he returned from Lourdes, Malepart went to his doctor for tests—and was given a clean bill of health.

"I was amazed and thrilled," he said. "My life had been spared! It was the greatest day of my life."

Said Dr. Ayoub, who's also director of the cancer center at Montreal's Notre Dame Hospital and director of clinical research at the Montreal Cancer Institute:

"While we did treat Mr. Malepart with chemotherapy and radiation, I don't believe treatment would have produced this remission on its own—especially so quickly. I believe his visit to Lourdes and his use of Lourdes holy water definitely helped save his life."

Added Malepart: "Every day now I say to myself, 'Thank you for answering my prayers.' "

## Man Comes Back to Life— Thanks to Religious Relic

Mariano Farinella's return from the dead after fifty days in a coma is one of only eleven miracles the

Catholic Church has deemed authentic in the past forty years.

Farinella, a seventy-year-old retired miner, had been declared clinically dead as he lay in a coma. But after a sacred religious relic was placed in his hands, he miraculously came back to life. After he walked out of the hospital feeling fit, the Vatican declared his recovery a miracle!

Even Farinella himself proudly boasts, "I am living proof of miracles—a miracle brought me back to life."

Dr. Giuseppe Palmieri, deputy chief of the Italian hospital where Farinella made his remarkable recovery, has said: "He was clinically dead. His heart continued to beat, but there was no hope for him. I am a man of science. I have never believed in miracles. But I can give no scientific explanation for his extraordinary recovery. I must admit some higher power intervened."

Three years ago, Farinella was rushed to Sant'Elia Hospital in Caltanissetta, Sicily, with severe heart and respiratory problems. "I fell into a coma. After twenty days, I showed signs of improvement. But then I fell into an even deeper coma," said the father of four. "For a month I was kept alive only by artificial respirator. I didn't move my head. I didn't open my eyes. My left arm was paralyzed. My face and body began to swell. My skin turned black. Finally, the physicians told my children, 'There is nothing more we can do for him.'"

Doctors declared Farinella brain-dead.

That's when hospital chaplain Monsignor Mendola stepped in with a relic from Giacomo Cusmano, a wealthy Sicilian landowner who left his fortune to the needy in 1884 and became a priest before he died in 1888. The relic, enclosed in a metal pin, is a piece of material from the garments Father Cusmano was wearing when he died.

Monsignor Mendola put it in Farinella's hands, and

amazingly, the stricken man began to improve immediately.

"Within days, I could use my left arm," recalled Farinella. "The doctors couldn't believe their eyes. After only one week, I was able to walk out of the hospital on my own two feet."

Vatican authorities organized a commission of doctors and theologians to investigate Farinella's cure. After questioning twenty-two witnesses over three years, the commission declared Farinella's recovery a "clear-cut miracle"—although the Vatican is not considering Father Cusmano for sainthood.

Farinella's family physician, Dr. Archille Ferreri, said: "It's an inexplicable healing—a miracle."

## Nun Who Died in 1938 Helps Cure Priest's Heart Problem

A young Polish nun who died in 1938 may have a shrine erected in her honor at a Roman Catholic church in Baltimore, Maryland, for the part she may have played in the miraculous recovery of a dying priest.

Forty-nine-year-old Father Ronald Pytel was stricken with a degenerative aortic valve and dire congestive heart failure and was perilously close to death—until skilled doctors and his prayers to a long-dead nun returned him to perfect health.

His full recovery after valve replacement surgery not only surprised doctors at Johns Hopkins Hospital, it set in motion an exhaustive inquiry by the Roman Catholic Archdiocese in Baltimore.

The archdiocese's investigation sent ripples of excitement through the Baltimore Catholic community. Had the faithful of Holy Rosary on Chester Avenue in Fells Point witnessed a miracle?

Father Pytel, a sweet, gentle man of Polish descent,

does give medical intervention some credit for his remarkable recovery. But he is unshakably convinced that the divine intervention of the Blessed Faustina Kowalska, a Polish nun who died six decades ago and was beatified in 1993—along with his own prayers and the prayers of his caring parishioners—played an important part in his astonishing recovery.

"I'm saying that I was healed, that I had an experience that was out of the ordinary—but I haven't used the word miracle," Father Pytel told the *Baltimore Sun.*

The dedicated priest chose his words cautiously, in obvious deference to the fact that the Roman Catholic Church does not use the word "miracle" lightly.

To the Church, the authentication of a miracle is very serious business. It's regarded as the most rare of events, caused only by the hand of God and not explicable according to natural laws. And miracles are what saints are made of.

For that reason, officials at the Baltimore archdiocese are reluctant to discuss the details of Father Pytel's case. But if his so-called miraculous healing is established as such, it could become the second authenticated miracle needed for the canonization of the Blessed Faustina.

Already the 1630 optimistic parishioners at the largely Polish Holy Rosary parish are dreaming of building a shrine that one day could attract religious pilgrims. Their hope that Blessed Faustina will be elevated to sainthood is still a long shot, especially when you consider that the internationally famous shrine at Lourdes has had only sixty-five of the many thousands of miracles claimed since 1862 authenticated by the Church hierarchy.

The Church's definition of a miracle, as I mention elsewhere, is extremely strict. In the case of a healing, the recovery must be sudden—"instantaneous" is a word often used—and directly attributable to divine intercession. Also, it must be unexplained by any other measure, medical or scientific.

No one doubts, however, that Father Pytel's heart condition was considered by some doctors to be irreversible and certainly life-threatening. The speed of his healing was also astonishing.

Father Pytel's medical problems began in November 1994, when he came down with a cold that just wouldn't quit. After that, he was stricken with a series of spring allergies. He had respiratory problems, and the once-active cleric soon found climbing stairs to be a hardship.

In May of 1995, he collapsed. His doctor detected unusual heart noises and ordered further tests. His close friend and fellow priest, Father Lawrence Gesy, sent him to respected Johns Hopkins cardiologist Dr. Nicholas Fortuin.

That's when the obstructed aortic valve was discovered. Father Pytel was also diagnosed with an enlarged heart and fluid in his lungs. He was, said Dr. Fortuin, "in very real danger of sudden death."

On June 13, 1995, Dr. Peter Greene, a Johns Hopkins surgeon, replaced Father Pytel's diseased heart valve with a mechanical one. "I expected he would improve immeasurably because he was so desperately ill," Fortuin told the *Baltimore Sun*. "But I did not expect his heart function to return to normal."

It was left to Father Gesy to break the bad news to Father Pytel. He told him that his medical condition had left him very weakened and uninsurable—and there was no way he could resume his old schedule, attending to his flock. Early retirement was his only option.

But, undaunted, Father Pytel gained strength. And by October 5, 1995—coincidentally, the anniversary of Sister Faustina's death—he was strong enough to officiate at a twelve-hour celebratory prayer service in preparation for Pope John Paul II's visit to Baltimore.

The Holy Rosary Church is designated as an archdiocesan shrine to the Divine Mercy—a devotion that preaches the mercy of Christ and encourages followers to seek Christ's mercy and practice mercy toward others.

The Divine Mercy message was originally published in a 697-page journal kept by Sister Faustina, who was born Helen Kowalska, a simple woman with scant education. At the time, Sister Faustina was not believed to have been capable of writing such a work. But she claimed she penned the Divine Mercy under guidance from Jesus.

In her journal, Sister Faustina, who died of tuberculosis at the age of thirty-three, also described a vision of Christ. Her vision has since been translated into a painting that has become the symbol of the Divine Mercy movement.

The writings of Sister Faustina have had a profound influence on Father Pytel, who carries with him at all times a small glass vial containing a tiny bone fragment from Faustina's body. When he prays, says the priest, he feels her presence—"like a friend."

During the October 1995 prayer vigil, Father Pytel experienced discomfort in his chest area. But these symptoms lessened when he reduced the medication prescribed to improve the function of his heart.

Then on November 9, 1995, Father Pytel visited Dr. Fortuin for a follow-up examination. Amazingly the "galloping noise" in his heart area had abated. An echocardiogram revealed that, for some inexplicable reason, his heart function had returned to normal!

When the doctor asked him what he had been doing that would account for this dramatic improvement, Father Pytel replied, "A lot of prayer—prayer and science."

Today Father Pytel firmly believes his rapid and unexpected recovery was the direct result of his prayers for intercession from the Blessed Faustina.

Dr. Fortuin, a dedicated man of science and a Protestant, does not discount Father Pytel's faith.

"I do not deny that his getting well has a lot to do with faith," said Dr. Fortuin. "I would say that spirituality is important for healing."

The doctor does add the caveat that Father Pytel's recovery, though certainly exceptional and unanticipated, was still within the realm of medical possibility.

Nevertheless, the distinguished cardiologist was so impressed by his patient's faith and the role it may have played in his recovery that he invited Father Pytel to speak with him before medical students and physicians at a Johns Hopkins cardiology seminar.

"I thought that bringing him in to discuss his faith would be enlightening to a group that is scientifically based," said Dr. Fortuin. "Hearing him, you believe in his absolute dedication to his faith."

Whether or not Father Pytel's recovery was in fact due to miraculous or medical intervention, it underscores the fact that faith in relation to healing is being discussed seriously in religious and medical circles.

In the past decade, many studies of the subject indicate that people who have strong spiritual beliefs not only lead healthier lives, less troubled by chronic complaints, but also often have swifter recoveries from serious illness.

Dale A. Matthews, an associate professor of medicine at Georgetown University Medical Center and a senior research fellow at the National Institute of Healthcare Research in Rockville, has participated in a study of 212 cases that so far found a "positive linkage" between faith and health in seventy-five percent of the cases.

"When we just use a medical approach and don't use a spiritual approach, I think patients suffer," Dr. Matthews, an evangelical Protestant who often prays with his patients, concluded from his study.

There is even a medical qualification for these impressive results. From a scientific point of view, noted Dr. Matthews, "religion probably does produce natural opiates in the brain."

A 1995 article in *Time* magazine backs up this theory. It reported on studies that suggest that praying induces a relaxation response in the body and lowers the production of so-called stress hormones. That, in turn, leads to lower heart rate, blood pressure, and respiration.

The Johns Hopkins University School of Medicine is actively exploring this theory. There, Dr. Stuart Varon, medical director of child and adolescent psychiatry at Baltimore's Sinai Hospital, teaches a course called Faith and Medicine.

The course is designed to teach young doctors to be sensitive to their patients' spiritual needs and to seek out hospital chaplains when questions arise.

"Just as a person who needs a particular medicine won't heal as well if he doesn't get it," says Dr. Varon, "so, too, if a person's sense of spirituality is not addressed, when appropriate, that, too, can be a detriment."

Nevertheless, to satisfy the Catholic Church's high criteria, a patient's recovery must be beyond medical explanation, which leaves Father Pytel's recovery still open to much theological scrutiny and debate. To date, a small army of priests, doctors, canon lawyers, and others have spent months taking sworn testimony and questioning witnesses. Even cardiologist Dr. Fortuin has testified before the fact-finding body. He speaks highly of the investigators' seriousness and thoroughness.

Bearing in mind that it took more than eleven years for the Catholic Church to authenticate the first and only miracle so far attributed to the intercession of the Blessed Faustina, Father Pytel's healing is not likely to be resolved anytime soon.

The first miracle attributed to Faustina also involved

an American. In that case, Maureen Digan, a Massachusetts woman suffering from lymphedema melroys—a rare disease that causes massive swelling—was inexplicably cured while praying at the tomb of Sister Faustina in March of 1981.

Then thirty, the young woman had undergone fifty operations, lost her right leg, and was in danger of losing her left leg when, at her husband Bob's urging, they traveled to Sister Faustina's tomb in Krakow, Poland.

At the tomb, Mrs. Digan claimed she heard a voice tell her, "If you want something, ask for it."

She responded weakly, "If you're going to do something, do it now."

Instantly, she said, the pain and the swelling in her left leg disappeared.

"I didn't have faith. I didn't think it was a healing," Mrs. Digan, a lapsed Catholic, recalled. "I thought I was having a breakdown."

But over the next few years, the young woman—who now works at the national shrine of the Divine Mercy, established by the Congregation of the Marians of the Immaculate Conception in Stockbridge, Massachusetts—was examined and questioned by medical experts who were at a loss to explain what had occurred in Poland.

Eleven years later, a commission of cardinals confirmed Maureen Digan's healing, which led to Pope John Paul II confirming Sister Faustina's beatification on April 18, 1993.

"I've wondered, 'Why me?'" says Mrs. Digan today. "And I've never come up with an answer. Maybe it is to show that God's mercy is for everyone, not just the holy people. And I wasn't holy."

Devotion to Faustina's Divine Mercy movement has gained momentum throughout the world in the past decade. Their utmost faith was evident among the fifteen thousand pilgrims who gathered at the Stockbridge shrine in 1995 on the anniversary of Sister Faustina's beatification.

"The cause (for canonization of Blessed Faustina) has proceeded quickly since her beatification because of the spread of the message of Divine Mercy," says the Reverend Shaun O'Connor, M.I.C., superior of the Marian Scholasticate in Washington, D.C.

And among church hierarchy and laymen alike, it is openly acknowledged that the pope, who has canonized a record 273 saints during his eighteen-year papacy, has a special affinity for the Polish nun and the devotion of Divine Mercy.

Back at Father Pytel's Holy Rosary Church, devotees of the Divine Mercy are, indeed, hoping for a miracle.

Father Pytel's friend, Father Gesy, has authored a book on amazing healings, *The Hem of His Garment.* And, as expected, one of the chapters details Father Pytel's experience.

Proceeds from Father Gesy's book go toward the $60,000 the church needs to erect the proposed shrine at Holy Rosary, which will house a painting of Blessed Faustina's vision symbolizing the teachings of the Divine Mercy.

One of the driving forces behind the establishment of the shrine is Holy Rosary parishioner Dottie Olszewski, who prayed for Father Pytel's recovery during a pilgrimage to Poland at the height of his life-threatening illness.

"I made a deal with Blessed Faustina," Mrs. Olszewski reveals. "I said if you go to Jesus and get Father Pytel healed, I will spend the rest of my days spreading the message of Divine Mercy and working for you to be canonized."

Regardless of what the Church ultimately determines, Dottie Olszewski is unwavering in her belief. "Was this a miracle?" she says. "Oh, absolutely."

# Priest's Amazing Healing Hands Cure Pain That Doctors Can't!

A priest with amazing healing powers cures people of everything from severe back pain to shingles—simply by laying his hands upon them, say astounded patients and doctors.

Father Andre Allemant of Avignon, France, has had such incredible success that doctors actually refer their most difficult cases to him.

"I have had patients with migraines, dermatitis, and back pain who are not reacting to traditional medication," declared local physician Michel Bonavaron. "I suggested they see Father Allemant. Often, his treatment works. He has a definite gift for healing."

Despite the seventy-one-year-old priest's impressive results, he asks no payment—except that his cured patients ease the suffering of other people.

"I start a chain of help, love, and goodwill," the priest said. "That's the real miracle."

The humble priest sees about twenty cases a week in his small two-bedroom apartment. One woman, secretary Marie Laure Sala, has a painful cyst on her wrist that doctors repeatedly removed—but it kept growing back.

After one session with Father Allemant, her wrist pain disappeared. Within a week the cyst was gone for good. "It's a miracle," she rejoiced.

More recently, Thierry Pignocchi, an insurance clerk, was suffering so badly from shingles on his left side, he couldn't move. None of the medication he was taking was helping.

"Father Allemant held his hands over my body and I felt a burning sensation," said Pignocchi. "The next day, the shingles didn't hurt—and gradually they disappeared. I was cured."

European kick-boxing champion Brigitte Pastor

thought her career was over in 1989 when she ruptured a disk in her back.

"I was in excruciating pain and barely able to walk," Pastor told the *National Enquirer*. "I was living on painkilling injections."

The priest moved his hands over her back. After three sessions she suddenly felt a searing pain rush up her spine.

"It was terrible," said Brigitte. "I thought, 'He's made it worse.' But as I yelled out in pain an immense wave of calmness flowed over me, then there was no pain whatsoever. I rushed to the hospital for an X ray—and there was no trace of a ruptured disk! It had totally cleared up.

"I went back to my boxing the very next day and became European champion in 1991. And now I'm training underprivileged children in my sport."

The elderly priest believes he heals people by channeling energy from his body into theirs.

"I feel a surge of power flood through me as I concentrate on my patients' illnesses," he explained. "I sense their own natural defenses are blocked, which is why they become ill. I send them waves of God's love and power, which restores their own ability to heal themselves."

Father Allemant, who was ordained in 1946, discovered his healing power in 1975 while working as a plumber.

The priest took on the full-time job in addition to his religious duties in order to be close to working people.

One day a secretary was complaining about severe pain in her arm and shoulder when he suddenly got the urge to take her arm in his hand and pass his other hand over it.

"She flinched, saying: 'Oh, that's very hot.' Then suddenly her pain was gone," he revealed.

Soon others were coming to him, and before long he was getting visitors from all over Europe.

"He relieved me of my crippling migraines," testified Robert Moles, codirector of the Passerelle Foundation, an organization founded by Father Allemant to help the poor. "He's a priest who stepped off his pedestal and practiced what he preaches—the love and power of God."

## She Walks Again After Miracle at Shrine

Heather Duncan was crippled for five years—but when a priest told her, "Stand up and walk," she did!

"A day never passes that I don't thank God for healing me," says Heather, a thirty-six-old mother of one.

Her longtime physician, Dr. Catherine Legg, agrees the miracle mom's sudden recovery was unexpected, and admits: "I can't offer a medical explanation for what happened."

Former nurse Heather was paralyzed from the waist down in 1985 when she fell while struggling to lift a two-hundred-pound patient at an Aberdeen, Scotland, hospital where she was working. The disks and nerves in her lower spine were severely damaged. She was in constant agony and relied on painkillers to ease her suffering. After several operations, doctors told Heather she'd be in a wheelchair for the rest of her life.

But in October 1990, Heather made a pilgrimage to the shrine of Medjugorje in Yugoslavia—and it changed her life forever.

She was at a prayer service in a graveyard when Father Peter Rookey, a Catholic priest from Chicago, laid hands on her.

"Father Rookey gave me a crucifix and told me to look at Jesus," recalled Heather. "He laid his hands on me a second time. After that, I could see Jesus! I wasn't seeing Jesus on Father Rookey's crucifix; I was seeing Him in a vision and could see nothing else. Father Rookey asked me, 'Do you believe that Jesus can heal you?' I said, 'Yes.' Then he said, 'Silver and gold I have not, but what I have I give to you. In the name of Jesus, stand up.' And a voice in the back of my head said, 'Stand up . . . stand up. . . .'"

And, incredibly, she did! Then even more incredibly, Heather walked around the graveyard!

"Everyone around me was cheering and laughing, clapping and crying," she recalled. "I laughed and cried at the same time. I kept asking, 'Am I standing straight?'"

When she got back home, an ecstatic Heather decided to surprise her husband, Brian.

"When he came in, I walked up to him and said, 'Hello, Brian. How has work been?'" recalled Heather.

Brian, thirty-eight, said: "All I could say was, 'You're walking beautifully. I don't believe it.'"

Heather, who now runs and swims, is convinced her recovery is nothing short of a miracle. "My five years of pain are over and I've never looked back," she said with joy. "For me, to walk is a gift from God."

## Priest Stuns Experts with Miracle Cures

- A policeman with incurable throat cancer is healed overnight!
- A wheelchair-bound housewife gets up and walks!
- A taxi driver on crutches for four years throws them away—and is now an enthusiastic jogger!

Those are just three of the many amazing cures credited to Father Serafino Falvo, a Catholic priest who conducts regular healing services in Pontassieve, Italy.

"That priest has extraordinary healing powers," Dr. Mario Lo Cascio, an Italian physician, told the *National Enquirer.*

Dr. Lo Cascio said he thoroughly studied the three seemingly miraculous cures of housewife Rosetta Cardella, cabbie Gilberto Vivarelli, and policeman Ferruccio Zara.

"I personally checked their medical records—and much to my astonishment, I had to conclude that their healings were not explainable from a scientific point of view," he said.

Taxi driver Vivarelli, sixty-one, severely injured his spine after falling from a ladder in 1985. "I had been on crutches four years," he said. "I couldn't take a single step without them."

But in 1989, friends talked him into attending a healing service conducted by Father Falvo.

"He laid his hands on me and prayed and I felt life coming back into my legs. I threw my crutches away and walked up and down in front of the crowd. Since then, I've even started jogging!" said the cured cabbie.

Rosetta Cardella said that for almost three years her life was just torture. She suffered from a severe form of diabetes that led to a bone disease and an ulcer on the sole of her right foot. Every movement caused her tremendous pain.

Doctors told her that she would have to resign herself to a wheelchair existence. Then someone told her about Father Falvo and urged Rosetta to attend his meetings in 1988.

"When the priest stopped in front of me, smiling, and laid his hands on me, I was immediately able to get up from my wheelchair and walk away without any pain at all. My foot ulcer quickly disappeared and my bones didn't hurt anymore," remembers Rosetta.

"And when I walked into my doctor's office on my own two feet, he looked at me as if I was a ghost. He couldn't believe his eyes. He examined me thoroughly and had to admit I had entirely recovered—but he was unable to give any scientific explanation."

Police officer Ferruccio Zara said doctors told him in 1988 he had only one or two years to live because of incurable throat cancer. But one day two years later, after attending a healing service conducted by Father Falvo, he says he was cured.

"He laid his hands on my shoulders and prayed out loud to Jesus to help me," Zara said. "I felt like a fire was burning in my throat. I went home feeling very strange.

"The next morning I got up and realized a miracle had taken place. The black patch in my throat, where the tumor was, had disappeared. I rushed to my doctor, who couldn't believe it. He put me through various X-ray tests. Then he said to me: 'The cancer has completely disappeared and I can't explain how it happened.' But I know how it happened. It was Father Falvo's prayers."

Dr. Pietro Prestifilippo, another Italian physician who has witnessed astounding healings performed by Father Falvo, said: "I've seen an old paralytic throw away his crutches and walk off briskly. I've seen a child with polio get up from his wheelchair and run into his astonished mother's arms."

Father Falvo, who's been practicing healing since the early 1970s, said: "It's not me who performs the miracles. It's man's faith and the power of God that performs miracles through me."

# A Humble Man with Miracle Hands

Brother Solanus Casey was a humble man, born in a modest three-room log cabin south of Prescott, Wisconsin, in 1870. But during his lifetime he became known to thousands of people as a man with a mysterious power for healing.

Hundreds of healings have been attributed to this Catholic monk, who was declared "venerable" by Pope John Paul II—the first man in the United States to be so honored.

When he worked as a porter at a monastery in Detroit, he became known as a man with miraculous hands. People used to line up at the monastery door, seeking his guidance and prayers. Hundreds of healings have been credited to him.

Brother Casey kept meticulous diary notes about his "patients." Among those healed were a woman dying of pneumonia, a woman who recovered her memory after a concussion, a man in a mental hospital who was released and returned to work a few months after his family interceded with Casey for him, and a woman whose cataracts reportedly vanished without surgery.

And a Detroit woman claimed—twenty years after Casey's death—that prayers to him cured her of arthritic pain in her hands. In 1995, Brother Casey was declared venerable—the first step toward sainthood—by Pope John Paul II. This is a singular honor, considering there is only one American saint as of 1996, Sister Elizabeth Ann Seton.

Brother Michael Crosby, who wrote an eight-hundred-page book about Casey's life for the Vatican's Office for Saints' Causes, says it was not the miracles that impressed him most about Casey.

"Everybody looks at him for all the unbelievable

things he could remember and the miracles," Brother Crosby says. "But for me, the most impressive thing was, he had a one hundred percent trust in God. He's been a real model for me."

## Thousands Flock to See Man Who Bleeds Like Christ

For years, devout Christian Giorgio Bongiovanni has been bleeding from mysterious wounds in his hands, feet, and side—just like those Jesus Christ suffered on the Cross!

The miraculous wounds—called stigmata—have drawn thousands to the holy man's house for his blessing. And a team of government-appointed doctors who examined the twenty-eight-year-old from Porto Sant'Elpidio, Italy, have no explanation for Giorgio's condition or why he doesn't die from blood loss.

"These wounds are definitely not self-inflicted," declares Dr. Stanis Previato, head of the psychiatry department of Rovigo, Italy's university hospital, and a member of the government team of doctors. "It would be impossible for someone to inflict these wounds on himself. They are deep and a person would lose consciousness from shock long before he was able to inflict them. We can also tell by the angle of punctures that he could not have done this to himself. His wounds are very painful."

Dr. Frederico Finatti, an official with Italy's National Health Agency and head of the team, is amazed that there are no signs of infection. He told the *National Enquirer*: "My colleagues and I concluded that the wounds weren't explainable in light of known medical experience."

Added Dr. Maria Luisa Viel: "I examined Bongiovanni but couldn't scientifically explain the origins of the wounds, or why, despite constant bleeding, he didn't suffer from serious anemia."

Giorgio said he started bleeding in 1989 after a series of visits from the Virgin Mary.

"One day I left the shoe factory where I worked," recalled Giorgio. "All of a sudden, I had a vision of a beautiful woman levitating above the ground. It was the Virgin Mary.

"I fell on my knees. I heard her voice: 'Don't be afraid, son. I am Mary, and I have a mission for you.' "

But just as suddenly, the woman disappeared.

He says he was visited again by Christ's mother in September of the same year while praying at her shrine in Fatima, and she gave him this message:

"You, Giorgio, must suffer to remind people of my Son. You must travel the world to evoke the pain of Jesus, suffered because of the sins of the world."

Then a bolt of light shot from the image of Mary and struck him, causing his hands to bleed, recounted Giorgio. Soon after, blood started to flow from his feet as well.

"I began to journey around the world, as the Virgin Mary told me," said Giorgio. "I went to Russia, where I was interviewed by journalists. More than 150 million Russians heard my message on TV.

"I went to Spain, where I met Queen Sophia, who introduced me to Mikhail Gorbachev and his wife, Raisa."

And wherever Giorgio goes, thousands flock to see him go into a trance and communicate with Mary. Many claim to be healed by him, but Giorgio says he's not responsible for the cures—God is.

"I keep saying to all of them that they owe their healings only to their prayers to the Virgin Mary and their faith in God."

# Miracle Cure
# After Twenty-seven Years

After twenty-seven years in a wheelchair, crippled grandma Jean Neil went to an evangelical service where she sprang to her feet and ran to the stage—totally cured of all the ailments that plagued her!

Even more mysterious, the fifty-seven-year-old Englishwoman says she foresaw her miraculous healing six weeks earlier when she met the presiding evangelist, Pastor Reinhard Bonnke, in an eerie dream!

Exclaimed her amazed doctor, orthopedic surgeon Stephen Eisenstein of England's Oswestry Orthopedic Hospital: "I've examined Jean and she is completely cured as a result of a religious experience. She has no pain and ran up and down hospital corridors to show me she has no limit to her movements."

Before the 1992 service, Jean suffered not only paralysis but near-blindness, severe heart problems, chronic pain, and other ailments.

Today, incredibly, she goes hang gliding!

"The minute I saw Pastor Bonnke, I knew he would heal me. I recognized him from my dream," said Jean, of Rugby, England. "Praise the Lord—it's a miracle!"

Dr. Colin West of Rugby, who treated her for five years, declared: "I can confirm that Jean Neil spent twenty-seven years in a wheelchair and now is cured. How this pastor succeeded where I failed will remain a complete mystery to us. It's unbelievable!"

Jean's spine was broken when a practical joker pulled a rug out from under her feet, causing her to fall hard to the floor.

"It was the start of more than a quarter-century of excruciating pain and despair," said the married mother of four. "So many times I wanted to kill myself. It was only my loving family that stopped me from committing suicide. I had fifteen operations, none of which helped. I was taking painkillers but was in constant agony.

"Then in 1981 I was in a car accident. My head went through the windshield, leaving my sight damaged. I also injured my leg. Later I developed angina, bronchitis, and a hernia, and eventually I had three heart attacks. I became totally blind for six months. At times my pain was so bad, I'd black out."

Then, in February 1988, Jean dreamed of being healed in a stadium by a "tall, large man with a foreign accent," she said.

Six weeks later, she and her husband accompanied a group of youngsters from their local church to a Pentecostal youth rally in Birmingham, England. She immediately recognized the German evangelist, Pastor Bonnke, as the man in her dream.

During the service, Pastor Bonnke kept looking around as if searching for someone. He began running through the crowd, pushing people aside until he got to Jean.

"He put his hands on my shoulders and suddenly a surge of warmth and energy flooded through my body. A pain like a hot knife shot into my spine," recalls Jean. "I heard the pastor say, 'Get up and walk in the name of Jesus.' I stood up—and walked! Then I began to run and run and run. I ran through the crowd to the stage with tears running down my face. I was so happy! I jumped and danced and touched my toes as twelve thousand people cheered."

Declared Dr. West: "Jean is now totally cured of ALL her illnesses—her eyesight has improved, she has no more heart problems, she can walk. I can't explain it."

Several years after she was healed, Jean is still as healthy as a teenager. Before her cure, she says she was so helpless she had to have other people bathe her and even take her to the bathroom.

"But now I swim, jog, play football, ride horses, do

gardening, and go hang gliding. During a trip to South Africa I even rode an ostrich!"

When contacted by the *National Enquirer,* Pastor Bonnke explained: "Jean Neil was cured by a miracle from God. I wasn't the least bit surprised. The Holy Spirit had told me, 'That woman will be healed tonight.' "

Jean added joyously: "After the rally, I went to see my local doctor—and when I walked in he almost fell off his chair. He said, 'Which doctor have you been to see?' I told him, 'Dr. Jesus.' "

## Thousands Flock to Grave of Louisiana Miracle Worker

Four decades after the death of a saintly twelve-year-old, thousands of pilgrims are flocking to her grave site, hoping for miraculous cures.

So many inexplicable healings have been attributed already to "Cajun Saint" Charlene Richard that the Catholic Church has taken the first steps toward canonizing her as America's next saint.

"She is already a saint to me," declared one "pilgrim," Billie Jo Dodson, whose daughter Nicole was healed of cancer after prayers to the little Cajun saint.

In yet another miracle healing, a respected doctor claims one of his patients literally came back from the dead after her family prayed to Charlene. And a cancer-stricken woman was transformed into a picture of health after touching the dead child's tombstone.

Charlene herself died of leukemia back in 1959. But even as she lay dying, the deeply religious twelve-year-old spent her last days devoutly praying to God to ease the pain and suffering of other sick people.

The cure of Billie Jo's daughter—little cancer patient Nicole—is among the most illustrative and most dramatic proof of the wondrous powers of the deceased Charlene Richard.

Nicole was barely two when she was stricken with the rare cancer neuroblastoma, which attacks the central nervous system. For nine months, little Nicole underwent painful chemotherapy.

"Then one night Nicole said she wanted to speak to Charlene," recalled her grandmother, Miriam Price, fifty-five. "We didn't know any Charlene, so I asked her where Charlene was. 'In heaven—with Jesus. She told me to be a good girl,' answered little Nicole."

Two weeks later, Mrs. Price, after making extensive inquiries, was told the story of Louisiana's saintly Charlene.

"So we took Nicole to Charlene's grave, but didn't tell her where she was going," said Mrs. Price. "When we got there we showed her Charlene's picture on the tomb and asked Nicole who it was. She told us right away, 'Charlene!' How could she have known?"

The family spent three hours at the graveside, praying fervently for Nicole's recovery. Today, she is a strapping, lively eleven-year-old—a living miracle.

Cancer specialist Dr. Jerome Broussard of Lafayette, Louisiana, became convinced of little Charlene's miraculous powers after a baffling experience with a twenty-five-year-old pregnant woman in his operating room.

"Her heart had stopped. She was blue, and I had to operate immediately to save the baby. The anesthetist tried to perform CPR on her, but it seemed hopeless," Dr. Broussard, fifty, later recalled to a reporter. "Then she started to breathe again! After the procedure, her family, who had been waiting outside, told me they had been praying to Charlene while I carried out the operation. They said they were convinced everything was going to be okay.

"I've got to be honest—they had a lot more faith than me that she'd make it. What happened comes about as close to a miracle as you'll ever see. That woman literally came back from the dead. It made a believer out of me."

Rocke Roy of Lafayette also is certain that "the little saint" worked a miracle for his daughter Tara, who developed a deadly form of colon cancer at age twenty-one.

"Even after surgery, Tara was in a terrible way— weak, pale, and sick," recalls fifty-four-year-old Roy.

"We prayed at Charlene's grave for help . . . and an incredible transformation came over Tara. As she knelt touching Charlene's headstone, suddenly it was as if electricity ran from the tomb into her entire body!

"I saw her neck redden with color and she was transformed from a pitiful physical wreck into an erect and vibrant young woman filled with life! Now she's twenty-five and completely free of cancer."

Father Joseph Brennan, the hospital chaplain who comforted dying Charlene, observes: "Yes, I'm convinced she has been responsible for a whole series of miracles."

The respect that is growing for Charlene—and the fact she's being considered for sainthood—has brought joy to the heart of Charlene's now seventy-one-year-old mom, Mary Alice Richard. She says: "It gives me a lot of comfort to know that she's still with us—and still thinking about and helping others."

## Tiny Greek Island Is a Miracle Mecca

For miracle seekers, the tiny Greek island of Tinos is a magnet. A religious shrine there draws thousands of worshipers each year—and it is credited with astonishing recoveries.

Greeks both rich and poor stream across the Aegean Sea by ferryboat to pray at the Shrine of the Annunciation, which contains an ancient picture of the Virgin Mary. And many leave behind gold and silver gifts—expressions of thanks from the paralyzed who can suddenly walk, the deaf who can once again hear, and the blind whose vision was miraculously restored.

"Every molecule of this shrine is living proof of the Virgin's miracles," said Father Anthimos, abbot of the monastery of monks who look after the shrine.

One of the most remarkable recent recoveries reported in the *National Enquirer* involves Nektarios, a twenty-five-year-old man from northern Greece whose legs had been paralyzed for sixteen years. His parents pushed him in his wheelchair into the shrine, where they stayed and prayed for three days and nights. On the fourth day they wheeled their son up close to the picture.

"As they began to lift him so he could light a votive candle, Nektarios pushed away his parents' helping hands and walked slowly by himself—trembling and unsteady at first—through the crowd of worshipers," said Father Anthimos. "Many fell to their knees, openmouthed and in awe as Nektarios walked past. Some cried out in wonder and prayer. This is something I saw with my own eyes."

To get to the sacred shrine, the devout slowly and painfully inch their way on their knees up a seven-hundred-yard steep incline as an act of penance. Then they continue on their knees up a series of marble steps covered with carpet until they can gaze on the precious picture, which is a thousand years old and made of hammered gold and silver.

"I've made that painful climb myself as a pilgrimage of faith," Chris Eliou, a journalist from Athens, reported.

Sometimes the sacred picture travels to the sick. In 1915, King Constantine I of Greece was seriously ill and doctors feared for his life. The picture was put by the king's deathbed.

"Barely conscious, the king kissed the picture," said Eliou. The illness instantly began to recede and within a few days the king was again in full health."

## Paralyzed Man Walks for First Time in Sixteen Years

"It's a miracle! It's a miracle!"

That was the ecstatic cry of Jean Salaun, who moved his arms and legs—and even jumped for joy—for the first time in sixteen years, after a visit to the famed Lourdes religious healing shrine.

Stricken with multiple sclerosis in 1977, the fifty-eight-year-old milk worker was left almost completely paralyzed—unable to walk and as helpless as a baby.

Today he walks, totes groceries, rides a bike, and even visits other sick people.

"I have investigated Jean Salaun's healing—and there is no scientific explanation for it," declared Dr. Roger Pilon, chief of the Lourdes International Medical Bureau, which examines healings reported at the shrine. "There is no doubt in my mind that a true miracle has occurred."

"I couldn't do anything by myself," Salaun told reporters after his healing. He recalled: "The government paid for a person to help me shave, get dressed, and do everything else."

Desperate for a cure, Salaun—who lives in La Loupe, France—visited Lourdes in August 1992. But his condition didn't change, so he went back to Lourdes for another try the following year. While staying at a hospital near the shrine, Salaun was praying one morning when the Virgin Mary suddenly appeared to him.

"She was very young and beautiful, dressed all in white, but barefoot," he recalled to the *National Enquirer*. "She had blue eyes and was smiling at me. She said, 'Stand up! Stand up!' But I was petrified. I couldn't move."

Later, Salaun's son helped him bathe at the shrine in a pool filled with holy water. But he failed to improve.

Deeply disappointed, he went home the next day. He was resting when an icy chill shot through his body. Then a burning heat consumed him.

"Suddenly I realized I could move my hands and my arms," Salaun recalled. "Then I stood up by myself. Next I stretched my left arm, then my right arm, and then my legs to make sure I was cured. I began jumping for joy, crying and hugging my wife. She was crying, too. We thanked the Lord and the Virgin for my miracle.

"Now I am perfectly well. I walk with my wife and carry the groceries. I even visit other sick people to give them hope."

Dr. Pilon added: "Mr. Salaun's healing is much more than a remission. Multiple sclerosis remissions occur fairly gradually, usually over several months. Salaun's recovery happened literally overnight. That's unheard of."

Father Joseph Hercouet, who organized Salaun's trip to Lourdes, declared: "There is no medical explanation for this miraculous cure. It's truly extraordinary."

## Miracles of the "Floating Nun"

A remarkable Buddhist holy woman known throughout her native Thailand as the "Floating Nun" miraculously heals the gravely ill and dying on a daily basis.

This is the amazing message from hundreds who have witnessed and felt the awesome powers of soft-spoken eighty-four-year-old worker of wonders, Sister Chan Rueylae.

Every year she is visited by thousands upon thousands of people suffering incurable illnesses, from cancer to paralysis. All have but one hope—to be cured by the nun who prays for her power to work while floating in a lotus pool for several hours each day.

And thousands say they have been healed!

"I am absolutely convinced of her ability to cure the sick. I've seen it with my own eyes," confirms Dr. Decha Sookarom, medical director of Decha General Hospital in Bangkok, Thailand.

The sick who visit Sister Rueylae come from all faiths and many travel hundreds of miles to her home, the Temple of the Golden Dragon's Cave in Nongyassi, Thailand. Some say their ailments vanished after they rinsed their hands in the pool where the nun floats. Others say she has healed them with potions. And still more swear they've been cured by her touch.

Farmer Wirat Chumsaeng, fifty-two, said he'd be dead if it weren't for Sister Rueylae. "Treatment was unsuccessful," says Wirat, who visited the Floating Nun a year ago at the suggestion of friends. "She touched my arm and blew smoke she inhaled from a candle directly at me.

"Then she gave me an herb medicine and told me to take it every day, followed by a prayer she gave me. In two months, a medical exam showed I had no tumor, and a recent checkup shows it's still gone."

Sugarcane grower Sanit Samaikong, forty-seven, suffered permanent nerve damage after tumbling down a ravine in 1984. Her arms and hands shook violently and her right leg was paralyzed.

"I had to hobble about with a cane I could barely control because of my trembling," she said.

After six years of suffering, Sanit visited Sister

Rueylae in 1990. The nun rubbed holy oil onto her arms and massaged it into her bad leg.

"In three weeks my shaking was completely gone," says the sugarcane grower. "What's more, my bad leg got better, and within two months, I was back to work."

Dr. Decha talked with the physicians for both the sugarcane grower and the farmer and verified that the patients were "mysteriously cured after being treated by the nun."

Sister Rueylae says a revered Buddhist nun taught her healing techniques and how to float on water while meditating.

She began her wondrous ways five years ago. The nun said people have told her they've been cured simply by rinsing their hands in the pool.

"Above all, I remind people to have faith. Many thousands have returned to say, 'Thank you for saving my life,' " she said.

Dr. Sumon Keanpintong, a government public health officer in Thailand, confirmed there's no scientific explanation for Sister Rueylae's power to heal. And he added: "There's no doubt people have been cured by this nun."

# Grandmom's Miracle Hands Cure Hundreds

A remarkable grandmother whose body spontaneously erupts with stigmata—the wounds of Jesus Christ—has cured hundreds of people with serious illnesses, including cancer, say researchers.

And each year thousands of the sick and dying still flock to the farm of sixty-six-year-old Maria Esperanza de Bianchini in Betania, Venezuela, where they, too, wait for their own miracles.

"There is no medical explanation for hundreds of cures attributed to Maria's intervention," Father Bernard Heffernan, who heads the Catholic Diocese of Petersborough, Ontario, Canada, and has investigated Maria's amazing abilities, told the *National Enquirer.*

Remarkably, a Harvard-educated surgeon with deadly cancer made a pilgrimage to Maria's farm and says he was cured by her.

"I was devastated when I found out that my prostate problem was the result of a malignant cancer that had spread to my lower spine," said Dr. Vinicio Arrieta, who lives in Maracaibo, Venezuela. "It was causing me great pain and I was given only months to live. My wife encouraged me to go to see Maria."

Dr. Arrieta joined five thousand visitors at Maria's farm and prayed with the holy woman. "I suddenly felt an infusion of heat within me that went straight down into my spinal column and prostate," he said. "I knew at that moment I was cured."

Medical examinations showed he was cancer-free, and Dr. Arrieta says he has not had a recurrence of the disease since he made that fateful pilgrimage in 1989.

"An unexplainable cure took place in Dr. Arrieta's case," said Dr. Vinicio Pax, chief of the nuclear medicine department at Maracaibo's Clinico Hospital. He verified the results of tests done on Dr. Arrieta after the surgeon visited Maria.

Josie Jackson, fifty-eight, of Marina Del Ray, California, traveled to Maria's farm recently after all medical attempts to treat a severe skin disease failed.

"The rash on my skin covered my arms, shoulders, and neck. I looked like a reptile," Josie said. "I prayed with Maria. She took my head in her hands and blessed me and I could feel this deep warmth coming into me. That day, my skin cleared up completely. I was astounded."

Although visitors seeking cures visit Maria's farm

all year round, stigmata only appear on her body every Good Friday, the anniversary of Christ's Crucifixion.

"Blood pours slowly out of her palms and drips off her hands," said Father Heffernan. "You see on her face that Maria's in great pain, yet she continues to minister to people. At the end of the day, the wounds heal and there are no scars."

Despite the special gift she has, Maria is a typical housewife. She and her husband Leo have seven children and twelve grandchildren.

Maria was twelve when she revealed that the Blessed Virgin appeared to her and told her to marry and live among the people, said Father Heffernan. Said the priest: "Maria is a person with fantastic God-given powers."

# Chapter Three

❦

# Skin-of-the-Teeth Miracles

A skin-of-the-teeth miracle is exactly what it sounds like—a miracle that comes along at the eleventh hour . . . when you've given up all hope and are resigned to the worst of fates.

These kinds of miracles happen every day, as you'll see from the following collection of miraculous escapes and survival—some of which made headlines over the past few years.

## White-water Miracle in Costa Rica

An anxious group of tourists and their guides watched fearfully as a young ex-cop with tears in his eyes worked frantically to revive a young woman who had just been miraculously plucked from certain death in the raging white-water rapids of a Central American river.

The resuscitation efforts of thirty-nine-year-old Robert

Angelino paid off. After giving CPR for several ago-
nizing minutes, he leaned over the lifeless body and
urgently called her name, "Cynthia! Cynthia!"

Amazingly, her eyes flickered open. She even gave
a shy smile in response.

The teary-eyed group standing around spontaneously burst into a round of applause. All agreed they
had witnessed a miracle. Only a few minutes before,
Cynthia, a twenty-nine-year-old mother of three, had
been close to death. When pulled from the water, she
was ice-cold and unconscious, bluish in color and unable to breath on her own.

As a member of that tour group from Florida, this
is a truly dramatic miracle story to which I can personally attest.

It was an amazing series of fortunate coincidences
that led up to the rescue and resuscitation on the
banks of the treacherous, fast-flowing River Pacuare
in the rugged, desolate mountains above San Jose,
Costa Rica.

It began on July 6, 1997—a day rescuer Robert
Angelino of Palm Beach Gardens, Florida, and his
companions will never forget.

"The memory will stay with me for the rest of my
life," said Robert. "What's particularly amazing is how
a series of fortunate accidents enabled us to be in the
right place at the right time."

It began for Robert and his Florida tour group companions early on a Sunday morning when they left the
Balmoral Hotel in San Jose for a white-water rafting
adventure. Bob had mixed feelings when he left his
hotel. He was looking forward to the rafting trip. But
he had another, sadder mission.

He hadn't originally planned on joining his companions on that particular July 4 excursion. His beloved
cousin, veteran Palm Beach County sheriff's officer
Captain John McGuire—who had been a regular on

previous trips—had died just a few months earlier. Robert had pledged to scatter his ashes in the picturesque vacation spot his cousin had loved so much.

Robert's thoughts were with his late cousin and the happy times they had spent together on previous vacations as he sat on the tour bus heading into the mountains above San Jose to the white-water departure point.

That trip was in itself an eventful one. The bus was fifteen minutes late picking the group up at the hotel. Then they were further delayed because a road had washed out and the bus was rerouted.

On the long bus trip, members of the tour group passed the time exchanging stories about unforgettable moments in their lives. The story Robert Angelino told had particular relevance. He recalled an incident that happened in 1983 when he was a police officer in Palm Beach Gardens, Florida.

"I don't know why that story was so vivid in my mind that day. Perhaps it was because that also happened on a Sunday morning," remembers Robert.

"Back then I was called upon to give emergency CPR to a three-month-old baby girl who had taken a seizure. I worked on her desperately. But I couldn't save her life. I felt really bad about it, although doctors told me later the baby had been dead about ten minutes before I started working on her."

"I remember one of my fellow bus passengers—a young American tourist called Michelle—asking me how it was possible to stay calm and retain your composure in an emergency situation like that. I told her you have to, because you might be the only person capable of saving another person's life at any given moment, and people are depending on you."

His own words were still echoing in Robert's mind a few hours later when he was given a second chance to save a life under eerily similar circumstances.

Arriving at the white-water rafting starting point

several hours late—fortuitously, as it turned out—the group split into crews and, under the supervision of skilled rafting guides, suited up in life vests and helmets and were assigned to three different rafts.

The rafts were guided by an advance man in a kayak—in this case an experienced river guide named Sebastian—whose job it was to scout ahead and warn of any dangers.

The American group's first quarter of a mile wasn't without incident. A young woman paddler took a spill and had to be fished out of the torrent by Sebastian. She was so shaken up that the group had to pull ashore for ten minutes so she could calm down. Then they continued their adventure downstream.

Three miles into the excursion they heard faint cries for help. Peering through the dense spray from the rapids, Robert and his companions could see a child about eleven years old clinging to a large rock about three times his size that jutted out in the river.

The boy was desperately yelling for help. Fearing he was about to be swept away at any moment, their boat guide and instructor, Luis, yelled for the group to paddle "hard forward." But as the raft approached the boy, they saw him manage to scramble up the rock, leap to another set of rocks, and make it safely back to shore.

"My heart jumped to my throat when I saw the little boy in danger. I thought immediately of my own son Danny, who is six," remembers Robert. "My heart filled with joy when I saw him reach the shore and safety.

"I stopped paddling for about one second, and began to relax. Then I could see the boy pointing downstream. He was yelling in Spanish, 'Save my mama.' I didn't understand what he was saying, but our guide Luis did. He began yelling for us to paddle harder.

"When we paddled past the rock the boy had been clinging to, I saw her. She was so small in that big

raging river . . . floating facedown with her arms at
her side and her feet and legs together. I guessed she
was about four feet six and seventy pounds, and—at
the time—she appeared to be a dainty little girl about
ten years old. I knew if we didn't get to her soon she
would die.

"We began paddling as if our lives depended on it.
She was approximately 150 yards in front of our raft.
We began to close the gap fast.

"Sebastian in his kayak got to her first. He managed
to pull her onto his kayak. I saw him trying to give
her mouth-to-mouth as his flimsy craft swirled and
tossed in the angry rapids. The kayak spun around
and flipped in the churning rapids. Sebastian lost his
grip on the girl and she slid off the front of the kayak
and back into the rapids.

"Her body disappeared completely beneath the turbulent waters. We couldn't even see Sebastian and his
kayak. We thought they were gone too.

"Horrified, we paddled toward the spot, putting everything we had into our effort. My heart was in my
throat as I prayed for them to surface, and for the
energy to keep paddling long enough to catch up to
them.

"Already I was thinking about CPR. I was conscious
of going over the procedures in my head. *Look, listen,
feel. Two breaths, check for pulse. No pulse, start compressions; if there is a pulse, no compressions . . .*

"Then Sebastian and his kayak reappeared ahead.
Then the girl's body, still floating facedown, propelled
by the strong current. Then the river calmed to the
point where Sebastian was once again able to pull the
drowning girl from the water onto the front of the
kayak.

"Another raft guide, Ivan, took off his life jacket
and dove off our raft to swim over to assist Sebastian
in getting the girl to shore.

"At this point, we had paddled so hard we were

cramping. I'm a big guy, but I felt as if my arms were about to fall off. When we saw they had the girl, we turned our raft toward shore about fifty yards ahead.

"As we beached the raft on a very rocky bank and jumped out of the raft, my foot slipped on a rock and I felt my left ankle collapse. Down I went on the rocks.

"My buddy from Florida, Michael Cusick, was beside me in an instant. He grabbed my right arm, threw it over his shoulders, and began carrying me toward the bank.

"The adrenaline was flowing. It must have given Mike superhuman strength—I weigh 275 pounds and Mike weighs around 175. But we were aware that every second counted if that young girl was to live."

Mike Cusick of West Palm Beach, Florida, remembers: "I could tell Robert was relentless in his efforts to get to the side of the girl. His story about once being unsuccessful in saving a young girl despite his efforts at CPR was still fresh in our memories.

"It was only natural he was the most intense and concerned among us. I was sure he had seriously injured himself when he jumped over the bow, onto the rocks, falling to his knees in shock and pain. But as I followed him out of the raft, all he could say was, 'I think I broke my ankle (it turned out to be a severe sprain). Help me to get to her!'

"Despite his injury and pain, he was still so focused on the task that I just had to help get him to the dying girl. Together we hobbled to the team of guides crouched over the small, still form on the beach.

"When we arrived, I took her wrist and immediately found her pulse. She was still alive!"

Robert Angelino continues: "When they reached her she was stretched out on the bank, unconscious and not breathing on her own. The others had begun to work on her. But I saw her neck wasn't properly elevated, nor was her nose properly pinched closed. I saw bubbles escaping from her nostrils.

"I eased myself beside her and closed the girl's nostrils with my fingers, lifted her neck, tilted her head back—to clear an airway—and gave her two short breaths.

"She responded—almost immediately I saw her stomach move up and down. It was obvious she had a pocket of water bloating her belly. When I thought she was starting to breathe on her own, I rolled her on her side to get the water out.

"She still wasn't out of danger. Her eyes were rolled back so only the whites showed through half-open eyelids. She was stark white, ice-cold to the touch, and light to medium blue around her eyes and mouth.

"I asked for someone to find out her name so I could see if she would respond to it. Her name was Cynthia. I called out her name a foot from her left ear, and her eyelids opened slowly. Her beautiful brown eyes rolled back down into place.

"Her eyes began focusing, her pulse became more rapid, and when someone asked her in Spanish if she was all right, Cynthia started to smile."

At that point the rafters standing around clapped their hands and cheered. Her family gathered around her. That's when Bob and his companions learned that the angelic-looking little girl they had rescued was in fact twenty-nine years old and the mother of three children.

It turned out that Cynthia had jumped into the water to save their small black family dog, which had slipped from a rock and was swept away by the current.

Drained of energy after the tense rescue, Bob Angelino limped from the rescue spot where Cynthia was being hugged and comforted by family and friends and found himself a quiet sandy spot where he could kneel and pray.

"As I prayed, tears of joy and thanks streamed down my cheeks. I remember thanking my late cousin

John McGuire for his help," said Bob later. "I could feel his presence with me that day. I knew he was beside me giving me the energy to paddle when I was totally exhausted. And I knew he was beside me as I worked to revive the dying girl."

Mike Cusick is also convinced that there was a higher power looking out for Cynthia and her rescuers that memorable Fourth of July weekend.

"Robert's efforts were commendable, but we should also be grateful for the strength and courage of all of the river guides who allowed us to save that woman's life.

"But, above all, it was the will of God that we should have timed our journey on that river so that their abilities and ours would be there when they were needed. If we had passed three minutes sooner, we would have only waved to the family playing on the riverbank. Three minutes later, and we would have pulled her dead body from below the next rapids. Praise be to God."

Adds Robert Angelino: "I felt guilty about leaving Cynthia that day. In fact, I will always feel guilty until I see her again, and she tells me everything is okay in her life.

"That rescue was an intensely moving experience for me. In fact, it was for all of us. On the road back, everyone felt they had been witnesses to a miracle. It was an experience that bonded us together like steel bridge cables, never to be frayed or separated."

## No, Miracles Are Not a Once-in-a-Lifetime Occurrence!

Most people are allowed only one miracle in their lifetime, but electric company repairman Randall Champion has had *two* in his life.

Both times, while working as a troubleshooter for Florida's Jacksonville Electric Company, he survived massive jolts of electricity. The second one zapped his body with a whopping 26,000 volts of electricity, the same amount of power a death row inmate gets in the electric chair!

Randall's first electrifying experience was in 1967 when he was an apprentice electrician working atop a utility pole. He accidentally brushed against a 4,200-volt power line and was knocked unconscious, leaving him dangling precariously by his safety belt from the pole.

A quick-thinking colleague shimmied up to him and saved his life by giving immediate mouth-to-mouth resuscitation. He fully recovered after a short stay in the hospital.

His second brush with death was on September 9, 1991, when a sizzling 26,000 volts shot through his body as he stood in a lift bucket next to the top of a utility pole. He was rushed to the hospital with severe body burns, and doctors feared that his heart or lungs would give out as a result of the severe shock.

But again Randall rallied and went on to make a full recovery.

Clyde Montgomery, a spokesman for his bosses, confirms: "Randall's the luckiest, unluckiest guy I ever heard of."

## The Luck of the Reillys!

The Reilly clan are the first to admit that a miracle was at work the time their car plunged fifty feet off a bridge, landing upside down—and all five family members walked away from the wreck unscathed.

"It was a spectacular crash. It's remarkable the family survived," declared Lieutenant John Marcello of the Worcester, Massachusetts, fire department after the accident.

Their chilling brush with death happened when a drunk driver smashed into the Reillys' 1989 Buick Century on a Worcester bridge. The Buick was carrying David Reilly, wife Maureen, and their three children, a boy and two girls, aged seven, five, and two.

An oncoming speeding car swiped the Reilly car on the driver's side, sending it scooting up a snowbank, over a guardrail—off the bridge and into the air.

As it was airborne, the Buick flipped over. The windshield was shattered as the branches of a tree smashed through it, narrowly missing driver David as he huddled beneath the dash.

The car eventually came to rest upside down in a parking lot fifty feet beneath the bridge. The roof buckled, but amazingly didn't collapse.

David and Maureen squeezed their way out of the wreckage and pulled their kids to safety. Amazingly, apart from a few cuts and bruises, no one was injured.

David later summed up the incident: "I consider us terribly lucky. It's a miracle we survived."

## It's a Miracle She Survived!

Swept out to sea by an overpowering current, forty-four-year-old diver Vivienne Slear, an auditor from Edgewater Park, New Jersey, spent twenty-seven terrifying hours in shark-infested waters before she was able to fight her way to shore—twenty miles from her dive site!

"It's a miracle she survived—there's no other word for it," was how veteran Caribbean diver Donna Yawching described Vivienne's miraculous escape from death.

Friends were so sure that she was forever lost at sea that they were planning to hold a memorial service for her on the day she returned from the dead!

Vivienne was spending a carefree week's diving vacation off the island of Tobago with friends. On March 17, 1997, she and seven other divers back-flipped off their dive boat about a mile offshore. To her horror, when Vivienne surfaced after a thirty-minute dive, she discovered a current had swept her more than half a mile from the dive boat.

Frantically she tried to swim toward the boat, but it was hopeless. The current was too strong.

Still wearing her wet suit, oxygen tank, flippers, and buoyancy vest, Vivienne found herself being swept further out to sea. Soon she found herself at least two miles from the coastline.

Feeling totally abandoned, she began swimming toward the beach. But it was an exercise in futility. The powerful current was like a barrier, pushing her further and further out to sea. She almost gave up hope. She almost resigned herself to a watery death.

As the day wore on, she found herself buffeted by ten-foot waves. The strong eighty-five-degree Caribbean sun also pounded her mercilessly.

It was even worse when it turned dark. She remembered reading somewhere that sharks liked to feed at night. And she knew the waters she was in were home to many hungry sharks.

She felt like shark bait, just waiting to be eaten, as she bobbed alone on the surface in the eerie darkness.

Vivienne gave a prayer of thanks when dawn eventually broke. She found she was still in the grip of a powerful current—but this time it was propelling her shoreward.

At one-thirty that afternoon she reached shore. A fisherman returned her to her hotel twenty miles away, where her friends were planning her memorial service.

The group held a thanksgiving service instead!

# Lost at Sea—with Sharks
# Ripping Their Boat Apart!

It was only a series of fortuitous miracles that saved the lives of two young fishermen lost at sea for twenty-eight days—with man-eating sharks ripping so savagely at their flimsy rubber life raft that they had to blow it up by mouth every few minutes!

The ordeal for Richard Enslow, twenty, and David Summers, twenty-five, began when their forty-eight-foot fishing boat struck something in the water and sank about fifty miles off Kauai, Hawaii. Both young men managed to scramble aboard their six-person life raft.

On board the raft, they were glad to find supplies that included a few days' worth of biscuits and water, a small fishing kit, a hand pump, two sponges and a bailer, flares and smoke bombs, and a quart water jug. The young men settled down for an uncomfortable night. Little did they know their ordeal would last a month!

The first few days adrift were worrisome but uneventful. They were pleased to see plenty of fish in the surrounding waters and were able to catch several mahi-mahi, which they were forced to eat raw. They took advantage of frequent storms to gather water, which they kept in the quart jug. Unfortunately, the heat was merciless and there never seemed to be enough water.

The young men managed to stay levelheaded by communicating with each other as much as possible. They talked about their families, reminisced about past adventures together, talked about their hopes, dreams, and ambitions for the future. But most of all, they dreamed about having gallons and gallons of cool, fresh water to drink.

They rationed their water supply to half a cup

apiece a day—enough to keep them from dehydrating. They augmented their intake of liquid with the moisture from the raw fish they caught and ate.

After a while, they began hallucinating about food, particularly a feast of mouthwatering fruits. They talked to each other about which foods they would eat as soon as they were rescued.

Many times rescue seemed near at hand. They heard aircraft overhead on several occasions—and quickly let off smoke bombs that sent up big orange clouds. But the would-be rescuers failed to see their desperate signals.

Their tiny craft was at the mercy of the powerful ocean, which was pushing them further and further out to sea. They were in danger of being swallowed up in the expanse of the vast Pacific. But, thankfully, storms blew up that pushed them back in the direction of the Hawaiian coastline—and home.

Shortly after Christmas Day, 1996, the young survivors faced a new crisis when sharks began circling their boat, every so often ripping out chunks of the rubber fabric. Every twenty minutes, one of the men would use a hand pump to reinflate the craft.

The situation looked so grim that they decided to write farewell messages to their families. Using a tiny screwdriver, they scratched their farewell notes on the raft's plastic paddles. On one, David wrote, "I hope to see you in the next world." Richard scrawled, "Sorry to cause so much grief. Give the family my love."

By this time, each man had lost about forty pounds. They were continually light-headed and giddy from lack of sleep, because both had to stay awake and alert to keep their raft pumped up.

Both thought they were goners when three weeks into their predicament a whale flipped their raft! But their strong will to live enabled them to scramble back aboard to safety. However, what was left of their precious supplies was lost in the ocean depths.

No longer could they catch fish. No longer could

they use a hand pump. And their small stash of fresh water was gone.

"For the next four days, we took turns blowing up the raft by mouth every fifteen minutes or so," explained Richard. "It took us about five minutes to do this. It made us incredibly sick and dizzy."

Hallucinations became more frequent. In fact, it was shortly after Richard began "seeing" cold glasses of fruit juice in front of his eyes that he saw a fishing boat on the horizon. It was only after he blinked and pinched himself for a few seconds that he realized the fishing boat was real!

Minutes later, the young survivors were aboard fisherman Kevin Yamase's boat, guzzling juice and soda and telephoning their anxious parents.

Richard's mother, Aud, summed up the happy outcome to their shipwreck when she said, "A series of miracles saved my son!"

## Woody Cheated Death in Three-Hundred-Foot Plunge

Not many people can lay claim to surviving a three-hundred-foot plunge from a cliff top—the equivalent of falling off the Statue of Liberty.

Thirty-three-year-old construction worker Woody Woodward can boast that he did—although he did figure he was a dead man when his forklift careered over the seaside promontory near the home he was helping to build overlooking the English Channel.

Probably the only thing that saved him was the fact that he was propelled through the air one hundred feet into deeper water after the forklift smashed into shallow water at the foot of the cliff.

Although he lost his right leg, broke his right arm, and sustained severe chest and head injuries, Woody considers himself the luckiest man alive. He is convinced that a guardian angel in the form of his dead father was "up there looking out for me."

Woody had everything to live for. He had just gotten married a couple of weeks before the accident and had even postponed his honeymoon to work on this particular home construction project.

The burly six-feet-two-inch construction worker's nightmare began as he was maneuvering his forklift near the top of the cliff. Suddenly, the ground crumbled and his vehicle shot over the edge, spinning wildly in midair as it crashed into projecting rocks on the cliff face.

Woody remembered: "It was like being in a giant tumble dryer. I just crouched down behind the wheel and hung on for grim death as we went down."

As the forklift smashed into the shallow water below, Woody was knocked out cold and hurled clear of the sinking forklift. He floated facedown for two full minutes before a friend got to him and pulled him out of the water.

Once an enthusiastic lineman for an amateur football team, Woody realizes his playing days are over. "But I know how lucky I am," he says. "My playing days are over—so now I'll be a coach!"


## Woman Run Over by Train —but Miraculously Survives

Everyone standing on the crowded platform of a New York subway station thought the young pregnant woman who had fallen on the rails was dead.

No way, they thought, could she survive having a screeching subway train run over her inert body.

The cousin of twenty-two-year-old Carmen Genao, Olga Reyes, was among the many spectators convinced the young woman had been crushed to death seconds after she tumbled onto the tracks.

"The moment she fell, the train came," Reyes, still breathless and shaking hours after the early morning accident in Brooklyn, told the *New York Post.* "Everyone was screaming and crying. I was screaming. 'The train killed her! It killed her!' "

Miraculously, after it was all over, the young victim was able to sit calmly in a hospital waiting room, awaiting X-ray results, and recount calmly how she was unable to remember anything about the accident.

The last thing she remembered was standing on the platform and wondering if the Manhattan-bound B train was ever going to arrive.

Genao did not have the slightest recollection of falling.

Transit Authority officials said the train operator saw the woman pitch off the platform right into the path of his train. Fortunately, the train was only traveling at around ten miles an hour.

But even after engaging the brakes, one full sixty-foot, eighty-thousand pound car and a third of another had rolled over the woman before the train stopped, said a spokesman for the Transit Authority.

Genao said she remembered taking one step toward the edge of the platform, anticipating where the train would stop. Then everything went black.

When she woke up she was lying sideways on the track with her arms extended and her body feeling like it had just been grazed by the wheels all around her. She said she heard her cousin screaming somewhere above her. She heard screams echoing across the crowded platform.

"I heard everyone screaming and then I got scared," she said. "And then I just said, 'Thank you, God.' "

The train operator stepped out of his car to investigate—and was shocked to see Genao struggling to stand up between the first and second cars. He and other passengers helped lift her onto the platform.

Miraculously, she had fallen exactly in the trough between the rails and avoided the six hundred volts of electricity coursing through the third rail.

Later, transit officials said they did not have any specific records on such falls, but could remember only three or four in the last decade. "She is an extremely lucky young woman," added a transit spokesman.

The lucky young woman's cousin, Olga Reyes, thirty-one, said she could not bear to look after she saw her younger relative sprawled in the path of the oncoming train—she felt particularly guilty since she had asked Genao to go with her to a Manhattan appointment because she did not know how to use the subways.

"The next time I saw her she was safely back on the platform," said Reyes. "I was yelling, 'She's alive, she's alive.' The conductor kept telling me not to worry. God saved her life."

When Genao was pulled from the tracks, she sat on the stairs leading out of the subway station, unaided, awaiting an ambulance. There was a little blood on her lips, apparently because she bit them.

At Kings County Hospital Center, after extensive X-rays, doctors determined there were no broken bones sustained in the fall—just scrapes and bruises on her arms and legs!

Most important, her unborn child was unharmed.


# Miracle Man Walks Away
## —After Plummeting Three Hundred Feet

Thoughts of certain death flashed through Tom Kolinsky's head as his four-wheel-drive vehicle plummeted off a three-hundred-foot cliff, smashed into jagged rocks below, and sank into the sea—but miraculously, he survived!

The forty-nine-year-old British Coast Guard officer crawled onto a rocky ledge after the horror-filled plunge and calmly waited for his rescuers. When they saw his battered vehicle upside down and nearly submerged among the rocks, rescuers thought for sure he was dead.

"He must be one of the luckiest men alive," Coast Guard colleague Derek Reeves told local reporters later.

The nightmare drama came as Kolinsky and another Coast Guard buddy, Pete Morris, searched for a cliff-top site for a Coast Guard exercise near Cardigan, Wales. Morris got out of the vehicle to walk ahead, then turned in horror as the heavy vehicle began to skid on wet grass and careen out of control. He watched helplessly as it slid off the cliff backward—with his pal Kolinsky inside. Terrified, Morris raced to a farmhouse a mile away to call for help.

But after the vehicle landed upside down on the surf-washed rocks, miracle man Kolinsky managed to wriggle out of the wreckage and made his way to a small ledge ten feet above the rising tide. He waited until Air Force Lieutenant Richie Smith arrived in a helicopter and lifted him to safety. Kolinsky was rushed to a nearby hospital, where he was treated for a broken rib and punctured lung.

"It was truly a miraculous escape," said Smith. "The cliffs are three hundred feet from top to bottom and he had gone all the way down. The vehicle landed on very jagged rocks and it was almost completely submerged in the sea. But somehow he got out on his own!"

# Lightning Rips Through Her
# Body—but She Lives

Stunned eyewitnesses screamed in horror as clouds of smoke billowed off the body of a woman slumped in front of them—her white skin burned black by lightning!

Seconds earlier, Janice Poupard had been happily walking across a narrow footbridge in a park. Then a massive bolt ripped through her body, nearly frying her alive. The bolt was so powerful it melted her gold necklace and turned the metal underwire in her bra as hot as a poker . . . but, miraculously, she survived.

"She's the luckiest woman alive!" declared Dr. John Masterson, head of the burn unit at Alfred Hospital in Melbourne, Australia, who treated Janice. "Based on the extent of her injuries, it's clear that this was a huge bolt of lightning—many, many thousands of volts. It's an absolute miracle she survived."

The amazing drama began when Janice, a thirty-seven-year-old grade-school teacher, went on a beach outing on January 1, 1992, with her accountant husband, Ian, and their two children. Suddenly, dark clouds appeared in the blue sky and heavy rain came pelting down, accompanied by deafening claps of thunder.

"We packed up and started over the footbridge to the parking lot where we'd left our car," Janice told the *National Enquirer.* "Then I heard a loud *craaaccck!*—and that's all I remember. The bolt entered my back beneath the right shoulder, leaving a giant wound as if I'd been blasted by a shotgun. The skin on my back and shoulder turned black, like charred meat.

"My clothes caught fire, causing serious burns on my legs where my shorts were ablaze. My left arm also was badly burned. I also had severe burns under my breasts. The doctor told me the underwire in the bottom part of my bra must have turned red-hot to burn me like that."

Janice's daughter Candice, eight, had been standing beside her when the bolt hit. Horrified, the child ran across the bridge toward her father and five-year-old brother, Aaron.

"I heard a lady scream, 'Oh, God! A woman's been struck by lightning!' " Ian said. "I ran back onto the bridge, pushed through shocked eyewitnesses—and saw my wife lying motionless, with smoke pouring from her body. There was a smell of burning hair. I thought, 'She's dead!' But a lifeguard trying to revive her said, 'She's alive! She's breathing!' "

Luckily, the rain quickly extinguished Janice's burning clothes. She was rushed to the hospital, where she finally regained consciousness eight hours later, Ian said.

"She mumbled, 'What happened?' I told her she'd been hit by lightning. I'll never forget her faint reply: 'You're joking.' "

When Janice's necklace melted and fell off, it left a tattoolike circle around her neck. For three weeks she couldn't walk and was terrified she'd be left paralyzed for life. But during nearly a month in the hospital she regained the use of her legs. Janice also underwent skin grafts beneath her breasts and on her thighs.

"Now I'm fully recovered. I don't even walk with a limp," she said. "I have scars on my legs and beneath my breasts, as well as the bizarre black ring circling my neck, but the doctors say they'll gradually fade as the years pass.

"Now, when I stare at lightning in the night sky, I think: "Wow! Something so powerful struck me down—but I'm still alive to tell the tale. God sure must've wanted to spare me!"

# His Pocketknife Stopped Life-Threatening Bullet

Navy veteran Elbert Nash joined the miracle survivors' club after he was shot by a desperate bank robber with a deadly .357 Magnum gun—and escaped unharmed because the bullet hit his pocketknife.

"It's a miracle!" confesses Elbert in an *Equirer* interview. "The slug shattered my trusty Buck knife, but left only the bruised imprint of the knife on me!" he said.

Elbert, fifty-two, was withdrawing cash from an automated teller machine outside a Chula Vista, California, bank in the spring of 1994 when three young men came running out of the building. They'd just robbed the bank—and a security guard was in hot pursuit.

As they ran, one of the robbers fired wildly in the direction of the security guard, said Elbert. "One bullet hit the ATM machine, another hit a nearby car— and the third hit me!"

But the bullet hit Elbert on the one spot of his body that was safe—his hip pocket, where he kept his faithful knife. The deadly .357 slug tore through his pants, through his checkbook, driver's license, and credit cards, and slammed into the old six-inch Navy Buck knife he'd carried for thirty years!

At first, Elbert thought he'd been hit by a hammer. The impact spun him around and he hit the ground. His backside throbbed. Gingerly, he reached inside his pants and felt for blood. When he withdrew his hand, he was amazed to find none!

Then, as he scrambled to his feet, he felt inside his pocket and was astonished to find a bullet—a .357 Magnun slug—flattened against his knife!

"My butt was sore—but I was alive!" added Elbert. "I bought the knife three decades ago for $5.25. The bullet shattered its wooden handle, blew out the rivets, and bent the blade. But I have a new Buck now. Officials of Buck Knives, Inc. heard about my escape and invited me to their headquarters to receive an honorary pocketknife!"

One suspect was arrested in the case and charged with robbery, according to Chula Vista detective Jon Heggestuen, who added: "Elbert Nash was saved by his pocketknife. He's the luckiest guy I know!"

## Falls 110 Feet, Lands on His Feet —and Lives!

"I guess there were angels on my shoulders," said construction worker John Reeves of Cincinnati, Ohio, after he plunged 110 feet off the top of a roller coaster, hit the ground feet first—and survived!

The twenty-year-old bachelor broke several bones in his eleven-story fall, but he went on to make a full recovery. His miraculous escape astounded Dick Gilgirst of the U.S. Occupational Safety and Health Administration (OSHA), who investigated the accident.

"It's unbelievable. I've never heard of anyone surviving an eleven-story fall. He is a very lucky person," Gilgirst, a twenty-year veteran of OSHA, told the *National Enquirer*.

The accident happened in February 1996 while John was working on the roof over the new Flight of Fear roller coaster at King's Island amusement park in Cincinnati. His safety line was attached to a construction hoist at the edge of the roof. Suddenly the hoist toppled over the side, dragging him with it.

About twenty-five feet above the ground he struck a ledge, helping to break his fall. He bounced off, landed on his feet, and topped forward onto his abdomen.

"I don't remember the fall," he admitted. "It happened so fast. In two seconds I was on the ground."

John tried to get up, but another worker held him down and told him not to move.

"I was pretty calm," John recalled. "The pain wasn't that bad. I was alert and didn't go into shock."

His survival was "a miracle," declared Assistant Fire Chief Char Cornett of the Mason Deerfield Joint Fire District.

"When we got there and were told he'd fallen 110 feet, we thought for sure he'd be dead," said Cornett. "But he was conscious and talking to us the whole time."

John suffered broken heels and hips, a broken left leg, a crushed right foot, and a shattered pelvis. He spent nineteen days in Cincinnati's University Hospital, then was transferred to a rehabilitation center where he spent the next few months.

The young man said the fall has given him a deeper appreciation for each day: "Don't take life for granted, because it can be over just like that."

Asked it he plans to ride the roller coaster he was helping build, John shook his head and said, "I've had my ride!"

## Falls Three Thousand Feet out of Jet Plane—and Lives!

In a feat worthy of inclusion in any historical record of astonishing miracles, a man fell out of a plane and tumbled three thousand feet to the ground . . . surviving without serious injury!

The plunge was "thirty seconds of sheer terror," says survivor Des Moloney. "I must be the luckiest man on earth!"

Des had been enjoying a thrilling ride in the cockpit of a former Air Force jet, as his pilot brother flew upside down at 250 miles per hour in an acrobatic maneuver. Then the passenger's ejector seat suddenly broke loose, sending Des crashing through the glass canopy of the plane and hurtling toward earth!

Des's parachute failed to open completely, trailing behind him like a giant sock. Incredibly, the fluttering chute slowed him down just enough so that he wasn't killed when he landed in a grassy area near a supermarket parking lot.

"It was a miracle—an amazing escape," said a police spokesperson, after the heart-stopping incident in the skies over Colchester in Essex, England.

Des, twenty-eight, who works in his brother Tom's aviation supply company, suffered only minor injuries, including scrapes and whiplash.

The aerial drama occurred as Des and brother Tom were taking an Easter Sunday pleasure ride in Tom's twenty-five-year-old two-seater Jet Provost, once used as a trainer by Britain's Royal Air Force.

Tom practiced some fancy moves, twice rolling upside down.

"The second time, Des's ejector seat broke from its mountings," said Tom, thirty-one. "There was a sickening crash and he disappeared through the cockpit canopy—he exploded through it like a rocket!"

Luckily, Des's helmet kept him from being knocked unconscious by the impact.

"It was a huge shock when I suddenly found I wasn't in the plane anymore—I knew I was in big trouble," he said. "I was scared, but I knew I had to stay calm."

Des's safety belt had broken and the ejector seat fell away. "I was in the seat for two or three seconds before we parted company and I became aware that I was free-falling."

He hurtled toward the unforgiving ground at about 120 miles per hour.

The only thing between him and death was his parachute. "I reached for the rip cord and pulled it," he said.

Then he got a horrifying shock—the chute had been damaged when he went through the canopy. He twirled around and around like a top beneath the parachute.

Christine Twigg, forty-nine, watched in disbelief from the ground. "I thought it was a dummy on the end of the parachute—it didn't seem real at first," she said.

The ground raced up toward Des. "I couldn't breathe for the last twenty seconds," he recalls, "but I never gave up hope that I would survive the fall."

Des slammed into the earth with a tremendous thud. He found he was still alive—saved by the soft ground. He was even able to stand up and dust himself off before stunned onlookers rushed over to help.

The ejector seat came down half a mile away—landing right outside the front door of a flabbergasted homeowner!

Frantic brother Tom set down at a nearby airfield and raced to the scene. "It was the worst fifteen minutes of my life. I thought Des was a goner," he revealed. "When I heard he was alive I couldn't believe it. I went straight to the hospital and he was sitting up with a brace around his neck, joking with the nurses.

"His first words were, 'I'm afraid reports of my death are premature.' I cracked up and kissed him with relief. Then we both cried."

Des was released from the hospital the next day. He said: "I'm a little sore, but apart from that it feels great to be alive!"

## Newlyweds Take the Plunge —off a 150-Foot Cliff

To say that newlyweds Joe and Colleen Rhine's marriage got off to a rocky start when they honeymooned in the Rocky Mountains is an understatement.

The just-married couple's car plunged off a 150-foot cliff—but miraculously they survived!

"We were flying through the air," Colleen, sixty-four, told the *National Enquirer.* "I saw boulders below—and said a quick prayer!"

Divorcée Colleen and seventy-five-year-old Joe, whose first wife had died seven years earlier, tied the knot in Tulsa, Oklahoma, in June 1993. Their skin-of-the-teeth brush with disaster came four days later, as they were on a hazardous road touring fourteen-thousand foot Pikes Peak in Colorado.

The couple now believe that Joe might have blacked out momentarily from the lack of oxygen. Colleen was looking at the mountains when suddenly she heard Joe gasp, "Oh, my Lord."

She was shocked to see the front end of the car jutting out into midair and the back end still on the road. There was nothing the frightened couple could do.

Seconds later the car was plunging down the cliff face. A huge boulder loomed in front of them. The passenger side smashed against it and the car continued its crazy descent.

Fortunately, the car stayed upright as it slid down the hillside, bouncing up and down as it hit rocks along the way. Each time it hit, it threw Joe and Colleen around like rag dolls. Colleen remembers Joe crying out "Oh, my Lord" again and again.

The car eventually shuddered to a halt when it hit a bunch of pine trees. And Joe croaked with relief, "Thank you, Lord." A passing motorist dashed down the cliff to help the couple, and the police was summoned.

Amazingly, Joe only suffered back pains, and Colleen was hospitalized for four days with a chipped neck bone, bruised spleen, and lacerated liver.

Joe said later: "One of the officers who helped rescue us said we'd just lived through the toughest part of our marriage—and everything else would be down-hill from there! I told him, 'Don't ever mention hills to me again.' "

## Survivor Erects a
## Monument to His Miracle

Thankful to be alive after he miraculously escaped death when he accidentally sawed through a power line, Jim Studer has erected a memorial to his mira-cle—a one-hundred-foot cross.

The shimmering steel cross, which cost $65,000, stands on a hillside near Ballinger, Texas, and can be seen from more than nine miles away.

As tall as a ten-story building, the impressive fifty-ton structure is lit up at night by three floodlights that make it appear to be floating over the brush-covered hills.

Studer, fifty-eight, will never forget the 1991 brush with death that led to his unusual "thank-you" to God.

"We were visiting my mother in Florida and she asked me to prune back the limbs on her fruit trees," the soft-spoken rancher-businessman told the *National Enquirer.* "My son-in-law and I attached a saw to a long aluminum pole, and the saw sliced through the power line going into my mother's house.

"There was this very loud POW! It was followed by a louder crackle. I froze, knowing that at any moment hundreds of volts of electricity would go shooting through my body."

Studer doesn't know what happened to keep the killer voltage from reaching him. But he's convinced there was divine intervention.

"God was protecting me," he declared. "My wife and I had been talking about building a forty-foot cross before this happened. But after surviving the near-electrocution, I looked up in the sky and said, 'God, I owe You another sixty feet!"

Studer immediately sketched the cross, and a local contractor in Texas built the huge religious symbol. Pilgrims have begun trekking to the cross to pray.

Studer, a father of seven, says that over the years God had been very good to him and his family. He hopes his cross will "give others a chance to reflect on the good things that have happened in their lives."

## Trapped Woman Survives Two and a Half Days—Eating Mints!

For two and a half days a Texas woman, trapped in her wrecked pickup, survived by eating mints and using her purse to scoop water from a creek.

Jamie Peavy was so sure she was going to die that she used lipstick and jotted a note: "Nobody killed me. I had a wreck."

She ran off the road and plunged into a ravine on a Friday night. She lay trapped in her truck for a full weekend, her legs pinned in the wreckage.

Then on Monday her faint cries for help were heard by construction worker Robert Ryding, who happened to be inspecting a site near Dallas-Fort Worth International Airport.

He was walking toward the ravine when he heard the faint plea, "Help me." Within minutes, medical help was on the way for Jamie, who was found to have suffered two seriously broken legs, a broken wrist, and a broken rib, a punctured lung, cuts, bruises, and dehydration.

But, miraculously, she was alive.

After undergoing surgery at Baylor University Medical Center, her first words to her mother, Mrs. Martha

Peavy, were, "I'm glad to see you," and, "I thought you were never going to find me."

Her relieved mother told *Star* magazine. "This was truly a miracle—a miracle."

Jamie, a twenty-five-year-old cashier from Irving, Texas, took a wrong turn while driving to a friend's home and accidentally plunged ten feet into a small ravine. She lost consciousness for several hours, awakening in the early hours of Saturday morning. Her ordeal was just beginning. For the next two and a half days, she fought to stay alive.

Dressed in denim shorts and a short red top, Jamie endured near-freezing temperatures.

To slake her thirst, she tied her belt to her purse and threw it out the window to catch water from the small, trickling creek beneath her. When the water got too low, she took her shirt off and tied that to her belt and let it soak up water.

For food, she ate stale five-month-old mints she found in her purse.

"She's a very plucky young lady," said Dr. Alex Santos, one of her surgeons.


## Woman, Eighty-three, Survives Eight Days on Fruit Juice and Frost!

An eighty-three-year-old woman, stranded when her car got stuck in the mud in the desolate grasslands of Wyoming for more than a week, miraculously survived by living on fruit juice and the frost she scraped off the hood of her car.

To survive life-threatening temperatures that dipped into the twenties, elderly Mae Wardell layered on all the extra clothes she could find—a sweater, jacket, and a couple of pairs of pants.

She sustained herself by drinking the half-dozen or

so cans of orange, apricot, and other juices she happened to have with her.

"It's amazing," local police chief Gary Jackson said. "She did the right thing to stay with her vehicle. When you get into a week or so it begins looking a little grim."

Ms. Wardell left Casper, Wyoming, where she had been visiting her sister at a nursing home, and headed home to Gillette, about 130 miles southwest.

But she got lost and stuck in the mud. She wore her car battery down trying to get free.

Eight days later, a father and son out hunting about fifteen miles west of Midwest—a central Wyoming town of about four hundred people—came across her car and found her lying on the front seat, conscious and happy to see them.

"The first thing she said was that she was really glad," a police spokesman said. "She said it was quite an ordeal. She was afraid and just about had given up hope."

Ms. Wardell was taken to the hospital, where she was reported to be "weak, but alert and in real good spirits."

# Shot Between the Eyes— but Bullet Bounced Off

Shot point-blank right between the eyes by a callous robber, Memphis store owner Mohammad Jafari miraculously survived—because the bullet simply bounced off his head!

Not only did Mohammad, a father of two, survive— he fought back like a tiger, and the thief ran screaming into the street, nursing a bullet wound in his arm.

Incredibly, the heroic store owner was back at work

the very next day—and the accused assailant ended up behind bars.

The thirty-year-old Jordanian immigrant's close brush with death took place September 29, 1993, at the St. Elmo Mart, one of three convenience stores he and his brother own in Memphis.

Shortly after opening time, a young man burst into the store, brandishing a .22-caliber pistol. He had a mask over the lower part of his face. "Get on the floor—fast," he yelled, pointing the gun right in Mohammad's face.

The young store owner, playing it safe, instantly dropped behind the counter. There were no other customers in the store and little money in the register.

But when the gunman leaped over the counter and started banging on the cash register, trying to get the drawer open, he knocked the key out of the register and it got lost on the floor.

Unable to get to the money, the gunman grabbed Mohammad's arm and stuck the pistol against the back of the storekeeper's head, screaming, "Get up and open this register!"

Mohammad scrambled to his feet and tried to get it open. But he couldn't do it without the key.

Recalling the terrifying incident, Mohammad said, "He flew into a rage and started cursing me. I turned—and the gunman pulled the trigger from only inches away.

"I saw the flash, heard the sound, and felt a terrible pain between my eyes. I was stunned. I saw a gray nothingness. But within seconds the haze lifted and I could see again.

"The first thing I saw was blood pouring down my face. Then I saw my attacker's gun, still pointed at my face. He was just looking at me—waiting for me to fall down, I guess. I knew I had to act to save my life."

That's when Mohammad grabbed the gun and

started wrestling with the thug, all the time thinking, "If I don't get this gun, I'm dead!"

As they fought, the gun went off. God was still watching over Mohammed—this time the bullet hit the robber in the forearm. He screamed in pain and fled.

Dazed, confused, and praying to God that he'd survive, Mohammad first was convinced he had a bullet in his brain and was moments from death. He staggered to the phone and called 911.

"It wasn't until doctors examined me at the hospital that I found out the astonishing truth—the bullet had bounced off my head! I had a flesh wound requiring nine stitches, nothing more. Doctors kept me a few hours for observation, then sent me home. God and my hard head saved me from certain death!"

Memphis police captain Earl Harker later reported: "Doctors confirmed that the wound to Mr. Jafari's head was a gunshot wound. There were powder traces in the area. Mr. Jafari is very lucky to be alive. It's a miracle!"

# Chapter Four

*~*

# Prayer Miracles

As an internal medicine physician in Dallas, Texas, Dr. Larry Dossey was intrigued all his life by those patients who got healed—but some were never, ever able to pinpoint exactly what cured them.

Slowly, Dr. Dossey began to have more and more faith in the amazing curative power of prayer. He became *totally* convinced of prayer's potency, however, when he pored over the now-famous 1988 San Francisco study that showed that cardiac patients prayed for by others did much better than a control group that had no one saying prayers for them.

"The outcome of the study was as if the prayed-for group had been given some sort of miracle drug," said Dr. Dossey. "I had never seen a study like this showing that prayer worked. This really bothered me."

He was fascinated with the original ten-month-long study—a computer-assisted review of 393 cardiac-care patients by a California cardiologist.

As it turned out, the prayed-for patients turned out to be five times less likely than the control group to need antibiotics and three times less likely to develop pulmonary edema (fluid in the lungs).

The results were impressive enough to send Dr. Dossey on his own five-year quest to determine whether prayer was indeed a positive factor in healings. To that end, he gave up his medical practice and moved to New Mexico, where he began his research, poring over more than 130 scientific studies that explored the unknown area of prayer in relation to cure.

In his book, *Healing Words,* Dr. Dossey was able to document positive links between prayer and healing. Prayer, even from a distance, was able to change physical processes in a variety of organisms, from bacteria to humans.

As we mentioned earlier, a private agency, the National Institute for Healthcare Research, has already examined studies in this area and supports Dossey's assertion that there is strong evidence for prayer's effectiveness.

"I'd concur with that conclusion from what I have seen," said Connie Barry, the institute's vice president.

The president of the institute, David Larson, who also works for the new NIH Office of Alternative Medicine, conducted reviews of scientific studies in this area for the institute—with support from the Templeton Foundation, which awards the prestigious Templeton Prize for Progress in Religion.

From his research, Larson has also produced a book—*The Faith Factor: An Annotated Bibliography of Clinical Research on Spiritual Subjects,* which contains more than two hundred studies.

Whether fellow physicians agree or disagree with Dr. Larry Dossey's work, there is no way he is backing off from his assertions about the medical power of prayer.

"I don't think you can put this genie back in the bottle," he says.

From my own files and research, I have come up with these remarkable anecdotal records of the incredible healing power of prayer.

# Her Appeal to the
# Grey Nun Was Answered

Sinking fast with acute leukemia and virtually paralyzed from the waist down, twenty-nine-year-old Lise
Normand prayed in desperation for a miracle to a nun
who'd died two hundred years before.

And her prayers were answered.

Four months after her fervent prayers to Marguerite
d'Youville, founder of a religious order in Montreal,
Canada, called the Grey Nuns, Lise was examined by
astonished doctors who declared her in complete
remission.

Almost two decades later, the Hull, Quebec, housewife remains cancer-free. She recalls with joy the miraculous feelings that swept over her disease-ravaged
body after she began praying to the Grey Nun:

"I began to experience floating sensations, as if I
were hovering in the air above my bed."

Sister Jeanette Gagnon, a spokesman for the Grey
Nuns holy order, confirms that Lise's recovery was the
direct result of a miracle.

The Vatican supports the theory—so much so that
Marguerite d'Youville was canonized on December 9,
1990, as the first Canadian-born saint for healing miracles she performed after her death—including the
amazing healing of Lise Normand.

After Lise's remarkable recovery in 1978, the Vatican asked her doctors to supply them with her medical
records. At a subsequent hearing, medical experts
testified before a Vatican board.

Vatican spokesman Monsignor Dante Pasquinelli
later confirmed: "Marguerite d'Youville is being canonized because of the miracles attributed to her after
her death, including the miracle healing of Lise Normand of leukemia."

The wonderful story of Lise Normand is typical of the incredible healing power of prayer.

Lise was first diagnosed with leukemia in 1978. After traditional chemotherapy, the disease subsided—only to return with a vengeance two months later. Doctors gave her no hope. Leukemia specialists confirm that it's virtually impossible for someone with a relapse of leukemia to go into remission.

Lise was in despair. "As I lay dying in hospital, my pain became worse each day," she recalled with a shudder. "I couldn't eat or sleep and my body was covered with horrible sores. I was virtually paralyzed from the waist down."

Devoutly religious, Lise remembered stories she'd heard about the Grey Nun Sister Marguerite, and how she was quick to respond to the prayers of the sick and desperate.

Her pleas to the Grey Nun were answered with the weird but wonderful physical sensations. And early in 1979, four months after she was hospitalized, astounded doctors pronounced her fully cured.

And the Grey Nun was on her way to sainthood.


## A Sad Family Prayer Session Ends in Celebration

Stricken with a viral infection that swept southern Italy, killing many people, a sixty-four-year-old man was sent home by doctors to die in the company of his loved ones.

In a deep coma in his bedroom, Letterio Mangano was surrounded by his grief-stricken daughter and other concerned family members. They had been told there was no hope.

In voices choked with tears and desperation, the family group began praying to Sister Eustochia Calafato, a fifteenth-century Sicilian nun credited with a number of healings over the centuries, whose portrait happened to be on the bedroom wall.

Incredibly, Letterio suddenly came out of his coma, sat up in bed—and asked for coffee and pasta!

This 1964 healing in Messina, Italy, is one of more than thirty recorded miracle healings attributed by the Vatican to Sister Eustochia, whom the Catholic Church declared a saint in 1988.

The legend of Sister Eustochia will never die on the island of Sicily. For five centuries, her glass-encased body has been on display in the crypt of the local convent. Astonishingly, it has never decomposed. And it is so blessed that it has survived both wars and an earthquake.

During World War II, confirm local clergy, bombs fell twice near the chapel where she lies—and inexplicably failed to explode. An earthquake devastated an area around the little chapel. But Sister Eustochia's glass casket was unscathed.

That's why more than 100,000 devout believers attended the ceremony at which Pope John Paul II canonized Sister Eustochia.

One of the local doctors interviewed by the Vatican commission investigating the Messina miracles was Dr. Carlo Ciapinna, head of neurology at the town's Regina Margherita Hospital, who along with his colleague, Dr. Carmen Di Pietro, examined Signor Mangano before and after his amazing return from the dead.

Confirmed Dr. Ciapinna: "He was in a coma for days. Finally, we decided there was nothing we could do for him, and told the family they could take him home where he would be surrounded by his loved ones."

Both attending doctors raced to the Mangano home after hearing he had regained consciousness.

"It was a real shock to see that man—whom I

thought I would soon be filling out a death certificate for—calmly sitting up in bed drinking coffee and eating pasta," added Dr. Di Petro.

"We examined him—and realized he had recovered. We could not give any scientific explanation for it . . . as I readily confirmed to the Vatican commission on sainthood."

# Ninety Minutes of Prayer Ends Five Years of Torture

For ninety minutes, a thirty-three-year-old man huddled with his parish priest, praying for relief from the agonizingly painful tumor that had made his life a living torture for five long years.

The intense prayer session worked for Antonio Piras. After it was over, he was miraculously cured of the splitting headaches, epileptic fits, and partial paralysis that had made his life a living hell.

Antonio's story began in 1984 when, as a strapping construction worker in his mid-twenties in Arzana, Italy, he started getting dizzy spells and convulsions. The seizures worsened until he suffered paralysis and other sicknesses. Doctors diagnosed a brain tumor. He was operated on three times to have it removed, but it kept recurring.

The turnaround in Antonio's life came in January 1990, when his parish priest, Father Vincenzo Pirarba, visited his home to pray with the bedridden man's anxious family.

Father Pirarba brought with him several pebbles from the miraculous shrine to the Virgin Mary at Medjugorje in Yugoslavia, which he had visited recently.

After praying with Antonio for almost an hour, Father Pirarba urged the sick man to cry out the name

"Mary." In a weak voice, Antonio managed to gasp the name. At the same time, Father Pirarba gave him one of the pebbles to clutch in his one good hand, then the other hand, which was partially paralyzed.

As the priest folded Antonio's lifeless fingers around the precious pebble, he spontaneously rallied in strength. "He began to open his hand by himself," marveled Father Pirarba. "It seemed like a flower bud was opening for the first time. Then he raised his arm in the air by himself."

Within an hour, Antonio had rallied enough to get out of bed on his own. Soon he was sitting at the dining table with his overjoyed family—miraculously healed.

Today he still leads a perfectly normal life. "In my prayers, I always thank Father Vincenzo and the Virgin Mary for what can only be described as a true miracle," he says.

## Dead Priest Credited with 75,000 Miracles

An incredible 75,000 healing miracles are credited to Roman Catholic Church dignitary Monsignor Escriva de Balaguer, who was declared a saint in 1991, sixteen years after his death.

One of the most amazing healings—which clinched his canonization—was that of a seventy-year-old nun who recovered completely from what doctors had pronounced terminal cancer.

"We couldn't find any scientific explanation for her complete recovery. It is a case that will go down in medical history," said radiologist Dr. Fermin Munoz of the healing that gave Sister Concepcion Boullon Rubio of Madrid, Spain, a new lease on life.

Prior to her total cure, Sister Concepcion's fellow

nuns had prayed long and hard to the deceased priest and Opus Dei, the powerful Catholic organization of influential businesspeople founded by Monsignor de Balaguer during his lifetime.

Her prayers began in June 1976, a year after Monsignor de Balaguer's death. She had a tumor the size of a baseball on her shoulder, and she was further weakened by acute anemia, a stomach ulcer, and a hernia. Doctors gave her days to live.

Two of her loyal colleagues in the order, Sisters Josephina and Carmen, spent one entire night praying to the late Monsignor de Balaguer, asking him to spare their beloved sister's life.

In the morning, Sister Concepcion awoke feeling much better. Her physician examined her and was astonished to find her tumor had completely disappeared. Her ailments also vanished.

After a checkup, radiologist Dr. Munoz declared: "I can't explain this in medical terms. I was astonished to find her free of cancer."

Sister Concepcion lived for another twelve years. She died in November 1988 from unrelated kidney failure.

Just before she died she whispered to her fellow nuns: "Thanks to Father Escriva, God decided to prolong my life."

## Future Saint Heals Young Housewife's Crippled Body

"It's a miracle. A miracle!" cried young housewife Lidia Nastasi through her tears of joy as her deformed and crippled body, which had kept her in unbearable agony for three years, miraculously healed after she prayed to the spirit of a future saint.

For two long days of prayer, the thirty-two-year-old

Pachino, Italy, woman appealed to the gentle spirit of the late Father Francesco Spinelli to ease her life of pain and straighten her paralyzed and deformed limbs, misshapen by multiple sclerosis.

He responded. Two days into her prayer marathon, she was able to throw away her crutches and stand on her own two feet.

Confirmed her physician, Dr. Giovanni Comitini: "When I saw Mrs. Nastasi stride into my office I thought I was dreaming. Her pelvis had been twisted and deformed by the illness—but it straightened overnight, allowing her to walk perfectly.

"I gave her the most extensive tests I had ever given a patient, but I had to admit the woman was perfectly recovered . . . and there was no scientific explanation for it!"

From 1989 to 1992, Lidia suffered from the terrible, debilitating disease. Specialists told her there was nothing they could do for her and that she'd have to learn to live with her torment and pain.

In a last-ditch search for any kind of cure, Lidia visited a local convent, where the mother superior told her the story of a nineteenth-century cleric with amazing healing powers, known as Padre Francesco.

After the mother superior gave her a relic of Padre Francesco—a small piece of one of his robes encased in a glass locket—Lidia put her trust in her faith. That night she went home, praying fervently for forty-eight hours.

"When I awoke the second morning, I was astonished to find that I no longer felt that pulsing ache," declared Lidia. "I was able to lay down my crutches and stand unaided for the first time in three years."

Joyfully, she strode out of her home into the street, tears streaming down her cheeks, crying out praises for Padre Francesco.

Lidia's healing was added to the long list of healings

credited to Padre Francesco, who has since been approved by the Vatican to be canonized as a saint.

Lidia's local priest, Father Salvatore Giordanella, confirmed, "I have no doubt Mrs. Nastasi's healing was a sign from God."

## "Prayerathon" Brings New Lease on Life for Tot

There was nothing doctors and other medical specialists could do to help four-year-old Tyrel McAmmond. The killer cancer that he was suffering from had spread throughout his tiny body, so the caregivers sent him home from the hospital to die.

But thanks to the miraculous power of prayer, little Tyrel did not die. God granted him a miracle. And today the child who challenged and conquered astronomical odds to stay alive is a perfectly healthy, fun-loving schoolboy.

The future looked grim for Tyrel back in 1993 when he was diagnosed with deadly B-cell lymphoma in his liver and abdomen. Months of extensive chemotherapy took its toll on the brave youngster. For a while the treatment seemed to be working. The tumors shrank and he was released from the hospital to go back to his home in Grand Cache, Alberta, Canada.

But in just a few weeks a relapse almost claimed his life as his temperature soared to 105 degrees. Frantic, his parents rushed him back to the hospital. Doctors discovered the cancer had spread through his liver, spleen, and bone marrow. And the tiny tot was literally sent home to die—just two weeks before Christmas 1993.

His loving parents, Tyrel and Shelley McAmmond, were devastated. But they had to put on a brave front for their little boy . . . even buying him the Christmas presents he had asked for so he would not have an inkling there was something so wrong.

Devout churchgoers, Tyrel and Shelley turned to their friends in the local congregation for help. They asked all their church friends to say prayers for little Tyrel.

News of the little boy's predicament spread to other churches—and beyond. Soon thousands of people from all across Canada and the United States were praying for Tyrel!

"God must have heard us . . . Tyrel did not die," said dad Tyrel. "Instead, he seemed to gain a little bit more energy day after day." On Christmas morning, he was strong enough to rip open his own presents.

After Christmas, Tyrel returned to the hospital for more tests. Incredibly, they showed his cancer had disappeared! A doctor declared, "God has healed your son . . . there's no other explanation!"

On February 7, 1994, using Tyrel's year-old sister, Jenae, as a donor, doctors performed a bone marrow transplant on the child to ensure the cancer would not return.

A subsequent checkup showed he was in total remission. And says his father, Tyrel: "God looked down on us and worked a miracle—for that we'll thank him every day of our lives."

## Deathbed Prayer Brings Nun Back from the Dead

On her deathbed, young nun Sister Caterina Capitani was given the last rites. She had a massive, terminal illness, so she was prepared to die. But she prayed to a cleric whom she idolized, the late Pope John XXIII, to help her endure the terrible suffering.

And the gentle, loving pontiff—who had passed

away in 1963—answered her prayers from the beyond and brought her a miracle . . . the miracle of life!

It was the miracle performed on Sister Caterina in 1966 that led to the consideration of Pope John for the sainthood in recent years.

These days, Sister Caterina, now in her fifties, is alive and well and still working for the health and comfort of others as the chief of nursing staff at a large public hospital in her native city of Naples, Italy.

"Sister Caterina had one foot in the grave and had received the sacrament of last rites when Pope John appeared to her and miraculously cured her," confirms Giovanni Cairoli, who heads up the Vatican committee of inquiry that is preparing the dossier of evidence for Pope John's elevation to sainthood.

Sister Caterina was suffering from a rare ailment called "red stomach"—a heavy, strangling growth of varicose veins—when surgeons operated on her in 1966, removing her stomach, large intestine, and other organs in an effort to save her life.

Her condition failed to improve and her health worsened. Her fellow nuns rallied to her aid. They visited her bedside, joining her in her prayers to Pope John.

Her colleagues even obtained a fragment of the sheet that Pope John died on. They placed the tiny piece of cloth on an abscess that had formed on Sister Caterina's abdomen after her surgery.

The following morning, Sister Caterina felt herself being gently shaken in her bed. Her eyelids fluttered open, and leaning over her was this glorious vision of Pope John.

She remembered his placing one hand on her abdomen, then whispering: "Sister Caterina, you have prayed much to me. Don't be afraid. It's all over. You are well." The healing pontiff disappeared as mysteriously as he had appeared.

Sister Caterina rang for her fellow nuns. When they

reached her bedside, they were astounded to see her sitting up, smiling, in perfect shape.

When her attending physician, Dr. Giuseppe Zannini, checked her over, he was puzzled to find that the abscess and other scarring and wounds from her extensive surgery had totally disappeared. Skeptical, Dr. Zannini ordered X rays. They revealed that Sister Caterina's internal surgical wounds and general condition had totally healed. Dr. Zannini was later to testify about this amazing turn of events at the Vatican commission's investigation.

Says Dr. Zannini: "Not only was Sister Caterina's survival unthinkable, but in her condition it remained unthinkable that she could return to her life of complete devotion to her work. It's definitely a miracle."

## Dead Nun Brings Drowned Girl and Electrocuted Fireman Back from Death's Door

Prayers to a long-deceased nun are credited with bringing back from death's door an eleven-year-old drowned girl and a young fireman who was electrocuted.

These two documented incidents, along with many others, convinced a Vatican commission investigating candidates for sainthood that Sister Teresa of the Andes, a beloved Chilean nun who died in 1920, should be canonized.

The little girl who "drowned" had lain underwater for more than five minutes before physician Dr. Gabriel Ramirez of Santiago, Chile, saw her.

"I didn't think there was much hope for her," said Dr. Ramirez, recalling the 1988 incident. Even if he could revive her, thought Dr. Ramirez, there was bound to be extensive damage to her brain, kidneys, heart, and liver.

The little girl, Marcella Antunes, had been frolicking in a public pool with friends. Suddenly, she was spotted floating facedown in deep water, near the bottom. Lifeguards pulled her to the surface and tried to resuscitate her—to no avail.

As an ambulance arrived to whisk her to the hospital, Marcella's schoolmates knelt in a circle, holding hands, silently praying to Teresa of the Andes for their friend's survival.

Dr. Ramirez and his emergency team hovered anxiously over Marcella's limp body in the hospital; they were startled when her eyelids flickered—and she suddenly opened her eyes. Within minutes she was able to clamber from the examination table and stand up, smiling and in good spirits as if nothing had happened.

There was no explanation for this type of recovery (there was not even the remotest hint of memory loss or brain damage). A miracle had taken place.

Five years earlier, Sister Teresa of the Andes had come to the rescue when fireman Ettore Uribe was battling a blaze on a rooftop and accidently came in contact with a power line that zapped 380 jarring volts of electricity into his body.

Rushed to a hospital, he lay in a coma for four days. His desperate parents made a pilgrimage to Sister Teresa's tomb to pray for their son.

At almost the exact time they arrived at the tomb, Ettore showed his first signs of life. A few days later, he had totally recovered.

His doctor, Eduardo Rios Vergara, later said: "I still can't explain his sudden, total recovery. A charge that strong either instantly kills or leaves irreparable damage."

These two miracles ensured a Catholic Church sainthood for the legendary Sister Teresa—who had been a Carmelite nun for only eleven months when she died at age nineteen.

# The Watts Family's Healing Odyssey

Southern Baptist Foreign Mission Board missionary Nancy Watts credits a God-sent miracle in answer to her prayers with saving and healing her husband, Wade, and her nine-year-old son, Marcus.

Wade and Marcus were left in grave condition, in comas, their odds for survival slim, after the car the family was traveling in was destroyed in a head-on collision on a mountain road outside Lima, Peru.

A year later Nancy is still nursing her family through the slow process of healing back home in Memphis, Tennessee.

What began for her as a family tragedy is today a positive family miracle. "If people hadn't been praying, where would I be? Would we be this far along in the recovery process?" asks Nancy.

Recently one of Wade's therapists described Mr. Watts's fantastic progress "a miracle."

"I totally agree with that, and I think it's because God is answering people's prayers," wife Nancy told the *Baptist Press*.

The experience has drawn her closer to God. "As I look back, I can see how he has carried me each step. I realize that being faithful to God even in the difficult times is the best decision one can make," she says.

She finds miracles are also "little things, small blessings that accumulate day by day."

Her son Marcus's recovery has been particularly amazing. Physically and mentally he is back to ninety percent. He is adjusting well to the fourth grade at Baptist School, is making new friends, is dealing manfully—along with his brother, Joshua, eight—with the pain of missing his father.

Husband Wade's progress has been much slower. It

was weeks after the accident before he could be flown home, because of brain and internal injuries. Even as he improved, it was unclear whether his mind would heal. Nancy never stopped praying for that miracle. Every day she visited the hospital. She would converse at length with Wade, filling him in on daily events and family matters—all the time hoping she'd get a reply or some other kind of response.

She wasn't sure if he even understood what she was telling him, until one day there was a breakthrough. As she spoke, he began blinking his eyes. From then on they were able to work out a system where Wade would blink yes or no in response to her questions.

Nancy knew then that his mind was alert and his memory intact. It was the first hopeful sign that her miracle was progressing.

Encouraging signs like this have kept Nancy's situation bearable. But she has had to be strong in other ways—particularly for young Marcus's sake.

Although he's recovering steadily, he still has special needs. His short-term memory suffers—but he still wants things to come easily, as they did for him before.

His mother tries to be patient. She sympathizes with his frustrations. And beyond his frustration in not being able to do things is his need to understand why things are different.

"Marcus knows that God saved him, that he was very close to dying and that God spared his life," Nancy says. "But he misses Peru and his home a lot. That's where he's coming from: 'Why do we have to be here? Why did it have to happen?' It's tough for me. I have no answer for him. God did not cause it, but for some reason he allowed it to happen, and we just don't know why."

Nancy, too, is eager to return to the family mission in Peru. And she's confident they will one day. Meantime, she is finding strength in the prayers of friends and colleagues.

"The miracle is continuing," she enthuses. "First we got one in Marcus, and now it appears Wade is (healing), too. We're just going to keep on praying and working really hard, see how far we can get, because no one really knows."

## Priest Heals Sick and Dying

Sick and dying people flock by the thousands to prayer meetings held by Catholic missionary Emilien Tardif—and many of them leave miraculously cured!

"I know the Bible says the blind will see, the crippled will walk—but I never thought I'd see that with my own eyes," declared Belgian physician Dominic Hubert, who attended one of Father Tardif's prayer meetings in Paray-le-Monial, France.

"I was very skeptical of the so-called miraculous cures attributed to Father Tardif. But I saw paralyzed people on stretchers get up and walk. I saw seven people in wheelchairs stand up and walk.

"I examined one man who claimed he had been deaf for years but could suddenly hear perfectly. I realized he'd had surgery to remove his ear cavities and the bones in his ears. It was impossible for him to be able to hear again. Yet there he was in front of me, hearing my every word! Father Tardif has a definite ability to bring cures to people by the power of prayer."

And Dr. Francoise Bertrand, a Belgian pediatrician who also attended the prayer meeting, reported afterward: "I was part of a medical panel dealing with children who came forward claiming to be cured. One man held a six-month-old baby whose right arm had been paralyzed since birth. By the end of the prayer meeting, the baby was clinging to his father's jacket with his 'useless' arm—the first time he had moved it."

By the end of the day, almost two hundred people had made statements that they were cured of illnesses including chronic migraine, arthritis, paralysis, deafness, blindness, and more.

Father Tardif, sixty-eight, was born in Canada, but for thirty-eight years has been a missionary in the Dominican Republic. He says his powers of healing came to him in 1973 after he survived near-fatal tuberculosis.

"Doctors gave me two months to live," the missionary told the *National Enquirer*. "Five members of the Church came to see me and said, 'Have faith in the Lord and He will cure you.' They laid their hands on me and prayed.

"I felt a powerful heat rising in my lungs. It was the burning love of Jesus curing me. I knew my life had to be devoted to healing people."

Today, the healing missionary travels the world, holding prayer meetings. He says all he has to do is pray as hard as he can. The strength of his prayers produces an energy that others can pick up, he says.

In Lebanon in 1995, 45,000 people came to pray with Father Tardif and 410 afflicted persons were cured—thirty-two of them suffering from so-called incurable illnesses such as cancer.

"I am a priest who prays for Christ to heal people. It is Jesus who does the healing."

Jean Audras, a retired French railroad worker, was suffering from blocked arteries in 1988 and faced death unless he underwent a dangerous operation. Instead, he went to one of Father Tardif's prayer meetings.

"I sat about twelve feet away from the altar and started to pray," said Audras. "Suddenly, Father Tardif's eyes caught mine and he announced, 'Crippled people will walk and blocked arteries will open.'

"That night, a warmth seemed to spread through my chest. I went to my doctor and he was stunned to discover my arteries were completely clear and I had no need for surgery. I'm convinced Father Tardif is a saint. He works miracles!"

## The Forest of Miracles

High in the mountains of Bulgaria is a miraculous forest where the sick and dying go to pray—and emerge completely cured!

That's the electrifying report coming out of Krustova Gora, or Forest of the Cross, where legend has it a piece of Christ's cross was hidden during the Middle Ages.

Little Vasko Marinska was five years old—and his inability to talk baffled doctors. Desperate for a cure, his loving mom took him to pray at the chapel in Krustova Gora—and miraculously, he began speaking!

"I could not cure him—but God did!" said the boy's stunned physician, Dr. Penka Ivanova. "After visiting Krustova Gora, little Vasko began chattering like a magpie. It's a miracle!"

Another mute youngster, Angel Vulkova, four, also was able to talk after praying at the chapel. "We had no hope," said his mother, Petrana. "But God has given my child a miracle!"

Mayor Kostadin Nedev of the nearby town of Borovo declared, "Many people have received miracles in the chapel."

And Father Vasili Arininski, a Greek Orthodox priest at the chapel, confirmed, "Miracles happen here all the time."

Elena Sarahosheva, forty-five, from Smolyan, suffered a devastating stroke and was unable to walk.

After praying at the chapel, she says, "I stood up and walked away. God had healed me!"

Recalled Father Arininski: "One little boy who came here was paralyzed. I had him placed near the cross and I sprinkled him with holy water. Something moved me to say, 'Stand up and kiss the cross'—and he did. That little boy runs and plays with friends today as if nothing were ever wrong.

"With my own eyes, I have also seen a little blind girl regain her vision, three mute boys begin to speak, and a crippled woman rise and walk. Women who are unable to conceive have become pregnant after praying at our cross."

Until the end of the Cold War, the Communists had placed Krustova Gora off limits to worshipers, and the sick had to sneak there. But now, says Mayor Nedev, "Hundreds of people drive to Krustova Gora every weekend. It has become the most popular religious site in Bulgaria."

# Chapter Five

*Virgin Mary Miracles*

When one reads of sightings of the Blessed Virgin Mary, the mind automatically places it in some exotic location—usually overseas, like the shrines of Lourdes, Fatima, or Medjugorje in Yugoslavia.

But many American pilgrims don't have that far to travel these days as more and more Virgin Mary sightings and related healing shrines crop up on their doorsteps.

While the Blessed Virgin continues to make miraculous appearances around the world, in the U.S. alone she's been spotted:

- In Ohio over a period of nine months—in a chapel in Barberton and a field in Wadsworth—Mary was spotted dressed not in her classic white-and-blue garb, but in red, or in an outfit of white, gold, and tan.
- In the sun above a Denver hilltop. Thousands of believers come to watch visions of Mary in the heavens. They stare at the sun so long that doctors fear for their eyesight.

- In a field near Kettle River, Minnesota, a Virgin vision urges the faithful to erect a large church on the site.
- In Joseph Januszkiewicz's backyard in Marlboro, New Jersey, the Virgin has made several appearances. Police work overtime on crowd control.
- In a mud-smeared kitchen window at an apartment house in Oxnard, California, a likeness of the Blessed Virgin manifested, causing crowd congestion. A frustrated building manager had the whole window removed.
- In the 1980s, a young restaurant worker said Mary appeared on an outside wall of a Presbyterian church in Royal Oak, Michigan. More than eighty thousand people visited the site over the period of a year.

"We are seeing an incredible outpouring of faith. This is one of the most important times in the history of the church," says Janice Connell, a Pittsburgh author of several books about appearances of Mary at Medjugorje in Yugoslavia.

There are some critics who say many Marian followers are gullible, since the vast majority of the physical healings reported at shrines are never documented by doctors.

Many Catholics consider the Marian revival itself to be a miracle, but there are natural forces behind it, too.

Appearances by Mary can satisfy deep spiritual yearnings for reassurances, says Sandra Zimdars-Swartz, professor of religious studies at the University of Kansas. "They give a real sense that, even when there are chaotic events in the world, there still is some kind of divine plan and we still are all going to make it through."

Sometimes the messages from Mary are not exactly what the faithful want to hear. In the Akron, Ohio, area, visionary Tony Fernwalt reports that Jesus is very angry and eager to punish the world for its evil deeds, and Mary, in her messages, claims she is the only heavenly force holding Jesus back.

Visionary Fernwalt's controversial claims have not blunted his credibility. And sometimes skepticism of a visionary can strengthen his support, believes Professor Zimdars-Swartz.

Skepticism can be healthy, according to the Reverend Joseph Galic, a Croatian priest who grew up near Medjugorje, the Bosnian city where the latest and now world-famous shrine is located, and who is now pastor of St. Jerome Catholic Church in Detroit.

Even the Reverend Jozo Zovko, the parish priest in Medjugorje, was skeptical in 1981 when six children told him they had seen Mary. Father Jozo said, "Don't believe this. We don't know these children. They are not educated." Jozo thought it might be some kind of Communist plot to embarrass the Church.

"But then even Father Jozo saw the Blessed Mother," Father Galic said. "Then Jozo Zovko became the children's staunchest defender."

Father Galic has never seen a vision of Mary, despite ten trips to his homeland since the children spotted Mary. Still, he believes the visionaries are telling the truth.

The whole message of Medjugorje is to lead people back into church, back to the rosary, back to confession and prayer and the Mass," he says.

The following is a fascinating guide to Virgin Mary sightings, both at home and abroad.

## THE BIG THREE

Only three visitations by the Virgin Mary have survived the grueling authentication process of the Vatican. They include:

- The Virgin of Guadalupe
- The Lady of Lourdes
- The Miracle of Fatima

## The Virgin of Guadalupe

Historians believe the apparition of the Virgin Mary that first appeared in 1531 on a small hill at Guadalupe, just outside Mexico City, may have prevented a bloody civil war between Indians and their Spanish oppressors.

Like Juan Diego, the Indian peasant who first saw her, the Virgin had brown skin and black hair. Her appearance marked the beginning of the mestizo culture, created by the merging of Indian and Spanish ways in Mexico.

There are baffling aspects linked to the miracle, however, that even the most confirmed cynics cannot explain.

When the poor Aztec Indian reported the amazing supernatural encounter of Juan de Zumarraga, Bishop of Mexico, the skeptical church leader asked for proof.

When Diego next encountered the brilliantly shining apparition, he told her he needed proof of her divine nature. She directed him to climb to the top of the hill. Although it was the middle of winter, the Aztec found roses growing there.

He dumped the roses at the bishop's feet. As he did so, Bishop Zumarraga noticed Diego's rough cloak—a brilliantly colored image of the Virgin of Guadalupe had been spontaneously impressed on the cactus fiber garment.

The four-hundred-year-old garment is on display today above the altar of the Basilica of the Virgin of Guadalupe in Villa Madero, a suburb of Mexico City.

In 1895, the Church officially proclaimed the saint

to be the Queen of Mexico. The Virgin of Guadalupe is honored by Catholics throughout the nation as the patron saint of Mexico.

Divine intercession from the Virgin has been credited with thousands of spontaneous cures of the lame and ill, and with many other miracles.

Annually, in December, millions of Mexicans and Americans of Mexican descent flood into the giant Basilica of the Virgin of Guadalupe on the hillside site of the apparition for a pre-Christmas rite honoring the Queen of Mexico. Many crawl on their knees for miles, flagellating their bare backs in penance with thorny cactus before at last limping into the church to attend Masses led by a battery of priests.

## The Lady of Lourdes

The holy grotto in the foothills of the French Pyrenees, with its miraculous healing waters, attracts invalids and pious pilgrims from throughout the world who come to seek healings or merely to testify to and renew their faith.

An underground spring has become a fountain of faith and healing since it was revealed on February 11, 1858, to Bernadette Soubirous during a Marian apparition that appeared in a cave under a cliff. Nearly three million people a year make a pilgrimage to bathe in the healing waters of the Massabielle grotto where the fourteen-year-old girl was visited by the glowing figure of the Virgin Mary almost 150 years ago.

Incredibly, since the devout and the needy began flocking to the grotto to seek divine remedy in the sparkling waters, more than five thousand cures have been reported. Of those, a medical committee has determined that more than sixty appear to be so completely baffling, contradicting scientific expectations, that they deserve recognition as true miracles.

The sixty-fifth healing accepted as legitimate by the committee and by the Church was that of an eleven-year-old girl from Paterno, Italy, who doctors said had no more than three months to live because of a cancerous tumor in her leg.

Without telling her how grave her illness really was, her parents took her to Lourdes and immersed her in the magical waters. Doctors were baffled when the tumor disappeared. The girl, Delizia Cirolli, grew up to become a nurse.

## The Miracle of Fatima

Around midday on May 13, 1917, a powerful bolt of lightning struck in a cloudless sky and the Virgin Mary appeared before three awestruck peasant children at Fatima, Portugal, as they watched over their grazing sheep.

The apparition, that of a young girl wearing a white veil bordered with gold, shone from the branches of an oak tree. She was clearly seen by Lucia Santos and her cousins, Francesco and Jacinta Marto.

"I come from heaven," the vision informed them. The Virgin told them to return to the same location on the thirteenth day of each of the next six months, when she would make additional appearances.

By July, word had spread and a huge crowd was waiting to share the supernatural spectacle at the site of the appearances, the Cova da Irea, which formed an almost perfectly shaped amphitheater.

While the crowd watched, a white orb of light was observed suspended over a nearby tree and the Virgin Mary appeared, promising that a miracle would occur on October 13. Lucia also reported that day a terrifying vision of hell, and it was eventually revealed she was also given several prophecies linked to Russia and the end of World War II, which was still years in the future.

Seventy thousand people observed and listened in the rain on that amazing October day when the apparition again showed up and explained she was Our Lady of the Rosary and desired a chapel built in her honor. Many journalists were spotted among the crowd, as well as some photographers, although no good photographs were produced of the solar miracle that occurred that day.

For twelve long minutes a brilliant silver disc of light danced in the sky as flames flared and shot out from the circle. There was panic when it appeared for a moment as if the dancing disc were about to crash into the crowd, but moments later it simply disappeared.

Observers reported that despite the drenching rain that fell on them throughout the period of the miraculous occurrences later described as "the dance of the sun," their clothing remained dry.

When Lucia, the girl who had first seen the apparition, was fourteen, she entered a convent and eventually became Sister Mary Lucia of the Immaculate Heart. A few years after taking her vows, at the request of her bishop, Sister Mary Lucia wrote out a list of secrets Our Lady of the Rosary had revealed to her, including the early deaths of her cousins. Francesco and Jacinta died in 1919 and 1920 during the influenza epidemic that swept the world.

Other elements of the Fatima secrets included a warning that a second world war would descend on mankind if God's children continued offending Him, and that the conflagration would be heralded by a mysterious display in the heavens. Twenty months before the beginning of World War II, Europe was electrified by a spectacular display of the aurora borealis.

The nun reported that the Blessed Virgin also included a plea that the world pray for Russia, so that nation would not spread its evils throughout the world.

The final portion of the secrets of Fatima has never been publicly revealed, although the message was unsealed by Pope Pius XII and several cardinals in 1960. According to reports, they read it with "expressions of horror." Sister Mary Lucia continued her quiet devotions behind the walls of convents until her death.


# OTHER SIGHTINGS


## Georgia's Seer

On the thirteenth of every month the Blessed Virgin is said to meet with a middle-aged housewife in Conyers, Georgia, passing on messages of great importance to the world.

A native of Cambridge, Massachusetts, Nancy Fowler, forty-seven, is a former nurse married to an Air Force man. She began having terrifying demonic visions in 1985. But through her devout religious faith, she succeeded in exorcising the demons, who were replaced by visions of Jesus, then by the Madonna and other saints and angels.

Heavenly beings often appear to her in brilliant bursts of light or showers of gold dust, and are frequently accompanied by a strong odor of roses.

Today, thousands of pilgrims journey to her home east of Atlanta to leave petitions, messages, flowers, and other offerings around a statue of Our Lady of Fatima located behind Nancy's house.

Messages announced by the seer are repeated by a Spanish translator and sometimes focus on some matters as an earthquake in Japan, but others deal with more traditional spiritual affairs, such as urging more prayer, opposing abortion, and encouraging religious fealty.

Mrs. Fowler also answers questions from worshipers about matters ranging from such things as how Halloween should be celebrated to the possibilities and timing for Cuba's freedom from the yoke of Communist rule.

## The Madonna of Medjugorje

Very young children with their pure souls and minds uncluttered by tangled matters of philosophy are often more naturally sensitive to supernatural phenomena than adults, and are frequently chosen as the conduits for spiritual messages.

So it was at Medjugorje, in the wine and tobacco country of western Yugoslavia a few miles inland from the rocky coast of the Adriatic Sea, on June 24, 1981, when the Holy Mother appeared to six children and promised to confide a series of important secret messages about the future to them. Each child was to be blessed with ten secrets, which could be repeated only to a priest. Some of the children subsequently revealed their secrets, and therefore no longer shared in new visions with the others.

Most of the messages were simple and stressed the importance of fasting, prayer, faith, penance, and the need to bring people back to the Church. One of the messages, however, was a prediction of the Balkan War, ten years before it actually broke out, and a promise that it could be avoided if more people prayed.

Another, strikingly similar to one of the messages at Fatima, and revealed before the breakup of the old

Soviet Union and the fall of Communism there, fore-
told that Russia would eventually glorify God.

Ivan Dragicevic, one of the children, who was a
teenager when the apparition first appeared to him
and his companions, has said talks with the holy figure
have lasted as long as thirty minutes.

In 1988, one of the visionary children, Marija Pav-
lovic, journeyed to Birmingham, Alabama, and donated a kidney to her brother during an operation at
University Hospital.

While she remained in Shelby County, she continued to have daily visions of the figure she and the
others call the Gospa (Madonna) and shared her experience and ecstasy with huge crowds of worshipers.

## Ireland's Dancing Madonnas

A life-size plaster-and-concrete statue of the Madonna is one of the most revered religious icons in
Ireland. Thousands of people claim to have witnessed
the statue shimmying and shaking in its leafy hillside
grotto just outside the hamlet of Ballinspittle in
County Cork.

It was twilight on July 30, 1985, when Clare Ma-
hony, seventeen, looked up from her prayers to peer
at the statue of the Madonna that had stood in the
same grotto for thirty years.

It was swaying, and as the teenager, her mother,
sister, and neighbors watched in astonishment, it appeared to be about to topple off the cliff and onto the
shaken worshipers.

News quickly spread about the moving statue and
thousands of people, including television crews, hur-
ried to the shrine at Ballinspittle. Most of them agreed
that they, too, saw the statue of the Madonna move.

Worshipers at Mount Melleray claimed their statue

of the Virgin Mary, standing beside the Monavullagh River, not only was seen to move in 1985, but it also spoke.

That year, in fact, statues of the Virgin were said to be moving, blinking, and breaking into Mona Lisa smiles all over Ireland, and some were photographed in action by television cameras.

## Christiana's Vision

Virgin Mary miracles occur in even the most remote regions of the world, and her apparition appears to the most unlikely witnesses.

A prime example of this are the sightings in Nigeria, Africa, by a young girl named Christiana Agbo. Christiana lives in the remote village of Aokpe, which boasts a population of about five thousand—most of whom have accepted Christianity and the Catholic faith.

Christiana, reported to be in her early teens, first witnessed a vision in October 1992, when she was working on her mother's cassava farm with some of her sisters. She was attracted to a light flashing nearby. She asked her sisters if they could see the light. They could not, but reassured her it must have been the sun.

Later, Christiana went to the same spot to collect healing herbs for an ailing aunt. Suddenly, there appeared to her "a woman of very rare beauty, with fair hair."

Christiana's first impulse was to run away. But she noticed the woman was smiling at her in a comforting way. She saw the same vision in the same spot many times after that, until one day she summoned the courage to ask, "Who are you?" The vision responded gently, "I am the Blessed Mother. I will come next

time to tell you what I want from you." The vision
then vanished.

Christiana, dazed by what she had seen and heard,
ran home and told her mother. Her family's first reaction was that she was "possessed by ogbe (water
spirits)."

Then in May 1993, in the same spot, the Virgin
again appeared to Christiana and requested the awestruck young girl to "offer sacrifice, do penance, pray
for the whole world, and assist the sorrowful"—where-
upon Christiana went home and prepared a shrine to
the Virgin in her room, where she conscientiously
prays every day, often in the company of young
friends.

News of Christiana's visions soon spread. At first,
Edwin Ogbanje, the church leader in Aokpe, threatened to expel from the church any villager who chose
to validate the "so-called apparitions."

Church leader Ogbanje then told parish priest Father John Beirne, based in nearby Ugbokolo, about
the sightings. Father Beirne in turn referred the matter
to another priest, Father Samuel Ehatikpo, a local authority on Virgin Mary apparitions.

Father Samuel came to Aokpe and interviewed several villagers. Impressed, he began visiting Aokpe on
a regular basis, often joining Christiana and her
friends at their prayer sessions.

As word continued to spread, the number of people
visiting Aokpe, and joining Christiana and her companions in prayer, increased. Christiana was advised
by priests to pray for a sign that the vision and messages were indeed God-sent.

The Virgin vision responded that even if people saw
a sign, they would still doubt, but she promised to give
the sign.

On July 30, 1995, Christiana was instructed by a
heavenly voice to go to a certain spot on her mother's
cassava farm at around five p.m. and observe the sun.

In an astonishing event, very similar to the happening at Fatima in 1916, Christiana and her prayer companions watched openmouthed as the sun started spinning round and round, throwing out different colors such as red, yellow, blue, and sparkling green.

The incredible display lasted for almost a full hour and was witnessed by many visitors and would-be pilgrims to the village of Aokpe. Some witnesses reported seeing a vision of Mary in the sun, first alone, then with Jesus and Joseph. One woman recalled seeing a burning tree. Another witness swore she saw Mary holding the infant Jesus.

On August 4, 1995, the Blessed Virgin appeared in another vision to Christiana. During this apparition, Christiana was also confronted with a vision of Jesus, who told her, "I come today because of those who bear my cross but do not carry it well."

The vision then cautioned Christiana about two upcoming events—first, a warning that Satan would come to earth in 1998 and attempt to deceive people into believing he was Jesus. Second, that the world would experience three days of total darkness during which unpleasantness would befall those who did not respect and follow God's laws.

In subsequent prayer sessions at her homemade shrine, Christiana began going into trances lasting up to six hours. During her trances, she claims to have been shown heaven, purgatory, and hell.

On November 21, 1995, more than eight thousand people, including Archbishop Ganaka, gathered at Christiana's mother's farm—at the spot now called the Apparition Ground—to pray with Christiana. She relayed to the throng the following message from Mary:

"Say your Holy Rosary every day, every day. Pray and do penance. Pray because of the time that is coming that is so great. So great. The time of three days of darkness. It is because I don't want any souls to get lost that I am motivated to come down from heaven to reveal secrets to you so that prayers will be said to console Jesus. Jesus is annoyed greatly because of the sins of the world. The thorns surrounding His Sacred Heart are now piercing Him greatly, especially because of the three days of darkness, the time God will release His anger and the whole world will shake. Out of my love as the Mother of God, I now beg you not to sin again, and pray for the Grace to enable you to stop sin. Continue to do what pleases Christ. May He unite you in His love, and in the love of God. Those of you that keep the laws of God and the Ten Commandments, God will protect you against any problems and sufferings that will come during the three days of darkness. Assemble yourselves together and pray all the time."

## Jesus and Mary in Rwanda

Over the last two decades, the Virgin Mary has appeared to seven young people in the little cottage town of Kibeho, Rwanda, in Africa. Three of the young people are boarders in a college administered by nuns in a poor area. Three of them live in the bush. The apparitions began in November 1981, but as of early 1997, as hostilities in that war-torn country eased, they had ceased. In 1982, the apparition wept and the visionaries wept with Her as she showed the youngsters images of the future war, much bloodshed, corpses left abandoned, and a gaping abyss. The message she delivered to the young folk during her visits was a simple one: Set a good example for the world.

On August 15, 1988, the local bishop, a Monsignor Gehanay, gave official church recognition to the apparitions.

# "Miracle" in Unlikely Place
# Attracts Faithful in Florida

They flocked by the thousands to pay homage to what many believed to be a true Christmas miracle—a rainbow-hued outline resembling the Virgin Mary, shimmering on the side of a tall glass building.

Believers were convinced they were witnessing a God-sent miracle. Skeptics were equally convinced the image was produced by liquid chemicals cast high into the air by water sprinklers.

Whether earthly or spiritual, the "miracle" attracted the faithful. They prayed and sang their hearts out in a parking lot next to busy U.S. Highway 19 in Clearwater, Florida.

In one day, Clearwater police counted nineteen thousand people arriving in two and a half hours, said police information officer Wayne Shelor.

Twenty-four hours after the crowds started coming, Clearwater police had portable toilets on site and established street crossings and around-the-clock security that included twenty-five police officers and twenty-five city workers on duty during the busy daylight hours.

Believers left dozens of potted poinsettias, hundreds of rosaries, thousands of candles, and infinite heartache.

Pleas, hand-written in English and Spanish, many by children, asking for divine help for the dead, the dying, and the doomed, were left at the site.

"Find a place in heaven for my darling baby."

"Please bring my daddy home from prison, where he doesn't belong."

"Please help my father walk again."

Wallet-sized school photos of smiling children, presumably dead, dying, or missing, were posted prominently on a nearby wall. Visitors reading the pleas frequently began weeping.

Pushing baby strollers and relatives in wheelchairs, the faithful still flock to the building. Sunday is a particularly busy day. Pilgrims leave offerings like fruit baskets and chocolate cakes, as well as hundreds of flowers, rosaries, and candles. Alongside family photographs and hand-printed letters are heartbreaking requests.

"Mary, please bless my father, who committed suicide," one note says.

Another note is penciled on the funeral program of a toddler who died. The program features a picture of the smiling child sitting on a teddy bear's lap. "Bobby, we miss you in this life, but we'll see you in the next."

"I can't believe how moving this is," said a Clearwater resident, who stopped on his way home. "I'm not a believer and I'm not impressed with what that is up on the glass. But I never thought I'd feel like this. It's amazing."

"It's truly a miracle," said one tearful Hispanic woman, who made the pilgrimage with three friends from Naples, Florida. Carrying rosary beads, cameras, and video recorders, the quartet planned to make the three-hour drive back home with proof of what they'd seen.

"This time of year is the birth of Christ. And what better time for His Mother to come here and show herself?" the woman asked, fighting back tears of emotion.

The image covers a two-story glass panel on the side of the Seminole Finance Corporation, a used-car financing firm. After the story appeared on television, it attracted more than 200,000 people in five days, causing massive traffic jams.

The owner of the building is not the least concerned that his place of business has evolved into a religious shrine. A Catholic himself, he doesn't understand why nonbelievers—or naysayers, as he calls them—struggle to come up with antimiracle explanations.

"Any way you look at it, it's creating some wonderful feelings," he says. "These are people looking for hope. They're trying to increase their faith. I think it's wonderful."

This isn't the only "miracle" that has cropped up in unlikely spots across the country in recent years. Consider these extraordinary reports:

- In Phoenix, Arizona, the Virgin Mary, Jesus, a flock of angels, and a dove appeared on Raymond Rodrigues's bathroom door.
- In Stone Mountain, Georgia, a forkful of pasta on a Pizza Hut billboard revealed Jesus's face to the faithful.
- In New York City, thousands lined up in a driving rain to see what believers said was Jesus's image in a fifth-floor apartment window.

"It's contagious. If someone believes it and starts to feel it, those feelings are transferred to others in very complicated ways," says David Klimek, a psychologist in Ann Arbor, Michigan, and author or *Wisdom, Jesus and Psychotherapy.*

"People don't want a scientific, intellectual approach to their faith," Klimek says. "When people are hurting and desperate, they're not interested in science or logic. They need this from the inside."

## Statue of Mary Cries Bloody Tears

Thousands of devout pilgrims say they've seen a crude wooden statue of the Virgin Mary miraculously cry tears of blood!

"It did happen. I saw it," declared Catholic bishop Salvador Lazo, who heads the Philippine diocese where the two-foot-tall statue is located. "First there was a sweet fragrance. Then the tears of blood flowed from the statue's eyes. It's a miracle."

The incredible statue—on a hill in the city of Agoo—began crying tears of blood early in 1993, according to Philippine News Agency reporter Mon Francisco.

The site is where a young boy claims he saw the Virgin Mary four years earlier.

"She reportedly told him she would visit him on the first Saturday of each month and create miracles for the faithful if they'd gather there and pray for peace," said Francisco. "The crowds came by the hundreds. All said they could feel the heavenly presence. But there were no reports of miracles until February 6, 1993, when five thousand pilgrims saw the statue weep bloody tears!"

Added twenty-four-year-old Rowena Arcega, "I was standing next to the statue when I saw the Virgin crying tears of blood. A shout went up as others realized what was happening. Then a feeling of peace swept over us."

That night, about twenty people brought the statue to Bishop Lazo.

"We talked for a while, and as they were getting ready to leave, we noticed a sweet fragrance," the bishop said. "Then someone noticed the statue was crying blood. At first we were afraid. Then we sang 'Salve Regina,' a hymn to the Blessed Virgin. We all knelt and prayed. Afterward, we felt joy."

One month later, more than a million people showed up at the sacred hillside for a service that was shown on television in the Philippines, reports Francisco.

"Tens of thousands of people—including me—saw the figure of the Virgin Mary atop a tree," the newsman said. "I was not hallucinating. I am a trained observer and I am a skeptic about such things. But I know what I saw. She was dressed in a white-and-blue gown. It was a fleeting vision, only three or four seconds. But she was there. I found myself on my knees praying like everyone else."

The Vatican is investigating the apparition and the statue. Bishop Lazo says the visitations are similar to Mary's miraculous appearances to three children at Fatima, Portugal, in 1917.

"The message is the same," Lazo said. "Pray for peace."


## Boy Leaves Wheelchair and Walks After Pilgrimage

Thirteen-year-old Nicola Pacini thought he was destined to be confined to a wheelchair for the rest of his life—until he was completely cured after visiting a Yugoslav shrine to the Virgin Mary.

His five years of crippling pain since he was stricken and paralyzed with muscular dystrophy were erased in a matter of miraculous minutes.

"When I saw Nicola standing and walking in front of me on his return from the shrine, I couldn't believe my eyes," Dr. Rosella Mengonzi, the youngster's physician, told the *Enquirer.* "He has completely recovered from an incurable disease, and I cannot explain it medically!"

Says a joyful Nicola: "I had a weird feeling in front of the statue of the Virgin Mary—as if something were moving inside me. I suddenly felt an urge to get up and walk. An irresistible force was pushing me to get up from the wheelchair in which I had spent the last five years.

"I thought it was impossible—but I found myself

standing up without even knowing how. It's an incredible miracle!''

Nicola, who lives with his family near Florence, Italy, was forced into a wheelchair and a life without the use of his legs. Four operations did nothing to help.

Recently, before Nicola was to leave for the United States and a fifth operation, his parents persuaded him to visit the Virgin Mary Medjugorje Shrine in Yugoslavia.

Nicola didn't want to go at first. "There are millions of cripples in the world. What makes my parents think the Virgin will choose me?" he recalled wondering.

But one night he dreamed of the Virgin Mary beckoning to him. When he described the dream to his mother, Mrs. Pacini saw it as a clear sign to visit the shrine.

After a rugged bus and ferry trip, the family arrived at the holy place on December 8, 1990. Mrs. Pacini pushed her son's wheelchair right in front of the Virgin's statue.

"After a few minutes of praying, I felt my right hand, which was locked in paralysis, slowly open!" Nicola said. He returned to the shrine the next day.

"I prayed, 'Don't just do it for me, but for my parents.' That's when I felt that I had to get up and walk. After taking the first steps, I called to my mother and heard her cry out with joy. She tried to help, but I said, 'Leave me, leave me. I can manage on my own.' ''

As he kept moving, his soul filled with the wonderment of it all—and hundreds of pilgrims at the shrine burst into applause.

"For the first time in five years, I walked. Mary heard my prayers!" said Nicola.

When he returned to Florence, Dr. Mengonzi examined Nicola and was shocked.

"I was sure he would spend his life in a wheelchair,"

she said. "His muscular dystrophy had proved incurable."

But Nicola now romps with his friends, "like he's making up for lost time," said his thankful mom. "Since he came back from the shrine, he won't keep still for a minute."

Says Father Angelo Meliani, the Pacinis' parish priest: "I have no doubts it was a miracle!"

## Virgin Statue Cries Real Tears

An amazing small clay statue of the Virgin Mary enshrined in a small church in the heartland of Brazil actually cries on the thirteenth of every month. Scientists and paranormal investigators have confirmed that they are real tears—bearing all the similarities to human ones.

"This is truly amazing—I've never seen anything like it in my life," said Dr. Nelson Massini, a professor of forensic medicine of Brazil's Campinas State University. "I believe it is a miracle!"

The two-and-a-half-foot-tall statue—Our Lady of the Mystic Rose—was enshrined in late 1989 at San Sebastian Church in Louveira, Brazil. It suddenly began weeping on February 13, 1990, according to Father Antonio Spolardi, the church vicar.

Remembering that blessed day, Father Spolardi said a church painter came running into his office, excitedly yelling, "The statue is crying, the statue is crying!"

"I followed him and could scarcely believe my eyes—there they were, liquid tears dripping down from her left eye," the priest said. "I muttered, 'Holy Mother of God,' and dropped to my knees in prayer.

"Then tears began to drip from her right eye. There was no doubt in my mind it was a miracle. I rang the church bells to announce it to the whole town—and hundreds poured in to see her crying. Her tears didn't stop until midnight.

"Since then she has cried every month on the thirteenth day—the day consecrated to her by our church."

Thousands of people from all over Brazil have stood before Our Lady of the Mystic Rose since the tears began flowing, praying for relief from illness and disabilities. Among recent visitors were twenty scientists from prestigious Campinas State University on a research mission to test the tears.

"We found they contain sodium and potassium, which are components of human tears," said Dr. Massini. "And we are amazed at the volume of tears."

During an hour-long period on the thirteenth day of several months, the scientists collected as many as eighteen tears flowing from the eyes of the statue—and the Virgin's eyes remained moist the whole day.

"It's almost impossible to explain this through scientific principles," said Dr. Fortunato Badan, a forensic pathologist who's also on the research team. "It's hard to see any explanation except a supernatural one."

Lucia Finamori of Louveira has seen the statue cry more than ten times.

"Every time I've witnessed it, I've been filled with a great sense of inner peace and well-being," she said. "It's a beautiful experience. The tears fall just as if the statue were flesh and blood. I know that the Virgin is crying for the state of the world."

## Cancer Cured After Bathing in Shrine

Ravaged by cancer and given just three months to live, schoolgirl Delizia Cirolli made an astounding complete recovery after a pilgrimage to Lourdes, where her mother bathed her in the waters of the holy shrine.

In 1989—nearly thirteen years after Delizia was healed—the Vatican declared the girl's healing a recognized miracle following an intensive investigation involving scrutiny by more than twenty doctors and two religious commissions.

They all agreed that there was absolutely no way Delizia's cure could be explained medically!

Delizia, now twenty-four and a nurse in her hometown of Paterno, Italy, developed a cancerous tumor on her right leg in 1976 when she was just eleven.

Doctors wanted to amputate her leg, but told her parents she would die in three months even if they did the amputation.

"Her mother, a devotee of the Virgin Mary, refused to allow the amputation and decided to take her daughter to Lourdes," said Luigi Bonmarito, archbishop of the region where the family lives. "Friends collected the money for the long journey to France, and in August of 1976 Delizia was taken to Lourdes by her mother."

The girl's mom bathed her in the holy waters at the shrine of the Virgin Mary while praying fervently for a cure.

Delizia says that at the time she didn't know why she was in the water. "I wasn't particularly devoted to the Lady of Lourdes back then," she said. "My faith was only a child's faith. I didn't even know I had cancer and was facing death—my parents kept telling me I had only a knee inflammation.

"When my mother asked me to get into the Lourdes baths, I did everything to get out of it. Finally, I had to obey my mother.

"After my pilgrimage to Lourdes, my condition took a turn for the worse. But one day in December of that year, I suddenly felt better. I went out—and when I got back home, I found my doctor waiting. He examined me very carefully and took me straight to a hospital for X rays. When the doctors saw that my tumor had disappeared, they couldn't believe their eyes!"

That's when the intensive study of Delizia's case began. Over the following years, she made a series of trips to be examined by internationally known doctors in France and Italy.

In 1980 the Lourdes Medical Bureau—composed of highly respected physicians—declared her cure to be "scientifically inexplicable," said Dr. Theodore Mangiapan.

And in July 1989, Archbishop Bonmarito issued a proclamation declaring that her cure was "an act of God"—the final necessary step for the Vatican to recognize the healing as a miracle.

"Finally, we may officially announce that the healing of Delizia Cirolli is a true miraculous event," the archbishop said. "Three medical and two theological commissions that studied Delizia's case for thirteen years have asserted that beyond any doubt there is no scientific explanation for Delizia's recovery."

Added Delizia, who is now married: "It still seems impossible that this incredible event happened to me, a humble girl from a small town with no particularly strong faith. I now pray to Our Lady of Lourdes every day."

# Thousands See Virgin Mary on Road Sign

A busy highway intersection became even busier when an image of the Virgin Mary mysteriously appeared on a road sign!

Believers by the thousands flocked to a highway intersection near Sunnyside, Washington. Even the police are treating it as a very special happening.

"It's the full figure of the Virgin Mary," patrolman Chico Rodriguez told reporters. "You really can't make out the face—it's more of a profile."

Within hours of the first sighting, throngs of people forced authorities to close the road at the intersection of Washington State Highway 241 and the Yakima Valley Highway.

Many visitors prayed, while others hung wreaths, lit candles, and danced to the beat of a drum.

"There were so many people walking around out there, we decided to barricade it and set down some flares, just to be safe," says state patrol sergeant Curt Hattell. "They kept coming and going all night, looking behind the sign at the shiny aluminum part."

Blanca Rodriguez, of Grandview, was one of the faithful who witnessed the Madonna's image.

"She had her hands clasped together," said Rodriguez in an interview. "She was looking straight forward."

The crowds became so dense that even Grandview mayor Jesse Palacios had to help with traffic control.

"It was a religious, church-type atmosphere," he recalled. "I think this is a once-in-a-lifetime experience."

## Chapter Six

❦

# Miracle Kids

Goodness attracts goodness. That's why so many innocent children are the recipients of miracles or angel visitations.

Says angel expert Jennifer Sutton: "People can attract miracles into their lives—if they really want and really believe. But if you are a skeptic, tunnel-visioned, cynical, afraid of loving and being loved—all of those things and much more—then you can forget about enjoying any kind of spiritual experience.

"That's why children have the jump on adults. Their minds are open, their attitudes are receptive to all kinds of exciting emotions and feelings. Miracles land in their laps. And their angels are never far from their sides."

Consider these heartwarming stories of how a loving, caring power is taking care of our young.

## Toddler Plunges
## Seven Floors—and Lives!

Doctors and other witnesses are convinced the sky was crowded with angels the day twenty-three-month-old David Markotan fell from a seventh-floor window and survived.

"There can be no other explanation," Dr. Edward Barksdale, Jr., told the *National Enquirer*. "It's a miracle this boy is alive."

Little David's awful plunge took place one balmy day during the summer of 1996 while he was playing near a window secured by a screen. When the lively tot leaned on the screen, it suddenly gave way.

His mom Michelle was nearby in the kitchen when her three-year-old daughter, Becky, came running in, yelling, "Mommy! The baby just fell."

"When I rushed into that room and saw the ripped screen," said Michelle later, "I was scared to death. Then I looked out the window and saw my little boy lying on the ground far below. 'My God,' I prayed, 'please don't take my son!' "

The boy's dad, David, Sr., was outside working on his car when he heard a thud about thirty feet away. He turned and got the shock of his life.

There, in a tiny heap, blood trickling from his mouth, was his precious son. His heart leaped into his throat as he saw the boy lying there motionless.

Shattered, David, Sr., picked his son up in his arms and started crying. But what Dad didn't know was that a miracle had just taken place.

His son had missed a metal dumpster by just a few inches and landed without suffering any deadly injuries. Little David was rushed to Children's Hospital in Pittsburgh, where Dr. Barksdale, a pediatric surgeon, expected very grave injuries.

"I thought I'd be dealing with a tragic death or at least life-threatening injuries," said the physician.

A trauma team was ready to rush David into surgery—but when he was examined it was determined he didn't need any surgery. The youngster had suffered a slight concussion, plus a few fractured ribs and bruises. Soon he was on the road to recovery.

Says his grateful father: "I'm just thankful God sent angels to save our son."

And mom Michelle adds: "I may not have believed in miracles before, but I believe in them now. I tuck one into bed every night!"


# Pierced Through Heart
# —but Boy, Eight, Survives


"I didn't cry, Mommy . . . I didn't cry!"

With these plaintive words, little Justin Stiner looked up at his mother from his hospital bed—only hours after he had fallen off a roof onto a steel rod that impaled him through the heart!

Not only did the gusty third-grader survive against all odds, but here he was trying to console and comfort his distraught mom.

Throughout his ordeal he stunned his mother, rescuers, and doctors with his determination to be brave. "When he saw me at the hospital, he proudly told me, 'I was uncomfortable but I never cried,'" his mom, Amanda, later told the *Enquirer*.

"I know. You're a brave little trouper," she responded through a flood of tears.

The freak accident happened on November 12, 1990, in Sierra Vista, Arizona, where eight-year-old Justin, who loves to climb, scrambled up a tree and, from there, onto the roof of his neighbor's house.

His footing was precarious. Horrified, his sister Nicole, twelve, and other children watched as the eighty-six-pound youngster slipped and plunged twelve feet onto the steel rod—which was being used as a stake for coiling a garden hose.

Eighteen sharp inches of the narrow rod penetrated his chest and up his neck to his jaw. As the terrified children ran for help, Justin's body dangled facedown on the four-foot-long rod.

"I'd never seen anything like it in my life," said fire captain Bob Miller, who quickly arrived on the scene.

The rescuers faced a terrible dilemma: They couldn't pull Justin off the rod, because it was acting like a plug, and if it was removed he would bleed to death.

If they tried to cut it, the vibration and movement could damage his heart even more and kill him!

Their choice: Cut the rod while trying to hold the boy perfectly still.

The youngster remained in the tortured position for an eternity of twenty minutes while rescuers working feverishly stabilized him and sawed through the rod.

"Neighbors watched quietly and anxiously," Captain Miller later explained. "All you could hear was the whirr of the machinery, murmured instructions, and our efforts to distract Justin from his predicament."

The youngster and his rescuers made small talk as the minutes ticked by.

Through it all, the courageous boy remained conscious and his heart and lungs continued to work normally!

"There were no cries or whimpers from him the whole time we worked," said Captain Miller. "He set an example that few adults could copy in such a situation. This kid was truly a little hero."

After the rod was finally cut, his rescuers moved fast.

"We loaded Justin into the ambulance and he talked to me the whole time," said Captain Miller. "He talked about his sister and told me how much he loved his bike. Almost as an afterthought he looked at the rod protruding from his chest and said calmly, 'When can you guys take it out of me?'"

After reaching a local hospital, Justin was flown by helicopter seventy miles to the trauma center at the

University Medical Center in Tucson where doctors rushed him into surgery.

When they opened his chest and neck, they found that the half-inch-thick rod had pierced his heart and severed his jugular vein, becoming embedded a fraction of an inch from two major arteries.

"Had it struck either of those arteries, Justin would surely have bled to death!" said Dr. Phillip Richemont, a surgeon who operated on Justin.

Doctors painstakingly unscrewed the threaded rod from Justin's chest, repairing damage as they went. The surgery took over two hours, but went smoothly.

"He's incredible," said Dr. Richemont. "How many people get this kind of injury and survive? It's a one-in-a-billion miracle!"

That night Justin was hooked up to a ventilator, but by the next morning he was breathing on his own. And when Justin woke up, he surprised doctors again.

Said Dr. Richemont, "He looked across at a TV and asked if he could play Nintendo!"

The next day Justin got his wish—he could play the computer game. And just forty-eight hours after the accident, he was out of intensive care.

Said his mom, "I'm not sure I believed in miracles before—but I do now!"


## Tiny Tot Survives—After Freezing to Death!

Tiny tot Karlee Kosolofski was hailed by doctors as "a miracle child" after the hardy two-year-old froze to death in subzero weather—and was brought back to life!

Little Karlee's temperature plunged from a normal 98.6 degrees to 57.2 degrees—seven degrees lower than the lowest body temperature anyone has ever survived, according to *The Guinness Book of Records.*

Her heart stopped beating for nearly eight hours and her body was as hard as a "block of ice," but she was revived thanks to the efforts of a dedicated medical team who worked on her.

"We have witnessed a miracle!" declared Dr. Joy Dobson, an anesthesiologist at Plains Health Center in Regina, Canada, where Karlee was treated.

The toddler's ordeal began in the bitter Saskatchewan winter on February 23, 1994. Her father, Robert, had left their home for his job at a local dairy at two-thirty a.m. The always-curious Karlee tried to follow him out to the garage, which was forty-five feet away from the house. When she walked outside, the door closed behind her and locked automatically.

Shivering, Karlee huddled against the back door. She'd slipped on a coat and boots over her pajamas and diapers, but they couldn't protect her from foot-deep snow and a bone-numbing windchill factor of 40 degrees below zero. She froze within minutes.

Her mother, Karrie, woke up at eight a.m., went downstairs, and got the shock of her life. She found her only child frozen stiff on her doorstep.

"When I rolled her over, the look in her eyes, the way her body felt, I thought she was dead," Karrie told the *National Enquirer.*

Frantic, Karrie called an ambulance. By the time Karlee arrived at the hospital at around nine-thirty, she had no pulse, no heartbeat, and she wasn't breathing.

"Her legs were like something you'd find in a refrigerator freezer," said Dr. John Burgess, a cardiovascular and thoracic surgeon at Plains Health Center. "She was literally like a block of ice."

In a desperate bid to thaw her out, doctors connected Karlee to a heart and lung machine. For nearly five hours, the machine slowly removed Karlee's blood, heated it, then pumped it back into her tiny body.

Karlee's heart started beating when her body reached 77 degrees. Doctors shocked her heart twice to keep it going, and her body gradually warmed up to 98.6 degrees.

Ironically, Karlee's vital organs, including her brain, were virtually undamaged because she froze so quickly, doctors say.

Sadly, she lost the lower part of her left leg to frostbite. But the adorable toddler otherwise made a complete recovery after several weeks in the hospital.

Said Karlee's grandmother, Pat Kosolofski: "Karlee is a fighter—and we're so proud of the way she's come back from the dead. Karlee is our little miracle child!"

# Miracle Boy of Argentina

Often when children in Argentina fall seriously ill and doctors can do little or nothing to help them, their parents take them to see Miguel Angel Gaitan in the small town of Villa Union.

Not only does Miguel enjoy a national reputation as a healer, he is reputed to make other kinds of miracles happen.

Recently, an eight-year-old boy given just a few weeks to live visited Miguel Angel in Villa Union. Within weeks he made a full recovery. And when a woman from Buenos Aires desperately needed a car after her brother wrecked her old Ford, she traveled nine hundred miles by bus just to touch Miguel Angel. The next week she won a new car in a church lottery!

When an eleven-year-old girl wanted high marks on her spelling test, she, too, visited Miguel Angel. She was later able to send him a copy of her perfect score.

For more than three decades, Argentines by the thousands have been flocking to the remote northwest town of only six hundred people, seeking Miguel Angel's miracles. What makes their pilgrimages so remarkable is that miracle-worker Miguel Angel died in 1966, one month short of his first birthday, from meningitis.

On display in a glass-topped casket at the town cemetery is his small, wrinkled corpse, which is remarkably well preserved even after thirty years.

Every day, miracle seekers arrive at the graveyard, bearing such offerings as flowers, teddy bears, toys, baby clothing, and money.

"We call him the miracle child because God has kept his body from decomposing so that all the world can come and see him and be blessed," explained one town resident.

As a special favor to some of the believers who come to Miguel Angel's remains, the dead baby's mother, Argentina Gaitan, who attends his tomb daily, opens the locked coffin and allows them to touch the corpse's head.

"Normally they don't get to touch him, but if they ask, I unlock the case and let them," said Mrs. Gaitan, sixty-four, who has had fifteen children. "But you'll get a miracle whether you touch him or not."

Mrs. Gaitan supplements her family's income by selling cards and trinkets with Miguel Angel's picture for two dollars, along with booklets recounting his all-too-brief life story for fifteen dollars.

The dead baby's coffin is housed in a two-story concrete tomb filled with colorful artificial flowers and glowing testimonials from Argentines who believe the tiny corpse brought a miracle into their lives.

A typical testimonial reads: "Miguel Angel, thank you for the miracle—Jose proposed to marry me yesterday."

"Thanks to you, Miguel Angel, I got 100 on my neonatal exam," reads another.

Villa Union's priest, Father Ricky Alberto Martinez, says that while the Roman Catholic Church only officially recognizes those saints that have been canonized by the Vatican, the Church does not totally ignore the many "unofficial saints" like Miguel Angel.

"We can't negate the feelings that people have for this child and the faith that he has inspired in them," Father Martinez said. "You can't dismiss them as a bunch of uneducated people from the backwoods. This is a national phenomenon. People are reporting miracles all over the country."

Father Martinez would like to head up a full scientific investigation to determine why Miguel Angel's corpse has not decomposed. He would also like to begin a detailed dossier of the miracles that people have claimed.

If he gathers enough evidence, he said, he will apply to have Miguel Angel beatified—the first step toward sainthood.

The bizarre legend of Miguel Angel began with a violent rainstorm in 1973, seven years after his death.

The winds were so strong that they unearthed the baby's coffin. A curious cemetery worker peered inside the casket and was astonished to find the child's remains virtually intact.

He constructed a temporary tomb to house the casket until it could be properly reinterred. Mysteriously, the walls of the makeshift tomb collapsed overnight. It was rebuilt, but the walls kept collapsing.

By this time the whole town was aware of the coffin that refused to be buried. The citizens of Villa Union decided to leave the coffin out in the open.

Mysterious happenings continued. The lid of the coffin kept being removed at night.

"We don't know why this was happening. We even put rocks and heavy objects on the top of the coffin, but every morning we found the lid removed," Mrs. Gaitan said. "Finally we realized that Miguel did not want to be covered. He wanted to be seen, so we placed him in this coffin with a glass lid."

By this time Miguel Angel had been elevated to the status of "miracle child," and as word of the miracle child spread, droves of believers began flocking to Villa Union.

"We've got tour buses coming from all over the country," said Ramon Ricardo Poblete, a municipal official. "Miguel Angel has been good for the town and for the people. We all have to believe in something."

The miraculous modern-day legend of Miguel Angel is not that unusual in Argentina. Miracles are also attributed to the tomb of nineteenth-century mother Difunta Correa, who supposedly died of thirst in the desert—but was survived by her infant son, who lived for weeks on milk from his dead mother's breasts.

Appropriately, bottles of water are the most popular gifts brought to Difunta's resting place in San Juan Province. The gift-bearers, of course, are invariably in search of a miracle.

Anthropologist Iris Guinazu, who specializes in Argentine folklore, said such myths and legends about miracles are likely rooted in ancient Inca civilization. The miracle legends, she believes, were a vestige of an indigenous culture that has been all but wiped out in Argentina, the most heavily Europeanized of Latin American nations.

Ms. Guinazu believes the Difunta Correa legend is related to that of the Inca god Pacha Mama, or Mother Earth, who after becoming dust still generates life.

"These simple, small rituals help preserve the American identity," Ms. Guinazu said of the mixed-race people who predominate in rural Argentina. "For these people, Christianity is too much of an abstraction. They believe in what they see or touch. These rites help them to identify with their true selves."

## A Miracle Visited This Florida Vacation Family

Guardian angels were looking after spunky two-year-old toddler Hays Burton the day he plunged eight stories from a balcony onto an asphalt parking lot, say his family and friends.

Maybe so.

Whatever saved the tot's life was "a miracle," declared Okaloosa County, Florida, sheriff's department spokesman Rick Hord when asked by disbelieving reporters how on earth the kid survived such a horrendous fall.

One of the factors that lessened the boy's injuries— he escaped with minor scrapes and a big bruise on his face—was that he was wearing a padded diaper.

The Huggies disposable diaper he was wearing cushioned his fall. The boy landed on his tail, and as he hit the ground, little pieces of diaper were scattered like chicken feathers all over the parking lot.

Nevertheless, to fall from a height of eight stories without as much as a fractured bone in your body is nothing short of a miracle.

The miraculous drama began when Hays's mom, Velmarie, his brother Drew, seven, sister Ann Claire, three, and two of the children's friends arrived at the Destin, Florida, condominium building on August 7, 1993, for a family vacation. Hays's dad, Greg, an Isola, Mississippi, catfish farmer, was planning to join the group later.

The first morning they were there, brother Drew was up early and left a door open. Little Hays wandered through the unlocked door and onto a balcony, which was fortified by a solid stucco wall.

Curious to see what lay beyond the wall, the blue-eyed, strawberry-blond mischief-maker saw a luggage cart nearby and clambered on top of it to see over the wall.

Wearing only his diaper, he lost his balance, toppled over the wall, and fell eighty feet to the hard surface below.

A neighbor witnessed the fall and alerted Hays's mom. Hearing the yells and the banging on the condo door, Velmarie admits that her heart almost stopped as she realized what had happened.

She also collapsed when she looked down from the balcony and saw little Hays lying motionless far below. A nurse by training, Velmarie felt that there was no way anyone could survive a fall of that magnitude.

But as she raced for the elevator, she kept repeating in her mind, "God, let my precious baby be safe."

When the elevator stopped on the ground floor and the door slid open, she was met with a miracle. On the ground, not too far away, sat Hays . . . moving and crying!

Paramedics rushed the toddler to the hospital, where he was checked out and given the all clear. Velmarie is convinced God sent the family a miracle.

She says: "The night before Hays fell, we said a prayer, asking God to send down his guardian angels to watch over Hays and the other children and keep them from harm. And He did!"

## Just Why Did Toddler Survive Deadly 140-Foot Fall?

Perhaps it was the same angels that were looking out for another miracle highflier, nineteen-month-old

Lucas Pangracio, who plunged more than 140 feet from a fourteenth-story window and survived—with only a broken wrist to show for his pains.

Luckily—or was it miraculous or divine intervention?—Lucas plummeted into a canvas awning over the entrance to the apartment building where he lived.

The broken bone in his wrist and a few relatively minor bruises are the only legacies of his high-flying misadventure, which prompted pediatrician Dr. Lauro Linhares of the Evangelico Hospital in Curitiba, Brazil, to say: "It's simply impossible for a child to suffer such a fall and come out without any injury. Lucas and his family have been involved in a true miracle from God!"

Lucas's household was in a state of chaos on October 9, 1990. They were preparing to move. Boxes were strewn all over the apartment. Unfortunately, one of the boxes had been placed near an open window. Adventurous Lucas decided to climb onto the box and peer out the window. He lost his balance and, watched by his horrified mom, Elizabeth, toppled backward out of the window.

"My darling boy is dead!" screamed Elizabeth, as Lucas hurtled to the ground. She knew full well no mortal could survive a drop like that.

She ran to the elevator, grief-stricken.

At ground-floor level, doorman Jair Bueno de Deus heard the dull thud and the ripping of canvas as the toddler's limp body crashed into the awning above the front door.

The boy fell to the ground, where he lay motionless, his face turning purple from lack of air. The frazzled doorman gathered his wits and began giving the boy mouth-to-mouth resuscitation, massaging his heart at the same time.

Little by little, Lucas began to regain consciousness. His breathing became less labored. Then, he suddenly burst out crying.

That's when Lucas's mother arrived on the ground floor. His crying was music to her ears. "All I could think of was, 'My son is alive, and no one can change that!'" said Elizabeth.

For six days, disbelieving doctors in a local hospital checked the little fellow out for internal or other traumatic injuries. There were none . . . just the broken wrist.

How does one explain this remarkable story? "How do you explain a miracle?" counters Lucas's mom.

"The scene of my son falling is repeated over and over in my mind. Instead of it being a tragic reminder, the flashbacks only make me believe more and more in the power of God. And we thank Him every day for little Lucas's life."

## Four-Year-Old's Miracle Swim Through Shark-Infested Waters

It had to be the worst possible scenario.

A four-year-old girl falls off her parents' yacht in pitch-darkness into treacherous, shark-infested waters. The boat sails on for another five full minutes, her parents unaware that their daughter is missing.

But little Pauline Cullen beat the odds. She remembered some tips from a recent shipboard safety drill she'd witnessed. She didn't panic, but stayed calm. And despite being chilled and bone-tired, the brave little lass "swam and swam and swam," half a mile through the darkness to the shoreline and safety.

While Pauline deserves credit for her grit and courage, her family and friends are still thanking God for sending them a miracle that terrible night.

The worst moments for her parents were when they discovered little Pauline was not aboard their forty-foot yacht as it glided along Florida's Intracoastal Waterway in Palm Beach County the evening of March 27, 1994.

Earlier, she had been playing on deck with her six-year-old brother and another little friend. Unseen by the others, she slipped and slid under the guardrail, headfirst, into the murky water.

Her dad, David Cullen, turned his boat around as soon as they realized Pauline was missing. "We cruised back the way we came, continually calling her name," said David, a Lake Worth, Florida, dive shop owner.

He called in the disappearance as an emergency. Within minutes the Intracoastal was buzzing with action. Coast Guard . . . Marine Patrol . . . small boats from all over—everyone wanted to get in on the life-or-death search.

The armada of search craft combed the vast waterway for forty minutes, until David Cullen decided to act on a hunch. He saw a faint light on the shoreline about half a mile away from the deeper waters. He decided to sail toward it.

"Something called me to that spot," said David later.

As he drew nearer, he saw the light was at the end of a dock. And standing on the dock was Pauline!

David Cullen immediately dove into the water and swam the last two hundred yards to the dock, where he grabbed Pauline and swept her up in his arms. "At that moment I was the luckiest man in the world," said David.

Pauline credits her survival with words of wisdom she heard her daddy give at a "man overboard" drill he had supervised a week earlier. He had stressed, "Don't panic, stay calm." And that's what she did.

Pauline told her happy dad: "When I fell in the water, I used my brain like you told me. I knew I had to save myself. But I was so scared and sad I started to cry. Then I swam toward a light on the shore.

"I got so tired my legs wouldn't work. So I turned over and floated. After I rested, I swam again, then I rested some more.

"It was so hard and I was so cold. But I just swam and swam. Then my feet hit the ground and I knew I was okay."

There's no argument that little Pauline's determination and precocious common sense contributed toward her survival. But given her age and the conditions in which she survived, there's no doubt that some kind of miracle happened that night.

## Doomed Boy Prays for Miracle—Brain Tumor Disappears

Young Tommy Orr describes himself as "a living miracle" after his prayers to God vanquished a fatal brain tumor that threatened his life.

Doctors had told Tommy he had only one to eight months to live. His family had even started thinking about his funeral. And high school senior Tommy had drawn up a special "wish list" of things he wanted to do before he died.

But just three months after Tommy was hit with the devastating death sentence, medical tests revealed his tumor had vanished! As of January 1, 1997—a year and a half later—the eighteen-year-old is still disease-free and as strong as a horse.

"He's in school and working part-time," his delighted dad, Russell, told the *National Enquirer*. "He's an inspiration to us all."

His dramatic comeback also stunned family physician Dr. Henry Friedman. "Tommy's recovery is akin to winning the lottery," declared Dr. Friedman, professor of pediatrics and head of Duke University's Pediatric Brain Tumor Program.

An enthusiastic athlete, Tommy played on his high school football team and was the pride of Centreville, Virginia. Then, out of the blue, in August 1994 he suddenly began to have terrible headaches. A sophisticated scan discovered a brain tumor. The very next day it was removed and Tommy had follow-up radiation and chemotherapy.

"It was a nightmare," he said. "It made me feel awful."

Then a routine scan in February 1995 revealed his tumor had come back—and had spread to his spine.

Tommy was getting sicker and sicker—and he made the decision to stop treatments and accept that he was going to die. All that was left for him to do was pray to God for a miracle.

"Suddenly life seemed more precious to me than ever. I started noticing the little things we all take for granted—like sunrise. I treasured every day," recalls Tommy.

A few weeks after he was given his death sentence, he went back into the hospital so doctors could check the tumor. Everyone got the surprise of their lives. It had actually shrunk!

Another scan to check the progress of the tumor a few weeks after that showed him to be in complete remission.

"It was a miracle! I'd been granted a miracle! Doctors were shocked. Dr. Friedman told me he'd never seen anything like it before," said a joyful Tommy. "The physicians told me, 'Enjoy your life. You no longer have a mere eight months to live.'"

Grateful his prayers were answered, the courageous teen said, "It's just like a happy ending in a movie. Thank you, God. Thank you."

## "Little Mr. Lucky"
## Survives Explosion

They're calling fourth-grader Clifford Abeyta Little Mr. Lucky after he survived an explosion that blew the brick walls of his parents' home to bits and hurled him high in the air.

The ten-year-old Denver, Colorado, boy was staying home alone when the house exploded. Miraculously, he escaped unscathed.

Clifford stayed behind when his family decided to visit a relative in the hospital in November 1993. The youngster was sitting in his stepfather's favorite easy chair, watching television, when the floor started shaking.

All of a sudden there was a hiss—then a loud *boom*. Clifford watched his television, which shot up in the air in front of his eyes. Then he felt his chair fly up in the air with him in it!

"I saw white clouds all around me. I thought I'd died and was in heaven," the boy told the *National Enquirer*. "Later the firemen told me what I'd seen was just smoke and dust from the explosion."

The chair slammed back to the floor with Clifford still sitting in it. Terrified, he jumped out of his seat and ran through the dust. The boy didn't have to find the front door to get outside—the explosion had completely blown out the living room walls.

Clifford raced to his sister's home nearby. Amazed medics found him shaken but unhurt except for a few cactus needles stuck in his hand from brushing against a houseplant.

A deadly rain of debris, including pieces of brick wall, had landed all around the chair but somehow missed Clifford.

"One of the firemen told me I should go out and buy a lottery ticket," said the lucky youngster.

Recalled his stepfather, Joe Salazar, sixty-nine, a disabled military veteran, "When we found Clifford was okay, we knew it had to be the work of God."

Investigators believe the explosion was caused by a gas leak.

## Sisters Survive in a Snake-Infested Jungle

For a whole month, two young sisters were lost in a treacherous Amazon jungle—surviving a hair-raising series of life-threatening adventures that included outrunning a jaguar and evading poisonous snakes and crocodiles.

Their parents had given them up for dead. But the miracle sisters, just nine and thirteen, stayed alive on berries and their wits until they were found, covered with angry red mosquito bites, but otherwise unharmed.

Older sister Bertina Domingo said later that by far the most frightening moment was when a ferocious jaguar, intent on making the girls its next meal, charged at them.

The quick-thinking youngsters ran to climb up a tree to safety. There was a heart-stopping moment when younger sister Bernadette stumbled and fell.

"Climb! Climb! Quick!" Bertina yelled at her little sister. Bernadette reached the tree and safety with only seconds to spare.

The girls got lost in the jungle wilderness with their uncle, who was taking them to visit a relative's farm. The trip should have taken only a couple of hours by foot from their home in Apoteri, an Amazon village about two hundred miles south of Georgetown, Guyana, in early April 1995.

But their uncle lost his way.

One of the worst periods of their monthlong nightmare was watching their uncle contract deadly malaria, grow thin and weak, and die.

The girls, who belong to the Waphishiana, an Amazon Indian tribe, were no strangers to the Amazon. The box of matches, two hammocks, and machetes the group was carrying were their tools for survival.

With the machetes, the fearless youngsters hacked their way through the snake-invested forest. They ate berries and other wild fruits and, occasionally, fish.

Bernadette said they cooked the fish over the flames of the waxlike gum that comes from the Hawaii tree.

Water was plentiful—although Bertina came down with dysentery from drinking creek water.

At one point, they narrowly missed being rescued. Bernadette said later that she could hear the sound of an engine—she wasn't sure whether it was a boat or an aircraft. Quickly, they hacked their way through the undergrowth toward the noise. But the sound faded away before they could reach it.

Officials estimate that help finally came thirty-one days after the girls became lost in the forest, when they accidentally happened upon a remote mining camp.

## Chapter Seven

## Disaster Miracles

Not a day goes by that we don't pick up our newspaper and read a terrific survival story involving a fire, flood, earthquake, explosion, or some other kind of disaster.

"We love to read these stories, because we can relate to them. No matter where we live, we are all vulnerable to the capriciousness of Mother Nature," says psychotherapist Dr. Eugene Donahue, who has studied the survival syndrome.

"At any given time, we could be stricken with some kind of natural disaster. So when we read the stories about people who survive these events, we relate to them emphatically and emotionally."

Why do some people escape unscathed from horrendous disasters and others don't? "It would be right to say 'luck of the draw.' 'Miracle' is the only word to describe it," added Dr. Donahue.

Here are a few gripping survivor stories, plucked from recent headlines.

# "God's Hand Held That Cellar Door Shut!"

When a killer twister swept like the hand of death across the small community of Jarrell, Texas, on May 27, 1997, it destroyed everything in its path and killed dozens of residents—yet miraculously spared the lives of Maria Hernandez and her three children.

As the killer twister approached, Maria wisely sought refuge with her kids in the cellar of her home. When she emerged from that tiny storm cellar, her mind boggled at the devastation. Her house was totally gone, ripped from its foundations and hurled into oblivion.

Dozens of neighbors' homes had also totally vanished.

Grass was sucked out of the ground. Cars and trucks were strewn across the pitted landscape where they had been tossed like toys. Only a few trees in the neighborhood remained standing, but the bark had been totally stripped off them. And telephone poles lay scattered around like snapped matchsticks.

Maria broke down when she learned of the tornado's human toll. Neighbors Larry and Joan Igo and their three children, who lived immediately behind her, were dead. Ruth Carmonas and her two children, who lived across the street, were dead. Next-door neighbor Bernice Gower and her son were gone. Ten other neighbors whom she regarded as close friends also perished.

Said Marie: "I got down on my knees and hugged my three children, weeping tears of thanks for the miracle that somehow saved our lives."

Five minutes of hell for the Hernandez family—Maria, twenty-eight, and the children Gabriel, Jr., seven, Jimmy, five, and three-month-old Mariel—began when the twister struck at around three p.m.

When it was all over, twenty-eight residents of the small subdivision, Double Creek Estates, were dead.

Ironically, it was the memory of another tornado—a 1989 twister that destroyed their trailer home—that saved the Hernandez family's lives. That incident convinced husband Gabriel to build a cellar under the kitchen of their new home.

But Maria still had only seconds to act after she looked out her kitchen window and saw the twister—"a half-mile wall of darkness"—headed in her direction.

With husband Gabriel away at work, she hurriedly gathered her three children. Her friend and neighbor, Rosa Perez, ran through the front door to join her with her own three children.

Together, both mothers yanked open the door to the storm cellar underneath the house and all eight bodies piled in. Even as they were pulling the cellar door shut, all hell was breaking loose in the house above them. Windows were breaking and woodwork was splintering as the tornado ripped the house apart as if it were being broadsided by an out-of-control freight train.

Meantime, the Hernandez and Perez families huddled together in their underground shelter. Dust and debris poured into the cellar through the cracks between the boards on the door, making it almost impossible for them to breathe.

At one point, the door to the cellar snapped open and shut several times. For a few horrifying minutes, both mothers thought the tornado was going to totally rip the door off and suck them out to be smashed to bits.

Frantically, both women sat perched on a rickety ladder in the cellar, trying to hold the flapping door shut with all their might.

But they became too exhausted to hold on any longer. Resigned to their fate, both mothers dropped to the floor and shielded their children with their bodies. They were sure the end had come.

Maria glanced upward. To her relief, the door was in one piece and stayed shut. "I found out later that debris had fallen on it and was pinning it shut," she said.

After five dramatic minutes, the storm passed over and peace and quiet reigned again. Soon after, rescue workers cleared away the debris on top of the cellar door and both families were able to gulp fresh air again.

Remarked Maria: "It was as if God had reached down and held the storm door closed for us."

## Only One House Remained Standing!

Positive energy can make miracles happen.

That was proved conclusively when fire raced across southern California in the Great Blaze of 1993, consuming hundreds of homes, leaving thousands homeless.

There was one exception in the residential community in the hills outside the picturesque town of Laguna, where fire destroyed 380 homes, one after the other.

Like a safe haven in the middle of hell, one home stayed untouched. While the houses around it smoldered and crumbled in charred ruins, the home of civil engineer. To Bui-Bender was unscathed and intact.

"You could call it a miracle," agrees Orange County fire captain Dan Young. But he added that the miracle includes foresight on To's part, exceptional bravery, and a large dollop of good luck.

As the houses around him started to burn, Vietnamese immigrant Bui-Bender, forty-four, refused to admit defeat and evacuate with the majority of his neighbors.

He had confidence and pride in the $350,000 multitiered home of concrete, stucco, and fire-resistant glass he had personally designed.

Fearlessly, he stood on his roof with a garden hose, putting out burning embers. He stayed at his post until the flames grew dangerously near and he had no alternative but to get out of the area.

With remarkable foresight, just the day before the blaze he had cleared his garden area of shrubs and wetted the soil down. The wet earth acted as a fire barrier.

His efforts paid off. The day after the fire, he returned to the family home with wife Doris and their three young children.

His wife and children wept as they drove through their neighborhood and witnessed the rubble and devastation all around them. They closed their eyes to the ugliness and tragedy.

Suddenly, To cried out, "Open your eyes, sweetheart." She did, to a sight she'll never forget—their house, still standing . . . the only one in a sea of smoldering ruins.


# The Bibles That
# Refused to Burn

Hazel and Herbert Twilley realized they had been visited by one of God's miracles when fire ravaged their home, burning all their worldly possessions but leaving two precious Bibles totally untouched!

"Those Bibles should have burned. Everything else did. I've never seen anything like it in my twenty-three years as a firefighter," marveled fire chief Danny Johnson, one of several who fought to put out the flames that swept through the Twilleys' three-bedroom home on their chicken farm in Water Valley, Alabama, on November 18, 1993.

The Bibles that miraculously survived the vicious fire were both family heirlooms. One was a gift from fifty-five-year-old Hazel's grandfather, a preacher, which he had given her two months before he died. The other had been in her possession for thirty-five years.

Incredibly, the table on which both books sat was totally consumed and charred. The fire melted a lamp sitting on the same table. But it hardly touched the Bibles . . . all they suffered were two faint scorch marks on their leather covers.

The Good Books that survived hellfire and brimstone brought the Twilley family comfort and solace as they struggled to rebuild their lives after fire stole their home and possessions.

Looking back at the strange event, Hazel observed: "I'm a Christian lady and I believe the Bibles weren't damaged because it was meant to be—to show that God's word is going to stand for all time no matter what happens."

## "I Can't Believe We All Got Out Alive"

That was John Lowe's first reaction. He had never thought much about miracles until he had to live through one.

Along with many of his new neighbors, John and his wife, Helen, were left homeless when their trailer home in Charlestown Township, Ohio, was totally devastated when a propane gas leak triggered an explosion.

The house next door to the Lowes' actually totally exploded and splintered into fragments.

"What really amazes me is that there was all that devastation with all these people around, and no one got killed or really hurt," added John.

Six to twelve homes in the Lowes' trailer park were totally destroyed in a tragedy that caused damage close to $1 million. Fifty other homes were affected in one way or another.

John and Helen Lowe were asleep at the time when the trailer park around them erupted. They credit a large headboard on their bed with keeping debris and showers of glass from harming them. One of their cars was damaged; the other was totaled.

"We never thought much about miracles until this happened," Lowe said. "About everything we had, we lost. So much of what we had was either riddled with glass and plaster or smelled bad from the fumes."

Several hours after the explosion, the Lowes found their longtime pet, a Chihuahua named Speedy, curled inside a wastebasket in the ruins of their living room. Speedy was fine.

## He Tumbled Like a Rag Doll in One-Hundred-Mile-per-Hour Hell

For almost a mile, thirty-seven-year-old ski safety patrolman James Sweeney tumbled amid tons of snow and ice moving at one hundred miles per hour. Incredibly, Sweeney was trapped in the heart of an avalanche—a thundering sea of death that was sweeping him helplessly into a suffocating frozen hell.

Somehow a miracle intervened! "I can't believe he ever made it. He should've been ground to a smear," observed Tom Evans of the Alaska Mountain Rescue Group.

Patrolman Sweeney became an avalanche victim when a mountain ridge of snow suddenly gave way under his feet as he was checking snow conditions on the slopes of Alaska's six-thousand-foot Mount Dimond for the World Extreme Snowboarding Championships in the spring of 1996.

Sweeney thought to himself: *Conditions are bad. Six inches of new snow, and warm weather—perfect conditions for an avalanche!*

Seconds later he was being swept down the mountainside as helpless as a rag doll amid huge fragments of snow and ice, some of the chunks as big as houses.

He was sure he was going to be buried alive. He could only try desperately to stay on the surface of the plunging torrent and keep praying for a miracle. Fortunately, his prayers were answered.

But James didn't think he had much of a chance of survival. The odds were against him from the outset. He first knew he was in trouble as the ground under him, twenty feet from a steep cliff, cracked and sent him flying backward into space.

He could see the whole ridge above him—about the size of a block of houses—shear off and begin its one hundred mile-per-hour descent.

First it dropped one hundred feet to another ridge. Then a chain reaction began, as it gathered up more snow and ice in its path and thundered toward the base of the mountain—with James riding the eye of the storm!

The hapless patrolman remembers to this day the roaring and pounding of the avalanche. Snow swirled around him. At one stage it felt like a million marbles were striking his body. Like a rag doll, he tumbled over and over.

Suddenly, he felt his body being buried in a cocoon of snow. Frantically, he struggled to get to the surface and fresh air. But the snow was closing in on him, restricting his movements. He was dead for sure, he thought.

Somehow he managed to tap into a miraculous inner strength that helped him struggle to the surface. Even then, he was still in danger. On the surface of the mountain of snow, great slabs of ice and huge snowballs were still moving around.

James was just a tiny speck in that snow-white sea of deadly debris. He expected at any moment to be crushed by one of the moving chunks. He thought he was going to share the fate of his close friend. Wilbur Madsen, who had been killed three weeks earlier in a similar accident.

As the snow surrounding him continued to move, James started tumbling head over heels further down the slope. He struggled to stay on the surface of the wave of snow. His ski goggles were ripped off and snow caked his eyes. He couldn't see where he was headed.

Then the thunder of the avalanche faded. The snow surrounding him began to slow down, creaking to an eventual stop. James scraped the caked snow from his eyes. He saw he was safe.

Immediately he sat up, grabbed his ski patrol radio—which amazingly was still working—and yelled into it, "I'm alive! Get me out of here."

It was only then that he was racked with pain. He was to find out later that his leg and pelvis were broken. A rescue helicopter with emergency personnel was soon at the spot to transport him to the hospital.

So what is it like to tumble two-thirds of a mile in just sixteen seconds? Says Jim: "It's like shake, rattle, and roll!"

# Vision of Daughter
# Saves Drowning Mom

Powerful forces of the mind—primarily, the will to live—can make miracles happen.

That's what young mom Pam Crossan, twenty-nine, found out. She should have died minutes after the thirty-two-foot fishing boat she was on sank and plunged her into the wild, icy sea off the rugged Scottish coast.

But for four grueling hours, the courageous woman swam against the odds for her life. Her fiancé, Paul Blaikie, along with three other crewmen drowned that day.

Pam was heartbroken to leave him behind. But she knew she had to survive—for the sake of her six-year-old daughter, Kayleigh, who she knew was waiting for her on shore.

Pam was in the wheelhouse of the little fishing craft, Equinox, while her fiancé and his shipmates were working on deck. Without any warning, at about ten p.m., a gigantic icy wave swept over the boat, bursting into the tiny wheelhouse.

"Oh, my God, I'm drowning," thought Pam. There was no time to make a Mayday call or put on a life jacket. In seconds, Pam felt herself being dragged down into the murky depths as the craft sank like a stone.

As the boat went under, she felt her ears popping with the pressure. Her lungs were bursting. She made a lunge for the wheelhouse door—and miraculously shot to the surface.

Bobbing in the water near her were her fiancé, Paul, and his shipmates. Paul shouted words of encouragement, urging her to stay calm at all costs.

There was a moment of panic when one of the young crewmen grabbed hold of her. He was in trouble and dragging her down. But she used every ounce of strength to pull both of them back to the surface.

She couldn't get the image of her young daughter waiting for her on shore out of her mind. "Let's swim for it," she shouted to her companions. But fiancé Paul and his friend Derek, the skipper, said they were going to stay and help their other two friends, who were having difficulty remaining afloat.

Pam and Paul exchanged glances for the last time. There was no time for last words or any other kind of farewell.

Two miles off, Pam could see the twinkling lights of the coastal resort they had sailed from. She knew it would be a miracle if she made it. The seas were rough and freezing cold. But Pam knew she had to swim or die.

She was just a small speak in the vast sea as she struggled toward the mainland. At one point another boat passed near her. She screamed and splashed to attract attention, but her signals went unnoticed in the stormy, dark night.

Exhausted, she renewed her efforts. She kept seeing Kayleigh's face in front of her, encouraging her, guiding her toward shore.

At one stage during her ordeal she got cramps in her legs. It left her totally without feeling in her lower extremities and she felt she was a goner.

That was her darkest moment. She felt sure she was close to death. Again the image of Kayleigh flashed before her. A voice inside her head told her she could make it.

Using only her arms, she swam on. With the last breaths left in her body, she began shouting, "Help me! Help me!" in desperation.

The next thing she knew, two men were pulling her from shallow water. She had made it—the only survivor, as it turned out.

In the hospital later, daughter Kayleigh jumped

onto Pam's bed in the intensive care unit. "I cried as I hugged her," recalls Pam. "I knew I wouldn't have made it if it hadn't been for her."

## Mighty Mutt Saves Lives of Thirty People

Disasters have a way of bringing out the best in people—and animals, for that matter!

During the disastrous floods in southern California in the spring of 1992, an unlikely hero emerged—Weela the miracle dog, a four-legged superhero credited with saving the lives of thirty people, twenty-nine dogs, thirteen horses, and a cat.

The gutsy pit bull terrier's astounding total of seventy-three rescues earned her the Ken-L Ration Dog Hero of the Year award.

For a whole month during the height of the flooding disaster, Weela tirelessly performed one amazing feat after another. She waded across a swollen river carrying a heavy backpack of food to stranded dogs—and led a human rescue team safely around quicksand and deadly deep holes beneath the water's surface to an island where horses were starving.

And even though Weela weighs only sixty-five pounds, she pulled out people stuck in mud up to their waists!

In one amazing rescue, the determined dog planted herself in front of a group of about thirty Mexican men, women, and children on the edge of the Tijuana River—and kept them from crossing at a place concealing a horrible undertow. Somehow Weela knew there was a raging underwater current at that point—and it would've washed them all away to their doom!

"Weela was incredible," says her proud owner, Lori Watkins, of Imperial Beach, California.

The drama began when heavy rains triggered floods along the California-Mexico border. The water washed out roads, destroyed houses, and forced residents to flee for their lives.

"Our neighbor's ranch was demolished, and he was in the hospital," said Lori. "So my husband Daniel and I took Weela to get his horses and dogs out. The rain was falling in sheets and the night was so black we couldn't see ten feet. Trees, parts of buildings, and other debris raced past us. Weela helped us locate our friend's dogs, which were terrified and hiding under debris. We got them to high ground."

Soon after that, Lori and some friends spotted thirteen horses stranded and starving on a small patch of land surrounded by water. The rescuers didn't know how to safely wade across the treacherous water, which concealed quicksand and deep holes.

But where there's a Weela, there's a way.

"We let her lead the way in through the flood area," said Lori. "Then Weela found a path good enough to get the horses out. We went about a mile and a half before we got to a road, but we made it safely.

"Weela hadn't been trained for any type of rescue. She just knew what to do."

On another occasion rescuers spotted a group of dogs and one car stranded on a tiny island. The team put a backpack on Weela's back—and she toted fifty-pound loads of food to the hungry animals with Lori wading along behind her.

"Weela carried the food to those dogs every other day for about a month to get their trust," said Lori. "Then we attached leashes to them and got them out of there."

Weela even kept rescuers going by dragging them out of mud when they got stuck, said Lori.

"Once I sank into mud up to my waist. Weela tried to dig me out—then she just grabbed me by my coat and pulled me out! Pit bulls are incredibly strong animals."

Ken-L Ration awarded Weela a certificate, silver-plated engraved bowl, and a year's supply of Kibbles 'n' Bits.

"Weela won out of more than 250 entries," said Ken-L Ration spokesperson Jessie Vicha. "She was judged the most heroic dog of the year."

## Miracle of Woman in the Rubble

To reach trapped survivors, rescuers had to squeeze through holes not much bigger than their heads. Their mission of mercy was hampered by the stench of rotting flesh from dead victims in the collapsed Sampoong Department Store in Seoul, Korea.

As the death toll rose to 323, hopes faded that any more survivors would emerge. One rescue worker, An Gung Wook, refused to give up. He squeezed his way further into the precarious heap of rubble, inching forward into the pitch-dark, scraping with his hands at the steel wires and porous cement, which fell away in flakes.

After digging in the rubble for more than two weeks, An was exhausted. But he was convinced he could hear distant sounds emanating from dark crevices in the crumpled building.

Could these sounds be real? An kept wondering. Day after day he would call out, all the time praying someone would respond to his voice or to the beam of his flashlight.

Sixteen days into the rescue, An's optimism was rewarded. From the gloom of the debris, he heard a faint voice.

As he inched toward it, the voice became stronger.

Scraping with his fingers, An dug a hole in a mound of debris and—miraculously—found himself face-to-face with nineteen-year-old Park Sung Hyon, who had been trapped for nearly sixteen days under concrete slabs and crumbled boulders.

"I'm naked," she whispered to An. The poor girl had peeled off her clothes to survive the heat. "I'm not wearing any clothes. I want my mother."

"What's important is that you are alive," An recalled telling her. Then he quickly covered her with a blanket and pulled her from her cramped quarters—six feet long and sixteen inches wide.

Park's rescue astounded the medical community, which had believed it was not possible for people to survive so long without water. Incredibly, Park claimed she did not drink any water, although it had rained heavily while rescue operations were proceeding, and her tiny space was damp and humid.

Park's miraculous survival of July 1995 has since led to new thinking and new research into how long rescuers should persevere in searching for survivors after earthquakes, building collapses, and other disasters.

Although many rescue experts say that there is little chance of finding survivors of this kind of disaster alive after the first forty-eight hours—and no chance after the first week—Park's miracle rescue is changing their minds.

The Sampoong Department Store collapsed on June 28, 1995, when one to two thousand people were thought to be shopping. More than eight hundred were entombed and perished.

## Chapter Eight

Miracle Births

To many people, the term "miracle birth" is a misnomer. They believe that the act of birth under any circumstances is a God-given miracle.

I tend to agree. But there *are* many births that are more miraculous than others. Here are just a few that have made the miracles' record book.

### After Rearing 277 Kids, Peggy Gets Pregnant at Last!

For twenty-two years of marriage, loving mom Peggy Whitman helped rear 269 foster children, as well as adopting eight others.

You see, when she first married husband Charles in 1972, doctors told the couple that Peggy could never get pregnant and that they shouldn't waste their time trying for that large family they both desperately wanted.

After more than a year of trying for their own baby, Peggy and Charles decided instead to enroll in a foster care program and opened up their hearts and their home to abandoned and abused children who so needed the hugs of parents who care.

Over two decades, almost three hundred foster kids shared the roof of the Whitmans' comfortable nine-room home, with as many as thirteen kids in the house at one time.

Throughout the years, the couple adopted four boys and four girls. The eldest, April, is in her twenties and at law school; their youngest is five.

Then one day Charles, a fireman, was relaxing in an armchair at the couple's home in Abington, Massachusetts. Peggy asked him coyly: "Honey, how would you like to be a father again at forty-seven?"

"Okay—who do you want to adopt now?" answered her husband.

"No, honey—not adopt. I'm pregnant!"

Stunned, Charles blurted out, "How did it happen? I mean . . . you know what I mean!"

Peggy confessed that over the years she had never stopped trying to get pregnant. She visited seven different specialists for test after test. And she even tried fertility drugs.

On this occasion, however, conception was totally unexpected. Peggy explained that they were the recipients of a little miracle.

The little miracle was delivered a short time later, five weeks premature—a healthy package dubbed Josh, the miracle baby.

Peggy says today: "It's a dream come true. No one deserves this much happiness."

## A Heartbroken Mom's Medical Miracle

Through fifteen years, three husbands, and eight miscarriages, Rosslyn Pope never gave up hope that she would have a baby one day.

There were times when her heartbreak was soul-destroying. There were two failed marriages and devastating midterm miscarriages.

Then top surgeon Dr. Peter Wardle offered Rosslyn a medical miracle—a pioneering surgical technique that is now offering new hope to millions of women like Rosslyn. It involves placing a stitch around the cervix—the entrance to the womb—and drawing the stitch tight like a purse string. Repeated miscarriages in many women are caused by a weak cervix that opens too early in pregnancy.

After her marriage to third husband Chris Pope, thirty-eight-year-old Rosslyn became pregnant. She was afraid she would miscarry again. That's when Dr. Wardle tried his new technique on her.

Each week between the critical fourteenth and twenty-eighth week of pregnancy, Dr. Wardle used ultrasound to check that the opening remained tight. On three occasions he had to put in an additional stitch.

"I was so nervous after losing so many babies in the past," said Rosslyn. "When I arrived at the hospital for delivery, I even left the baby clothes in the car. After eight miscarriages, I did not want them brought in until I was sure the baby was actually here."

She was overjoyed when new baby Jessica arrived—one month early, but healthy and weighing in at five pounds ten ounces. "It was the happiest moment in my life when I held my daughter in my arms and gave her that first kiss."

That was four years ago. Rosslyn tried it again. And with the help of Dr. Wardle, consultant and senior lecturer in reproductive medicine at St. Michael's Hospital in Bristol, England, she had another lovely daughter, Megan! "My happiness is complete," she says.

Dr. Wardle's technique is neither expensive nor does it involve sophisticated surgery. "It is simple—something that can be copied by other doctors—and it's well over ninety percent successful," he explains.

"In some women, we may have to insert as many as four or five stitches over the course of twelve weeks."

In Rosslyn's case, she had a general anesthetic for her stitches, but some other women patients simply have an epidural anesthesia injected directly into the spinal area.

Dr. Wardle has conducted a study of nineteen women who, between them, had suffered a combined total of more than fifty miscarriages. He added: "But with the new technique, all gave birth to healthy babies beyond thirty-five weeks of pregnancy."

## Miracle Mom Has Baby Girl Docs Said She'd Never Have

Debra Bingham went to the hospital fearing her kidney transplant had failed—but the pain was really God delivering a miracle: the baby she thought she could never have.

After twenty-six years of marriage, childless Debra, who had no idea she was pregnant, was in labor. To her amazement and great joy, she gave birth to a girl, Robin Leigh.

Forty-three-year-old Debra was hysterically happy. Here she was, going into the hospital thinking her kidney was failing. And instead she walked out of the hospital—on air, of course—with her baby daughter.

Her joy was shared by her delighted husband, Johnny, forty-five, who told the *Enquirer:* "After years of not having the child we longed for, to have one now is a true gift from God."

The couple, from Lexington, Tennessee, were high school sweethearts and married in their teens. At first, they put off having a child, although that was their ultimate dream.

But fourteen years ago, Debra developed severe

kidney disease and doctors advised the couple not to have children because the stress of having a baby could be fatal to Debra and the child.

In 1987, Debra had a kidney transplant and was told that the drugs she must take to keep her new kidney healthy would make pregnancy virtually impossible. In other words, the chances of her having children were zero, said Debra.

Then the miracle took place.

In February of 1996, Debra began experiencing great pain. Thinking her kidney was failing, she went to a hospital in Jackson, Tennessee, where she went through a battery of tests.

Although doctors felt it unnecessary, they routinely gave Debra a pregnancy test. Amazingly, it was positive. Debra was in her seventh month! An ultrasound test confirmed she was pregnant. "We were astonished!" declared her kidney specialist, Dr. Lucius Wright.

Debra was carrying twins, but sadly, the ultrasound test showed one was dead.

Quickly, Dr. Wright made arrangements to get her to a Memphis hospital and phoned her husband, Johnny.

He recalled telling him: "Are you sitting down? I've got amazing news for you. Your wife's pregnant and she's in labor."

Johnny rushed to the hospital in time to welcome Robin Leigh Bingham into the world. She weighed two pounds, two ounces, and had a headful of dark hair. She was delivered by Cesarean.

## Miracle Birth for Mom
## Who Lost Thirteen Babies

When tiny Benjamin Roomes came kicking and crying into the world, not only did he make his mother believe in miracles—he made history!

Happy mom Cherry Roomes had lost thirteen babies before giving birth to Benjamin. And her newfound happiness is all due to a first-of-its-kind medical procedure.

"It's a dream come true," said thirty-nine-year-old Cherry after Benjamin was born May 25 at London's Kings College Hospital.

In the twelve years they were married, Cherry and her husband Geoff, forty-three, of Kempston, England, longed for a child of their own. She had two sons from a previous marriage and the couple adopted a daughter, but trying to have a baby together was proving to be a futile wish.

Cherry was rare Rh-negative blood and Geoff's blood is Rh-positive. That often is a fatal combination for children in the womb. When the unborn child has the positive blood type, the mother's negative blood sees that as a foreign invader and attacks.

For Cherry, the attacks were always deadly. In thirteen previous pregnancies, four children—Anne, Jane, Edwina, and Emily—died just after birth. Megan lived three days and Eleanor, who was born severely handicapped, survived the longest, seven months.

With the other seven, Cherry suffered miscarriages or the babies were born dead.

Fortunately, Cherry's physician is Dr. Kypros Nicolaides, a pioneer in the field of obstetrics and head of the renowned Harris Birthright Unit at Kings College Hospital. He, too, was frustrated and felt Cherry's pain. "We tried every medical advance in the previous pregnancies, but still her babies died," said Dr. Nicolaides.

When Cherry got pregnant a fourteenth time, Dr. Nicolaides took a gamble on an untried technique he'd developed. He injected bone marrow from Cherry's hip directly into the fetus during the twelfth week of pregnancy. That slowed down the attack of Cherry's Rh-negative blood.

As the child developed in the womb, Dr. Nicolaides injected seven transfusions of Cherry's blood directly into the baby, his brilliant medical mind telling him this would ensure that the child would be born alive and healthy.

On May 25, Cherry went into labor. Geoff held her hand as she was wheeled into the operating room just after noon for the cesarean procedure.

It was a tense moment. No one knew if Dr. Nicolaides's technique would be a success.

But at 12:26 P.M., a joyful sound was heard, the cry of a baby. Benjamin had arrived—alive and in good health.

A nurse broke the news to Geoff, who threw his arms around her and said, "After all these years, I can't believe it."

Benjamin was placed in an incubator so doctors could monitor him. He continues to thrive and his chances for survival are good.

When a beaming Cherry gazed at her son, she said: "I can relax and be happy. I know we are going to have Benjamin for a lifetime."

Doctors in the United States marveled at Dr. Nicolaides's breakthrough, which they feel can help other women in the same predicament as Cherry.

"I've never heard of this being done before. It has great potential," said Dr. Robert Gergely, director of the maternal fetal testing center at Cedars-Sinai Medical Center, Los Angeles.

As for Cherry, she often thinks of the thirteen children she lost, but when she looks at Benjamin she knows miracles happen. Said the delighted mom: "My heart bursts with pride every time I look at him. He's so wonderful, because he looks like all the others rolled into one."

# Mom Gives Birth
# After Liver Transplant

Maggie Jaycock was on the operating table, undergoing risky liver transplant surgery, when doctors made the startling discovery that she was four months pregnant.

The stunned surgeons were suddenly faced with a life-or-death dilemma. They knew the transplant procedure, with the antirejection drugs Maggie would need afterward, could kill her unborn child. But to halt the surgery to save the child would condemn her to death!

After consulting with Maggie's husband, Paul, the transplant operation continued. Incredibly, medical history was made and another miracle birth entered the record books.

Not only did Maggie come through the surgery with flying colors, she later gave birth to Rebecca—a healthy baby girl who beat tremendous odds to live.

"I thank God for the miracle of life—twice over," Maggie of Kent, England, enthuses today. "When I came to after the operation and Paul told me I was having a baby, I was in shock and prayed everything would be okay.

Dr. Roger Williams, head of the medical team that gave Maggie a new liver, called the survival of mother and child "a miracle" and "a first." "It's incredible the baby wasn't harmed," declared Dr. Williams.

Maggie, twenty-six, was plunged into a medical nightmare in 1992 when she caught hepatitis and it developed into a severe liver disease. Doctors said she'd die without a transplant.

Maggie and Paul had one child, daughter Hayley, now five. But they wanted another. Physicians told the couple it was very unlikely with a diseased liver.

Early in 1994, Maggie was weakening more and more each day. Then a liver became available. She was rushed to Kings College Hospital in South London for the transplant surgery—not realizing she was pregnant, because her illness hid normal signs of impending motherhood!

Her weight had bloated from 122 to 154 pounds because she was having a problem with fluid buildup. But nobody attributed the weight gain to a pregnancy. And nobody picked up a thing from her regular blood tests.

Maggie, who was sick round the clock at the best of times, did not have anything that could be recognized as morning sickness.

When she woke up from her surgery and learned she was pregnant, doctors told her the child had already passed one huge hurdle—surviving the trauma of the transplant. But they then warned that the anti-rejection drugs Maggie needed could still erase her dream of becoming a mom again.

They began pumping lifesaving drugs into Maggie. All the time she was aware that those same drugs could destroy the baby she was carrying. To make matters worse, she developed a virus—and even more drugs had to be given to her.

Miraculously, the strong dugs never harmed the unborn child, and regular tests showed the baby was developing normally. Maggie went on to give birth prematurely. Rebecca weighed only two pounds thirteen ounces. But she'd already proved she was a fighter and grew stronger and healthier.

At last check, mother and child were still both doing well. Comments Maggie: "Miracles really do happen!"

# New Mom Comes out of Coma After Three Months

Just days after giving birth, Janette Nadesan slipped into a coma in a Chicago hospital before she could even hold her new daughter.

Her prognosis was not good. Doctors were not optimistic for a complete recovery for Janette, who was suffering from severe preeclampsia, a hypertensive pregnancy disorder.

Only a miracle could save the day, and Janette's devoted husband, Aru, was determined to make that miracle happen. For more than three months, Aru sat at her bedside, playing tapes he recorded of the newborn baby's coos and gurgles . . . desperately trying to coax his wife back into consciousness.

Not once did he give up hope. His prayers and devotion were answered early in June 1995 when Janette slowly began to come to. And on Friday, June 23, Janette was able to hold her baby daughter, Anna Marie, for the first time.

"I see miracles every now and then," said Dr. Jesse Hall, professor of medicine at the University of Chicago Hospitals. "It kind of rejuvenates everyone."

Mrs. Nadesan was first diagnosed with severe preeclampsia at her local hospital, St. Margaret Mercy Health Care Centers in Hammond, Indiana, four months earlier. Still, she was able to give birth in an emergency cesarean section on February 28.

Two days later, doctors were obliged to perform a lifesaving hysterectomy in an attempt to stop massive internal bleeding. After the surgery, Mrs. Nadesan's condition worsened and she slipped into a coma.

She was flown to the Chicago hospital March 15, suffering from respiratory failure and problems with her kidneys and liver. Doctors placed her on life support. More than once, medical experts told Mr. Nadesan his wife was close to death.

But devoted husband Aru refused to accept that. There had to be a way he could bring his wife back to the family fold.

That's when he made the tapes of newborn Anna Marie and of the couple's other children, Nadia, five, and Narayan, four. Sitting at her bedside, he played them over and over to his comatose wife.

Days became weeks and weeks became months. Aru Nadesan did not waver in his resolve. His determination was rewarded when his wife's eyes flickered open.

For the first couple of weeks, the young mother was weak and delirious. But as she gained strength, she was able to recognize and smile for her loyal husband and the doctors.

All the young woman could remember of the family ordeal was being taken into intensive care in Indiana for the cesarean. As she slowly grasped what had transpired, she started asking to hold the baby she had never seen.

"I tell you, I am very blessed," Aru Nadesan told reporters from the *Chicago Tribune* newspaper after his wife came back to life. "What pulled me through this is my kids . . . just being able to come home and see them."

## Lifelong Pregnancy Wish Granted—at Forty-eight

New York lawyer Diane A. was forty-eight and still wanted desperately to have a child.

After repeated visits to her doctor over the years, she had failed to conceive. And she felt that, biologically, time was running out fast for her.

She decided that perhaps a spiritual approach was necessary. Diane brought up the matter during one of her annual visits to her local rabbi.

"I very much wanted to have a child," she remembers. "We'd been trying, but nothing was happening. We'd been seeing a doctor for six months, but still nothing.

"I hadn't even told my parents that, at my age, I wanted a baby. And though I'd met him before, I'd never said a word about it to the rabbi.

"He handed me a piece of honey cake and said, out of the clear blue sky, 'I give you a blessing for an addition to your family in the coming year.' "

Six weeks later, she was pregnant.

"People can form their own conclusions, but these are the facts," says Diane. "I had a nice, healthy baby. And another amazing thing: The night I went to the hospital, one of the rabbi's aides called our house. 'I just had a feeling,' he said."

## Chapter Nine

❧

# Miscellaneous Miracles

During my research, I came across a potpourri of miracles that just defied categorization. What type of miracle, for example, would you label Mother Teresa's image appearing on a cinnamon bun? Then there's the miracle mutt that flew through the air in a tornado like Toto in *The Wizard of Oz* . . . the woman who didn't eat for thirty-six years . . . the message from Muhammad in a tomato . . . the stone that floats like a feather . . . the list goes on and on.

Read all about these oddball miracles—and some in a more serious vein—in this fascinating chapter.

## Woman Who Wept Blood Fasted for Thirty-six Years!

For thirty-six years, Therese Neumann ate nothing but Communion wafers—and every Friday, her body would re-create the wounds of Christ.

She spoke in languages she'd never studied—and even wept torrents of blood, say Catholic Church investigators.

Today, more than three decades after her death in Germany, Therese is being considered for canonization as a saint.

Bishop Rudolf Graber of Regenburg, Germany, who is overseeing the investigation of Therese, has declared that her amazing powers were genuine. And church administrative official Maximilian Hopfner further confirmed that the Vatican process for Therese's sainthood is underway.

"Therese Neumann herself was a living miracle!" added Father Carl Strater, the man Bishop Graber put in charge of collecting documentation required for Therese's sainthood.

Born on Good Friday in 1898, Therese grew up in a poor family. Following an accident when she was nineteen, she was left blind and crippled from the waist down.

But then, four years later, her seventy-six-year-old brother, Ferdinand, recalls, "Her sight miraculously returned!"

What's more, before her family's astonished eyes, she got up off the bed and walked around the room!

More astonishing events were yet to come in Therese's life, said Italian author Paola Giovetti, who has written a book about Therese.

"On Good Friday, 1926, Therese had a vision of Christ's death on the cross—and wounds appeared on her," Giovetti said.

Therese's shocked family was dumbstruck—Therese had open, bleeding wounds on her hands, feet, and on her chest.

What's more, Giovetti says, "Two priests rushed to her bedside and reported her eyes were full of blood and she had two lines of dried blood on her cheeks."

The bleeding wounds and eerie visions returned every Friday for the rest of Therese's life.

"During her many visions, Therese spoke in foreign languages she'd never studied," said Giovetti. "She spoke Latin, Portuguese, French, and even Aramaic, the language Jesus spoke. Language experts and historians who studied Therese were astonished."

Late in 1926, Therese stopped eating, except for her daily Communion wafer, as a symbol of her faith.

For the next thirty-six years, the wafer remained her only source of food, say church officials.

Word of Therese's astonishing fast spread like wildfire—and church officials moved swiftly to determine if it was a hoax.

"The Church appointed a medical commission," said Giovetti. "Since experts said a person could live eleven days with no food or water, a period of fifteen days of surveillance was established. Four nuns took turns watching over Therese. During the fifteen days, no food or liquid intake was observed."

But Therese weighed exactly the same at the end of the study as she did at the beginning—121 pounds.

Therese was revered by thousands during her life—and when she died of a heart attack in 1962, her funeral was attended by a huge gathering.

Professor Andreas Resch, who teaches psychology at the Vatican's university in Rome, said that all the checks made at the time ruled out the possibility that Therese may have been eating secretly.

He declared, "It is an extraordinary phenomenon. I feel she will certainly be made a saint."

## Amazing Woman Has Lived More Than Twenty Years Without Food or Drink

An eighty-two-year-old Frenchwoman is being hailed as a living, walking miracle—because she has gone without eating or drinking for more than two decades!

Scientists and theologians are amazed by tests that

show she can live without food or liquid. What's more, since beginning the total fast in 1975, she's actually *gained* fifty-nine pounds!

Physicians have conducted four separate medical examinations on the Frenchwoman—dubbed Madame R. to protect her privacy. They've concluded that she maintains perfect health without taking in any sustenance other than Communion wafers.

Dr. Phillipe Lorron, a psychiatrist at the Salpetrierre Hospital in Paris, told inquisitive reporters: "I'm one of the doctors who supervised an experiment that kept Madame R. locked in a convent cell with no food or liquids for forty-seven consecutive days. I can't give any scientific explanation for the phenomenon. According to what medical science knows, no human being can survive such a long period with no food or liquid. But Madame R. made it and she is in good health."

Madame R.—who says God ordered her to embark on the fast to ward off Satanic influence—says she must resist constant temptations from the Devil to eat.

Her incredible story is recounted in her journal called *The Passion of Madame R.*, which is a bestseller in France.

Father Rene Laurentin—a theology professor at Paris Western University whose books have received four awards from the prestigious Academy of France—authored a paper on the case. He describes Madame R. as having been an "average wife and mother of three" before beginning the fast.

"Her family tried to force her to drink some water and eat something—but each time they did, it had catastrophic results," he wrote. "If she drank even a sip of water, she became violently ill. The only thing she is able to swallow is the Holy Communion.

"The extraordinary thing is that not only does she

not lose weight, she gained weight, going from 121 to 180 pounds!"

Medical experts are stunned and baffled.

The test supervised by Dr. Lorron, ran from April 22 to June 7, 1980.

"For forty-seven days, the woman was locked in a convent cell without running water and visited only by two doctors, her spiritual father, and the nun who held the only key to the room," said Father Laurentin. "During this stay, she had no food or liquid at all— even her toilet water was taken away. The conclusion was clear: Her survival was unexplainable."

## Mystery of the Miraculous Shroud of Turin

It's the most fascinating and mysterious religious relic of all time.

For centuries, debate and controversy has surrounded the Shroud of Turin. Exactly who is the bearded man with soulful eyes whose image is imprinted on the fourteen-foot sheet of faded yellow linen?

Many Roman Catholics firmly believe the image is that of Jesus, and that the faded cloth itself is his burial shroud.

As the debates are waged, miracles continue to be associated with the miraculous sheet. Why else was it not consumed in the mysterious blaze that ripped through the seventeenth-century baroque chapel built to house the shroud in Turin, Italy, on the night of April 12, 1997.

Although the chapel was gutted, the shroud was miraculously unharmed, adding more fuel to the legend that has fascinated millions for centuries.

Recent carbon tests to prove the authenticity of the shroud as a true biblical relic have been inconclusive. One test suggested that it was of an indeterminate age, while another suggested that the cloth dated no further back in time than the Middle Ages.

No further tests on the shroud will be permitted until after the year 2000. And these new tests will be mainly confined to discovering new and better preservation techniques.

Regardless of the age of the shroud, not even the most sophisticated of modern tests to date has come up with a satisfying explanation as to how the stark and clear image on the shroud was made.

Measuring fourteen feet three inches long by three feet seven inches wide, the image portrayed on the rectangular shroud is a disturbing one when you consider that it carries the image of a man recently cruelly beaten and crucified.

The cloth is believed to have been donated by Joseph of Arimathea as Jesus was being placed in his tomb. Indeed, the Bible carries a reference to a linen shroud in the New Testament book of Mark 15:46.

The fire of April 1997 wasn't the first time flames have threatened the priceless relic. In 1532, during a fire at Sainte Chapelle in Chambery, France, the shroud's silver container melted. The blaze ignited parts of the cloth at its folds before it was doused with water. It was repaired with patches.

The cloth has been at the Chapel of the Holy Shroud in the Cathedral of St. John the Baptist in Turin, Italy, since 1578.

One carbon dating done in 1987 determined it was no more than 750 years old. But those who are convinced of its authenticity claim the scorching and repairs on the shroud after the fire in France in 1532 corrupted the results of the carbon test.

# Miracle Mutt Falls
# One Hundred Feet—and Survives

Judy, the miracle dog, came back from the dead—after plunging over a one-hundred-foot seaside cliff onto a bed of jagged rocks below.

A rescue team failed to find her; then a series of fierce storms whipped the coast. Heartbroken, owner Darrel John gave his beloved pet up for dead.

Then, nearly three weeks after Judy disappeared, a bird-watcher scanning the cliff focused his binoculars—and spotted the spunky pooch, half-starved yet alive on a sunny rock!

"Cats, not dogs, are supposed to have nine lives—and Judy has used up at least eight of them!" gushed John, thirty-one, to TV and news reporters. "It's a miracle she's alive."

The drama unfolded when John and some pals took his fourteen-year-old tail-wagger along on a walking vacation of England's rugged Cornish coastline. Things were fine until Judy, a city dog all her life, spotted her first sheep. The fleet furball took off like a shot, chasing the sheep across an open field toward the cliff's edge.

"The sheep went over the edge, then I saw Judy tumble over too," said John. "By the time we got there and looked down, we couldn't see a thing."

Frantic, John dashed four miles to the nearest village to get help. A Coast Guard team scrambled down the cliff searching for his dear dog.

"We found the sheep's body, but not Judy," said team leader Steve Tregear. "For the next two weeks, severe gales hammered that coastline. We thought Judy had been washed out to sea.

"But nearly three weeks later we got a call from a bird-watcher who'd spotted her on a rock. God knows how she survived those gales. We think maybe she sought shelter in a small cave and drank from a stream that runs down the cliff."

Amazingly, Judy suffered only a few cuts and bruises in the fall.

"She was very, very lucky," said veterinarian Stephen Sawyer. "Plenty of sheep, cattle, and dogs have gone over that cliff—and were killed outright. I gather Judy was a pretty pampered pet before the accident. Maybe those extra pounds cushioned her fall!"

John, her grateful owner, said: "When I walked into the vet's office to get Judy, I was in tears. She was as weak as a kitten, but she tried to lick me anyway. Now she's being spoiled again so she can build up her weight!"

## Miracle Dog
## Working on Life Number Seven

If there's any pooch that qualifies for the title "America's Miracle Dog," it's got to be Bullet.

Don't tell Bullet it's a dog's life: In just eight years, the poor mutt has been shot three times, hit by cars twice—and even survived a collision with a train!

"She's the luckiest dog in America!" Bullet's owner, Sharon Duvall, told the *National Enquirer*.

Added veterinarian Steve Mason, who confirmed the mongrel's mishaps: "She's extremely fortunate to be alive."

Bullet's brushes with fate began when the amazing pooch was just a six-week-old stray.

"My son John almost ran her over with his car one night," said Sharon, fifty-three, of LaSalle, Michigan. "We decided to keep her—but we had no idea what we'd be in for!"

A year later, the death-defying dog was accidentally shot by a hunter.

"We just washed out the wounds and she healed fine," Sharon said.

Next, Bullet was hit twice by cars.

"We thought she was going to lose an eye the first time, but she came through intact," said Sharon. "The second time she was hit, the veterinarian X-rayed her—and found more buckshot. She'd been shot again and we didn't even know it!"

Sharon was so worried about Bullet getting shot a third time that she started spray-painting her dog bright orange during hunting season. But that didn't stop Bullet from being hit by a train this past October!

"My son John was on the other side of the tracks when the train came by, and Bullet tried to get to him," Sharon said. "She broke her jaw and lost part of a front paw—but she's doing great!"

Unfortunately, the paint didn't protect the aptly named Bullet from hunters, either. When the vet studied the X rays after the accident, he saw a familiar sight—more buckshot!

"Bullet's just a survivor," Sharon said. "She's dog-gone lucky!"

## Miracle Saved TV Star from Being Scarred for Life

Popular television game show host Monty Hall, of *Let's Make a Deal* fame, has revealed how he once cheated death in a horrifying accident—and "only a miracle" kept him from being disfigured for life.

The accident happened when he was only seven years old and was playing in the kitchen of his home in Canada with his cousin. Hall, now in his seventies, revealed all in an exclusive interview in the *National Enquirer*.

The young boys were putting a chair on top of a

rocking chair near the stove—and the chair knocked over a pot of boiling soup. The pot landed right on young Monty's head!

"All I remember is intense pain and screaming in agony. My mother heard my screams from upstairs and ran down. The burns on my face and right arm were severe—third-degree. I was terrified," remembers the celebrity.

Doctors wrapped large bandages around the boy's entire head—leaving just a little opening for his nose and mouth. As there were no really effective pain relievers back then, the severe scalding left the boy in constant agony.

Doctors also wrapped Hall's right arm in bandages. He was kept in the dark like that for four long weeks. His devoted mother had to feed him through a straw.

After a month passed, the doctor took off the bandage on young Monty's arm. The limb was all black from the third-degree burn. It was like a piece of charcoal.

His parents didn't even dare think what they were going to see when the bandages were removed from their son's face.

"My mother and father prayed silently while the doctor was taking off the facial bandages," said Monty. "When he got them off, everyone screamed in delight. A miracle had happened! My face was flawless—like a newborn baby's skin. We were amazed."

But Monty was not out of the woods yet.

"While they were treating my arm, I became very weak and came down with double pneumonia," said Monty, current international chairman of the Variety Club, a children's charity. "There was no penicillin yet, so they put me in an oxygen tent for a week. I was terribly sick. But another miracle happened—I pulled through.

"What a horrible, horrible time. It was my most frightening moment. And I still get the shakes as I think about it. Today my arm has flesh-colored scars—but there's no scarring on my face!"

## Saved in Plane Crash by Tree He Planted Twenty-five Years Before

James and Marilyn Haney thought they were goners as the plane James was piloting plunged toward the earth—but in a fantastic miracle, they were saved when their crash was cushioned by a tree he'd planted twenty-five years earlier!

"It's beyond coincidence—God was taking care of us," Marilyn told the *National Enquirer* reporter who interviewed the couple immediately after the dramatic accident. "We were diving out of control nose-first into the ground when we somehow hit that pine tree and it broke our fall!"

The fateful drama unfolded on October 22, 1996, after the Haneys had flown twelve hundred miles from their home in Idaho Falls, Idaho, to visit friends and family in Silver Lake, Indiana, their hometown.

James, a fifty-nine-year-old physician and father of four, began circling the town to alert Marilyn's sister and her husband to pick them up at a nearby airport.

Then something went dreadfully wrong with their Piper PA-16. The engine just quit cold. They had been flying at three thousand feet when the plane suddenly went into a steep dive toward the town.

The engine cut out. It was suddenly eerily quiet—and terrifying.

Marilyn vividly remembers watching the plane plunge toward the house where husband James grew up. "Oh, my God, we're going to die in the room where he was born!" she thought.

Then she saw that they were headed directly toward

the forty-foot pine tree that Jim, with the help of their four sons, had planted twenty-five years earlier.

Incredibly, the plane plowed through the branches of the tree, sheared off a wing, and slowed dramatically before it hit the ground and skidded to a halt in a yard across the street.

For some miraculous reason the plane crash-landed relatively unscathed. The aircraft narrowly missed hitting light poles, phone wires, houses, other structures—everything!

Said Marilyn, "The only thing that saved us was hitting that tree. We thank God every day for our miracle."

The two were hospitalized with head and back injuries, but later released.

"It's an amazing story," said Sheriff Al Rovenstine of the Kosciusko County sheriff's department. "What are the chances of someone flying twelve hundred miles and then having their lives saved by a tree they planted twenty-five years ago?"

## Love at First Sight

It was love at first sight when a young man's sight miraculously returned and he was able to see his longtime girlfriend for the first time.

"My God, you're beautiful," gasped Simon Stain as he got his first glimpse of twenty-three-year-old Wendy Jackson's features.

The young couple had initially fallen in love and moved in together after their first meeting on a job interview. Now Simon fell in love with Wendy—who's also blind—all over again. He even asked her to marry him!

"I'm so happy. I couldn't have picked anyone lovelier," Simon, twenty-one, who was sightless for six months because of an eye disease, told the *National Enquirer.*

Wendy was worried, then overjoyed that Simon could see. She had feared he would leave her if his vision came back—but instead he pledged to love her forever.

"I know Wendy had doubts that I would stay with her once I got my sight back, but I will always be there for her," vowed Simon of Derby, England.

His incredible recovery came without warning in January of 1991. He simply woke up one morning with the draperies shut in the bedroom—but he could see the light of the sun shining faintly through the blue curtain material. He asked himself, "Is this a dream?"

Later that day he saw Wendy. His sight was clearer at that moment than it had ever been. He just had to tell her how beautiful she was.

Doctors were astonished when Simon told them his vision had returned. They had believed him to be suffering from a hereditary eye disease called retinitis pigmentosa, which worsens with age until there is no sight left at all, explained Professor Alistair Fielder at Birmingham and Midland Eye Hospital in England.

Simon's vision had been poor as a child. But by the time he was a teenager, he suffered from night blindness and could see things in the daylight only if he held them right in front of his eyes.

By July 1990, just a few months before he met Wendy, Simon was totally blind and needed a guide dog to get around.

Then came the recovery that's baffled his doctors!

"In Simon's case, his eyesight has returned miraculously," said Dr. Fielder. "But it could also go again. We just can't be sure."

Meantime Simon and Wendy were making wedding plans—and still thoroughly enjoying their romantic miracle.

# Are Fertility Gods Performing
# Pregnancy Miracles?

Stories about women becoming pregnant after coming in contact with so-called fertility images are so bizarre that they could come from Ripley's Believe It or Not.

In fact, they do.

They claim there are strange things happening at Ripley's Museum in Orlando, Florida, these days. Even the telephone requests they get are weird—just recently a woman in Texas called to ask museum officials if she came to Florida to touch Ripley's amazing fertility gods, was a pregnancy guaranteed?

And there's the story about the New Jersey man who couldn't wait for his planned visit to Orlando. He faxed in a photocopy of his wife's hand—and requested that one of the museum officials rub it on one of the five-foot African statues and fax it back to him.

But are miracles really happening at this Florida sightseers' museum? We can only present the facts. You must judge for yourself.

So far there have been thirteen pregnancies attributed to the museum fertility gods. As of the summer of 1996, officials claimed attendance at the museum was up by as much as thirty percent. The attraction? The display of ebony gods carved by the Baule tribe on the Ivory Coast of West Africa.

The fertility gods have become nationally known since they arrived in Orlando in November 1994. Edward Meyer, Ripley's vice president of exhibits, had originally bought them as part of a collection of African statues, masks, and jewelry, paying less than a thousand dollars for each.

At first, the statues were the source of office jokes. Don't get too close to those things, employees warned each other. You might get pregnant.

Before long, though, the snickering gave way to morning sickness. Three women who work at the corporate headquarters and three wives of employees got pregnant!

One of them, Kimberly Martin, twenty-four, was married in October 1994 and wanted to wait at least four years to start a family, she said. But she tripped on the female statue shortly after her wedding and—despite vigilant birth control—was pregnant in two months.

"I think it played a big part, I really do," she said as she cradled her baby, Jacob. "My husband played a part, too, but the statue was a big part of it."

The trend isn't limited to employees. Museum officials issued the following tally:

- The Airborne Express driver, a regular visitor to the office, got pregnant.
- So did the woman who does the office's camera work. Last week, it was the freelance computer operator.
- Two Ripley's employees from Gatlinburg, Tennessee, got pregnant after visiting the Orlando office during an accounting conference.
- And finally, two more became pregnant after coming to the office selling jewelry. One of them had been trying for nine years.

All had touched the statue.

# "Miracle" Mushrooms Grow on Nun's Grave

For more than fifty years a Catholic nun tried to grow mushrooms on her convent grounds without success—but, miraculously, three months after her death, mushrooms sprang up all over her grave.

And the simple grave site of Sister Stanislaus, who died about four years ago, is the only spot within the five-acre convent ground where mushrooms grow.

Not a single mushroom has sprouted on the other ten nearby graves.

"It is a miracle—the work of God," Mother Francesca, abbess of the Mother of God Convent in Hawarden, England, told the *National Enquirer.*

"There is no scientific explanation. Sister Stanislaus was buried in the same kind of coffin, in the same ground, and the same way as her colleagues. There was nothing different about her funeral.

"It was her dream to grow mushrooms. She started trying soon after joining our order at age twenty. But when she died at seventy-nine she still had not succeeded. Then, suddenly, mushrooms covered her grave. And they do every year for three weeks."

The eighteen nuns at the convent harvest and eat the mushrooms, which are of the finest quality and delicious. Mother Francesca added: "This is one of the proofs that God looks after us—giving each person something special to show us He loves us."

## Mother Teresa and the "Nun Bun"

The late Mother Teresa thought it funny when a Tennessee coffeehouse claimed a "miracle" when they found her likeness on one of its cinnamon buns. But she thought the joke went too far when the Bongo Java coffeehouse began merchandising the buns commercially.

She put pen to paper to personally tell owner Bob Bernstein: "My legal counsel has written asking you to stop, and now I am personally asking you to stop."

The "nun bun" controversy began in October 1996 when an alert customer spied Mother Teresa's likeness in the folds of flaky pastry.

The bun was immediately shellacked and enshrined in a permanent counter display in the coffeehouse. The shop even began selling T-shirts, prayers cards, and mugs with the "nun bun" image.

Mother Teresa's U.S. attorney, Jim Towey, said initially Mother Teresa was tickled over the incident when she read about it in a Calcutta newspaper.

"Mother has a great sense of humor and appreciated the story about the bun—until it got commercialized," said attorney Towey.

Meantime, coffeehouse owner Bernstein has removed the miraculous "nun bun" from display until he confers with Mother Teresa's legal advisors.

## Message from God
## Written on a Tomato!?

If you thought that story was a lulu, what do you make of the one about a sacred message craftily hidden *inside* a tomato bought by a family in Huddersfield, England?

The tomato in question—which made headlines in British newspapers, magazines, and television—attracted hundreds of awed pilgrims to the humble home of Noor Mohammed.

They crowded into his tiny kitchen to gaze in wonder at the tomato turned holy relic. They were convinced it contains an important message from God.

Shaista Javed, Mr. Mohammed's fourteen-year-old granddaughter, bought the tomato—one of a big bag—at a local greengrocer's. She diced two tomatoes before asking her grandfather how he wanted the third done.

"Slice it," he told her. And she promptly cut it in half. Then she stared in amazement at the two segments.

In Arabic script inside one tomato she could make out the words, "There is only one God." On the other half, the script seemed to spell out, "Mohammed is the messenger."

Shaista, a Moslem, believes she has witnessed a miracle.

"God made me buy that tomato," she insists. "Those words are a message from God."

Word soon spread throughout the Moslem community. Scores of people have since crowded into the small kitchen to view the holy tomato for themselves. For a while the family kept it on display while it was fresh. These days it's kept in the freezer—available for viewing on demand.

Shaista's mother, Shamim Javed, believes her daughter—devoted to helping her elderly relatives—was chosen to spread the word.

"It was an incredible twist of fate that the tomato ended up with Shaista," she said. "Someone else could easily have sliced the tomato the other way round, or even eaten it without noticing the message inside."

Shopkeeper Shahida Parveea, who runs the greengrocer store, has noticed a sudden upturn in demand for tomatoes. "There's no shadow of doubt that it was a message from God," he said.

The last word comes from a spokesman at the nearby Nadni Mosque: "We don't consider it a miracle, but it is certainly a blessing."

# Minor Miracles for Della

One of the reasons Della Reese is so believable as the supervising angel on the hit CBS-TV show

*Touched By An Angel* is because Della firmly believes that she has an ongoing working relationship with God.

The sixty-five-year-old singer-actress had made up her mind a few years ago to get away from the glitz of Hollywood and showbiz in general and concentrate on her Christian ministry.

But, according to Della, God had a special mission for her: the role of Tess in *Touched By An Angel.* God spoke to her and asked her to take on the demanding role.

"I went home, sat up in my bed, I prayed, and said to the Father, 'I wish I didn't have to do this.' And as clearly as I'm speaking now, God said, 'Do this for me.' "

Colleagues on location are also convinced of Della's special affinity with God. And some even believe God performs minor miracles at her behest.

Once, the whole cast and crew stood sweltering for hours in the desert outside Salt Lake City with the mercury sizzling above 104 degrees.

Della suddenly raised her hand to halt production, looked to the sky, and prayed out loud, "Lord, we're hot. We need a cloud."

Within fifteen minutes the sky clouded over, recalls executive producer Marianne Williamson. "I'm not exaggerating," recalled Williamson. "With Della, you don't get just one cloud. You get a sky filled with clouds."

## Amazing 198-Pound Stone Floats in Air Like a Feather

Faith *can* move mountains!

Or at least it can move India's incredible 198-pound "miracle stone"—a wondrous holy rock that rises into the air like a feather with just a gentle touch, according to stunned eyewitnesses.

"It's like a person in the sky pulls it up," said one recent witness. Abdul Karim, fifty, a bicycle shop owner who was awestruck after he made the mysterious rock rise.

And a university researcher who investigated the amazing event admits it defies the laws of physics.

"It's definitely not a trick," says Dr. A. S. Nigvekar, head of the department of physics at India's University of Poona. "I've examined the stone. It's an ordinary rock weighing just under two hundred pounds. There's nothing special about it."

The stone—a round hunk of granite the size of a small tire—is a revered relic at a Moslem shrine in the Indian city of Khed.

Ordinarily, it would take a weight lifter's strength to lift anything weighing 198 pounds into the air. But each day scores of visitors line up and easily make the "miracle stone" float.

Following an ancient tradition, a group of eleven men gather round the rock in the shrine's sandy courtyard. Each places the tip of his right forefinger at the bottom of the stone.

Then in one voice the men chant the name of Peerbaba Kamarali Dervish, an ancient Moslem holy man. And with just a slight touch of their fingertips, the heavy rock rises like a balloon.

Effortlessly, the men heft the amazing stone as high into the air as possible on their outstretched fingertips. And then, witnesses say, the boulder floats on its own to a height of ten feet, hovers in the air for a few seconds, and drops heavily to the ground again!

"I felt how heavy the stone really is when it was on the ground and I touched it with my fingertip," said Ubedulla Khan, a forty-five-year-old teleprinter who took part in the ceremony. "But as we chanted the name in one voice, there was no weight. The stone went up like a bird's feather."

The miracle stone dates back to the thirteenth century, when it was found during construction of the shrine of Peerbaba Kamarali Dervish.

"On the average day, ordinary groups of people make it fly up and down at least one hundred times," said Javed Mehboob Tambuli, the shrine's caretaker.


## Tornado Swallows Pooch—
## and Dumps Her Two Miles Away!

Like Toto in *The Wizard of Oz,* Sadie the Yorkshire terrier was whisked into the sky by a swirling tornado. But she landed safe and sound—two miles away!

"Sadie didn't get to the land of Oz, but it must have been one heck of a ride," marvels the dog's devoted master, Deputy Sheriff Sandra Davis, thirty-six, of Saginaw, Texas. "It's amazing she survived."

The twister touched down near Deputy Sheriff Davis's home on the morning of September 13 while Davis and her husband, James, thirty-nine, were at work and daughter Lindsay, eight, was at school. As the surging wind howled, neighbor Mary Powers, fifty-one, saw the twister pick up Sadie from the Davis yard and lift the startled four-pound dog twenty feet into the air.

"I could see all kinds of stuff swirling around," Powers told the *National Enquirer.* I saw this green kiddie pool. I could also see shingles from roofs. Then I saw this black-and-white furry ball.

"I thought: 'What the heck is that?' And then I went, 'My God, that's a little dog.' I could clearly see it. It was twenty feet up and it was being tumbled around like it was being bounced in a clothes dryer."

Within minutes, Deputy Davis, who works for the Tarrant County sheriff's department, got a call that a twister had hit her neighborhood. She phoned James, an assistant manager at a manufacturing plant, and they rushed home.

Their house suffered six thousand dollars worth of damage, but their first thoughts were for Sadie and her safety.

"She's like one of the family," Deputy Davis said.

So when the Davis family learned their beloved pet had been blown up, and away, they frantically searched the countryside.

Sadly, there was no sign of Sadie.

But the next day, a miracle occurred! They got a call from a man who said he had found their tiny five-year-old terrier shortly after the storm—and she was a full two miles from her home! Luckily, Sadie had been wearing a name tag with her owner's phone number on it.

The delighted deputy and her hubby drove to the man's office and reclaimed their windswept but unharmed pet.

"Sadie is so special to us," gushed the grateful deputy. "It felt like we'd lost one of our family and now we've gotten her back. We're overjoyed."

# Chapter Ten

## Saintly Miracles

For centuries, Christians have hailed them as heroic miracle workers. They are universally recognized as role models, and children are urged to emulate them in word, thought, and deed.

They are saints—devoutly religious people who have lived lives of heroic sanctity or holiness, and who are therefore worthy of imitation and respect.

Over the last two thousand years, tradition has also recognized many of these saints as being special pleaders for specific causes. They are called patron saints.

The martyr St. Lucy, for example, had her eyes gouged out in A.D. 304—and is today remembered as patron saint of the blind and all those suffering from eye problems.

And St. Anthony, as the patron saint of lost objects, is the one to pray to when you lose something.

Says Philip St. Vincent Brennan, author of *Miracles of the Saints,* "This may sound like superstitious folklore to many. But before you dismiss the miraculous powers of the saints, you should bear in mind that seeking the help of a saint has a very legitimate basis in theology.

"Look at it this way. If you had a friend who had

special influence with a VIP whose help you needed, it would only be natural to seek your friend's intercession with that person. It's known as having a friend in city hall.

"Well, that's what saints are—friends who can go to bat for you in that celestial city hall we call heaven!"

It's not easy to become a saint. Official church-sanctioned investigations are exhaustive, very rigorous, and can last centuries in some cases.

Only after they are fully satisfied with all the testimony, facts, and other credentials will the Church declare that that person is in heaven enjoying "the beatific vision"—being in the presence of God Himself—and can therefore be designated a saint.

It makes sense to pray to these people to intercede for us for a miracle—after all, we know they're in heaven, are very special in the eyes of God, and therefore have a lot of pull with the Almighty.

And when they were on earth, God showed his partiality to these saints-in-the-making by allowing miracles to be performed through them during their lives, or in their names after they died.

Just remember, as sincere Catholics believe, we do not pray to saints—that would be idolatry. We pray only to God: Father, Son, and Holy Spirit. We ask the saints to intercede with the Boss.

And over the years, there's been plenty of evidence that they do this for us!

In this chapter we will include recommended prayers for certain saints more commonly associated with miracles, as well as a listing of common problems we encounter in our lives, health-related and other, and the saints we should be praying to for intercessions on our behalf.

A common misconception about saints is that they are flawless, perfect beings—angels, in fact. Nothing could be further from the truth.

As Phyllis McGinley wrote in *Saint Watching,* "I

cannot repeat often enough that saints are not angels. They enter the world as human beings; arrive as ennobled or disfigured by mortality as the rest of us."

St. Augustine is one example. In his *Confessions,* he admitted to living a dissolute life in his younger years, even fathering an illegitimate child. But Augustine went on to become one of the holiest of men, a scholar who helped define the philosophical theology of the Church.

Another saint, Teresa of Avila, one of history's most miraculous figures, was a real-life flying nun—in fact, her ability to rise into the air was so powerful that she often had to hold on to the edge of her pew to prevent herself from soaring into weightless space.

But she had a zest for living. She enjoyed life—and good food—immensely. "I could be bribed with a sardine," she once said.

She had a sense of humor, too. When someone once said that God punishes those whom He loves the most, she had a ready retort: "That," she said, "is why he has so few friends!"

For over a thousand years, the Catholic Church has established itself as the only Christian body that hands out halos to its heroes—but only after it has examined the life of each candidate with a fine-toothed comb.

Petitions are submitted on the candidate's behalf and his or her good deeds are catalogued. Then a "devil's advocate" is appointed to challenge every item of evidence and try, if he can, to discredit the candidate.

Miracles that can be thoroughly documented and clearly attributed to the candidate's intercession must be proven to have taken place.

# How to Find Your Miracle Through the Intercession of the Saints

There are right ways and wrong ways to ask the saints to plead a miracle on your behalf.

First and foremost, you should never pray with the idea that you are manipulating or bribing God for self-serving reasons—"If you give me what I ask, I'll do such and such a thing, but only if I get what I want."

And there's no such thing as "foolproof" or "guaranteed" prayers. If that were the case, our churches would be filled with lottery winners.

In many cases, nine-day periods of prayer for a saint's help—known as novenas—are traditional petitions. There is nothing wrong with this, but it's not the amount of time spent nor the number of days involved that matters.

Explains *Miracles of the Saints* author Brennan, "There is no heavenly CPA (Certified Prayer Accountant) sitting up there in paradise pecking away at a calculator, ready to declare prayers invalid because the petitioner didn't complete some specified period of praying ('Scratch that one, St. Jude, he only prayed for seven days and didn't leave nine copies of the prayer in the church—he only left eight.')

"There is, however, biblical justification for hammering away and not giving up. Christ himself advised launching a sustained campaign to seek God's help when he told the story of the man who keeps pounding on a neighbor's door in the middle of the night to get something he needed. Sooner or later, the neighbor would get up and open his door to the petitioner, Christ said. And, he added, His Father would do likewise.

"Christ said, 'Knock and it shall be opened to you.' Sometimes you have to knock for a long time.

"In other words, don't give up."

# New Saint Cured Three People on Their Deathbeds

One of Italy's top doctors, who dedicated his life to serving the poor free of charge, is credited with miraculously curing hundreds of sick and dying people after his death.

His healings earned him the honor of becoming one of the Catholic Church's newest saints.

Pope John Paul II bestowed sainthood in October 1987 on Dr. Giuseppe Moscati in a Vatican ceremony watched by 150,000 people—including many who claimed they were healed after praying to the late physician.

Three incredible miracles attributed to Dr. Moscati were confirmed by the Vatican commission that investigated his life:

- A blacksmith, dying of leukemia, said Dr. Moscati appeared to him in a vision and told him, "You are well." He immediately underwent medical tests—and sure enough, all signs of his leukemia had vanished!
- Hospital doctors sent a man with terminal Addison's disease home to die. He prayed to a portrait of Dr. Moscati—and said he later dreamed the physician was operating on him. Next morning he rushed back to the hospital and doctors confirmed he was cured.
- With her teenage son dying of meningitis, a desperate woman prayed at the tomb of Dr. Moscati. When she returned to the hospital, she found her son's bed surrounded by excited doctors. The boy had suddenly recovered!

In all three cases, the physicians involved submitted written testimony to the Vatican commission saying there was no medical explanation for the recoveries.

"The miracles we selected can only be explained as the outcome of divine intervention," declared Father Paolo Molinari, who headed the commission.

Dr. Moscati—the first doctor in modern church history to be sainted—astounded people even while he was alive, often making diagnoses and prescribing treatments without even seeing his patients.

"His colleagues admired him for the almost prophetic way he could make diagnoses," Father Molinari said.

The kindly physician from Naples spent his life treating patients' bodies and souls before he died in 1927 at age forty-six—apparently from pushing his body beyond its limits, Father Molinari said. "You could say he died from devotion. He worked in a public hospital ward and devoted his free time to the poorest districts, where people received him like a missionary to their misery."

The deeply religious physician never asked the poor for payment. In fact, he gave so much of his own money to help others that he often was broke, despite his reputation as one of Italy's top doctors.

After Dr. Moscati's death, his remains were placed in a special tomb inside the Church of Jesus in Naples, and thousands of pilgrims visited every day to seek cures for themselves and their families.

Out of the countless miraculous healings attributed to Dr. Moscati, the Vatican commission selected three for investigation and documented them beyond a doubt, said Father Luigi Garofalo, deputy head of the commission.

The last of the three miracles involved the healing of Giuseppe Montefusco, who was expected by doctors to die of acute leukemia. As Montefusco lay close to death in a hospital bed, his mother says Dr. Moscati appeared to her in a dream and told her: "Trust in God and you'll see your son recover."

With his mother's help, Montefusco sneaked out of the hospital and prayed at the late doctor's tomb.

"Then one night, I had a vision of Dr. Moscati," Montefusco said. "He appeared in a long white coat and said: 'There is no need to occupy a hospital bed. you are well and can go home.' "

Montefusco was tested for leukemia by his family physician, Luigi Di Palma, and Professor Mario D'Onofrio, chief of hematology-oncology for Naples University Medical Center, and the doctors pronounced him in complete remission.

"We looked at it as an amazing happening," said Dr. Di Palma.

Concluded Father Molinari: "Saint Giuseppe Moscati performed God's work while he lived—and continued doing God's work after his death."


## Centuries-Old Hand Cures Stroke Victim

A Benedictine priest rapidly recovered from a stroke after the three-hundred-year-old embalmed hand of a saint—a religious relic—was laid on his forehead.

Roman Catholic parish priest Reverend Christopher Jenkins, sixty-three, of Hereford in England, went into a coma after suffering the stroke. Doctors didn't expect him to live. But a fellow priest, Father Antony Tumulty, took the hand—usually kept at St. Francis Xavier Church, where both clergyman ministered—to the hospital, placed it on Father Jenkins's head, and prayed.

Within a few hours, Father Jenkins had miraculously rallied. He was up and about and eating and talking as if nothing had happened.

"Nobody expected him to live, but he came out of

the coma within hours. It's not up to me to say whether his recovery is a miracle, but it's beyond our wildest hopes," Father Tumulty told reporters.

The miraculous hand was once attached to the body of St. John Kemble, a seventeenth-century Catholic priest who was hanged and drawn and quartered in Hereford in 1679—simply for being a Catholic priest at the time of the Reformation.

After the execution, the hand was severed and thrown to the crowd. It was rescued by loyal religious sympathizers and had been kept in the church for two hundred years before being removed to save the life of Father Jenkins.

## St. Mary, the Mother of God, Patron Saint of Peace, Enlightenment, Pilots, and Home Builders

As you will see elsewhere in this book, the Virgin Mary's name is associated with a multitude of miracles, some of recent origin, others dating back centuries.

That's one of the reasons Mary is so venerated by many Christian churches—but especially by Roman Catholics, who like to describe her as "the mother of all mankind."

They recall Jesus's words from the Cross to the apostle John: "Son, behold thy mother; mother, behold thy son." So Catholic believers venerate her as a heavenly mother, full of love and compassion.

As the mother whom Jesus loved, as any good son loves his mother, it's fair to assume she occupies a special place in heaven. And it's equally fair to assume that prayers to her have a special influence.

After all, it was for his mother, Mary, that Jesus performed his first miracle—at the wedding feast at Cana, where he transformed water into wine only because she asked him to.

Mary's own miraculous interventions are mentioned in the Memorare, an ancient prayer to Mary often used by desperate souls seeking her help. Also, countless miraculous cures have been confirmed by serious medical researchers as having occurred at the shrine at Lourdes in France, which became internationally famous as a mecca for the sick and dying after a vision of Mary appeared there to the young peasant girl Bernadette.

Mary's principal feast days in the U.S. are December 8, the Feast of the Immaculate Conception, and August 15, the Feast of the Assumption.

Prayer recommended for those seeking Mary's intercession:

Remember, Oh compassionate Virgin Mary, that never was it known that anyone who fled to thy protection, implored thy help, or sought thy intercession was left unaided. Inspired by this confidence, we fly unto thee, Oh virgin of virgins, our mother. To thee do we come, before thee we kneel, sinful and sorrowful. Oh Mother of the Word Incarnate, despise not our petitions, but in thy clemency, hear and answer them. Amen.

# St. Anthony of Padua,
# Patron of Lost Articles,
# Childless Women, and Amputees

If you've lost anything, this is the saint who will help you find it.

Once, with the mere power of prayer, a valuable

stolen relic reappeared in the church after Anthony prayed for its return.

Although he was known as St. Anthony of Padua in Italy because he lived there for a long time, St. Anthony didn't hail from Padua, nor was he even Italian.

He was Portuguese, born in Lisbon in 1195.

Anthony was originally baptized as Ferdinand. When still a youngster, he began his religious studies at the Roman Catholic Cathedral in Lisbon.

When he was just fifteen, he joined the Augustinian monastic order. After ten years in the order, he left to join the Franciscan order—much against the wishes of his fellow Augustinians, who didn't want to lose one of their best teachers and scholars.

Anthony, however, felt the need to go out into the world to preach God's word. After a stint as a missionary in Africa, he went back to teaching, basing himself in several European cities, including Padua.

Because the calling to preach was so strong, Anthony couldn't stay settled in one place for any prolonged period of time. When he could no longer resist the missionary urge, he would take to the road, preaching in cities all over Europe.

An inspired orator, filled with enthusiasm for missionary work, he became so famous for his spellbinding sermons that he was no longer able to preach in churches—no cathedral was large enough to hold the enormous throngs of people who came to hear him.

He became famous as an inspired outdoor preacher. He also won acclaim as a saintly miracle worker, capable of the most extraordinary feats.

One of his best-remembered miracles was the sudden and mysterious reappearance of a valuable prayer book that had been stolen. It miraculously reappeared in the church after Anthony prayed it would be found. It was this miracle that prompted the belief that his intercession could help find lost articles.

Anthony died in 1231. His feast day is June 13.

Prayer to St. Anthony:

Almighty, ever-living God, you gave your people the extraordinary preacher St. Anthony and made him an intercessor in difficulties. By his intercession, grant that we may live truly Christian lives and experience your help in recovering that which we have lost, and in all other adversities.

## St. Blase, Patron Saint of Those Suffering from Throat Disorders

Blase didn't start out as a holy man. He was originally a physician—but he found that he could heal with the power of prayer better than he could using medicines. So he turned to the priesthood and rose quickly through the ranks to become bishop of Sebasta, a region in fourth-century Armenia.

A controversial, outspoken character, Blase fell out of favor with the powerful governor of Sebasta and was placed under arrest. On his way to prison, Blase performed one of his most famous miracles. He was approached by a woman whose child was suffering from a serious throat disorder. Blase prayed over the child, who was miraculously cured. Since that time, the name Blase has become synonymous with the healing of throat disorders. Countless miraculous cures of throat diseases have since been attributed to St. Blase.

Every February 3, Catholics the world over have their throats blessed in the name of St. Blase. In the throat-blessing ceremony, a priest or deacon holds two candles in the shape of a cross and extends them over the person's throat while praying:

"Through the merits and intercession of St. Blase, bishop and martyr, may God deliver you from all diseases of the throat, and from every other evil. In the name of the Father, Son, and Holy Spirit, Amen.

His feast day is February 3.

Prayer for the help of St. Blase:

Lord, hear your people through the intercession of St. Blase. Help us to enjoy good health, prevent all disorders of the throat, and heal any from which we now suffer, and help us to find peace in this life and a lasting refuge in the next.

## St. Giles, Patron Saint of the Physically Disabled

St. Giles was so well known as a healer of the sick and crippled that the king of France asked him to become a permanent member of his court—an offer the devout Greek-born holy man had no problem refusing.

Giles is probably best remembered as the saint who talked to God—and hardly anybody else.

By birth a seventh-century Greek aristocrat from a noble Athenian family, he won fame and respect for his great piety and academic brilliance while still a young man. As a holy man, however, the public acclaim bothered him because it interfered with his desire to spend his life in solitude and prayer. To find solace, he fled Greece to live alone in the wilderness. He located himself in several remote areas of France, where he spent all his time conversing with God in prayer.

Many of those for whom he prayed reported miracle cures, particularly when Giles prayed on behalf of crippled people and others physically disabled.

Again, Giles's fame and reputation became wide-spread, this time throughout France. He became so famous as a miracle worker that the king of France begged him to leave his hermitage and come live at his court. Giles resisted, insisting that his sole desire was that he be left alone with his God.

In later years, Giles allowed several disciples to share his isolation. Before he died in 724, he founded a monastery.

His feast day is September 3.

Prayer for St. Giles's intercession:

Lord, amid the things of this world, let us be whole-heartedly committed to heavenly things in imitation of the example of the evangelical perfection you have given us in St. Giles the Abbot, and through his inter-cession, ease the burden of those who are physically disabled, and if it be thy will, heal them of their disabilities.

## St. Gerard Majella, Patron Saint of Expectant Mothers

Because he repeatedly assisted in the miraculous de-liveries of healthy babies to women in life-threatening labor, St. Gerard has historically been recognized as the man who helps out with difficult pregnancies.

Born in Italy in 1726, he took holy orders at age twenty-three. As a lay brother in the Redemptorist order, he was initially assigned such menial tasks as gardener, hospital attendant, and tailor.

It wasn't long before his superiors realized they had a very saintly man on their hands. Brother Gerard showed incredible piety and wisdom beyond his years. Above all, he had a remarkable gift of compassion. He had an almost miraculous ability to know exactly what was on people's consciences before they uttered even one word of confession.

Realizing that he was capable of doing far more important work than the menial tasks they had previously given him, his superiors assigned him the job of providing spiritual advice and guidance to members of female religious orders.

Gerard had yet another miraculous talent. Like St. Teresa of Avila, he was able to float himself in midair. He would do this from time to time without giving prior warning. And, like the late Padre Pio, Gerard is also reported to have had the gift of bilocation—he could literally be in two places at the same time!

Since his death at the age of twenty-nine in 1755, countless other miracles have been attributed to his intercession on behalf of women in danger of losing their unborn babies.

His feast day is October 16.

Prayer for the help of St. Gerard:

God, by your grace, St. Gerard persevered in imitating Christ in his poverty and humility. Through his intercession, grant that we may faithfully follow our vocation and reach that perfection which you held out to us in your son, and in your mercy help those expectant mothers to enjoy a safe pregnancy and delivery and give birth to healthy, normal children.

# Saint Jude Thaddeus,
# Patron Saint of Impossible Causes

Jude, a first cousin of Jesus, has long been regarded as the saint of last resort—when all else has failed you, Jude is the man to turn to.

If you are in desperate straits, you can call on St.

Jude to get you out of whatever fix you or a loved one are in. And the record shows that he frequently does!

In the book *The Power of Jude,* the authors describe St. Jude as "a mysterious figure in many ways."

"He moves in and out of the gospel story as a shadowy figure, almost as if he were deliberately seeking to submerge his own personality in that of Christ rather than draw any attention to himself.

"This very obscurity is one of the reasons why he remained unknown and forgotten for so many centuries."

The book says the reason Jude is relatively unknown stems from the fact that there were two Judes among the disciples—the other being the infamous Judas Iscariot, the betrayer of Christ.

"When St. Matthew and St. Mark wrote their Gospels, they attempted to avoid confusion between the two men by listing them apart. They called our St. Jude only by the name of Thaddeus," according to *The Power of Jude.*

Even in today's Catholic Mass, St. Jude is referred to as Thaddeus, not Jude. However, there is no denying his ability to perform miracles for those who call on him for help in the midst of their most serious difficulties.

St. Jude Thaddeus was born in Galilee. His father, Cleophas Alphaeus (Mark 3:18, Matthew 10:3, Jude 1:1), was a descendant of King David and a brother of St. Joseph.

His mother, Mary of Alphaeus, was a cousin of Mary, the Mother of Jesus. St. Jude was therefore a first cousin of Jesus, who was also his childhood friend and neighbor.

Together with his older brother, James the Less (Luke 6:16, Acts 1:13), he was one of the twelve apostles.

According to *Lives of the Saints* (Catholic Press), after Christ's resurrection, Jude traveled widely, preaching the Gospel in Judea, Samaria, Idumaea, Syria, Mesopotamia, and Libya.

According to Eusebius, a bishop and early church historian, Jude returned to Jerusalem in A.D. 62 for the election of his brother St. Simeon as Bishop of the Holy City. Later in life, he died a martyr's death in Armenia.

According to *The Power of Jude,* appeals to St. Jude are usually restricted to matters of a very personal nature. His reputation as a powerful saint has spread primarily by word of mouth.

"For example, when one person has successfully implored help from St. Jude for some intimate problem that apparently defied solution, that person passes the wonderful news on to a friend who has let it be known that he or she also has a serious problem," according to *The Power of Jude.*

"The recipient of St. Jude's help, in turn, relates his or her personal experience, tells someone else of the blessings received, asking, 'Why don't you take your problem to St. Jude? You won't believe the results until you talk to the Man yourself.'

"Thus, the story of St. Jude's powerful intercession and his help in the most difficult cases spreads by personal recommendation—a most effective way of popularizing devotion to him.

"The letters of gratitude and the petitions made public through the various shrines, churches, and newspapers all share a common bond: They express a strong belief in the power of Jude.

"Petitions ask for his intercession for such diverse personal matters as the quest for a happy marriage, success in business, finding a job, reconciliation with a spouse, cure of alcoholism, peace of mind, a happy death, a safe pregnancy, or return of an absent member of the family.

"Another distinctive feature of devotion to St. Jude has been the constancy with which his clients have thanked him.

"Nearly every regular reader of the classified and section of newspapers or magazines will find tucked away in the Personals or Card of Thanks section a little ad that says: THANK YOU, ST. JUDE.

Prayer Seeking St. Jude's Intercession:
Oh Holy St. Jude, apostle and martyr, great in virtue and rich in miracles, near kinsman of Jesus Christ, faithful intercessor of all who invoke your special patronage in time of need, to you I come. I humbly beg you to whom God has given such great power to come to my assistance. Help me in my present and urgent petition.

## St. Theresa of Lisieux, the Little Flower of Jesus, Patron Saint of Sinners, Priests, Ministers, Tuberculosis, Gardeners, Florists, and Aviators

She's also known as St. Theresa of the Roses for her miraculous ability to make sweet-smelling flowers materialize out of thin air.

Truly a saint for our age, this gentle, frail little nun lived a mere twenty-four years, yet her influence spread far and wide within days of her death. The ardor of her faith and her inspirational example as a model of humility and patience have inspired popes and millions of people throughout the world.

"Within a few months of her death, [such] a storm of interest and affection of Theresa began that a Vatican cardinal declared: 'We must hasten to canonize Theresa, otherwise we shall be anticipated by the voice of the people,' " writes Father Alfred McBride in the book *Saints Are People*.

And canonized she was, in record time. She was

named a saint in 1925, a mere twenty-eight years after her death—far less than the fifty years the Vatican usually stipulates should pass before acting on the canonization of a saint.

Theresa is one of a few saints to leave behind a memoir, *The Story of a Soul.* By 1932, it had sold an astounding 800,000 copies, in addition to 2.5 million copies of a smaller French-language version.

Few people have endured the suffering this French Carmelite nun endured during her short life. As she lay dying of a painful terminal illness, she was heard to offer thanks to her Savior for allowing her to share in the agony He endured on the Cross.

Theresa wrote: "After my death, I will let fall a shower of roses." She kept her word. After her death, many mysterious showers of roses were reported in religious circles.

"After that, people sought miracles and spiritual favors through her intercession," writes biographer Father McBride.

Her convent at Lisieux is literally buried in testimonies attesting to favors and miracles she performed for desperate people who sought her help. Among them are documents and medical affidavits that tell of cures for cancer, blindness, ulcers, and meningitis. Other believers have written about the great peace that entered their lives in the midst of turmoil after they prayed to St. Theresa.

Theresa Martin was born in Alencon, France, in 1873. She was the youngest of nine children. Her mother died when she was only five, and she was raised by her older sisters and an aunt.

Her father, Louis Martin, was a prosperous watchmaker and a devout Christian. His devotion to God was so strong that two of his daughters were drawn to a religious life by his example. Both entered a convent at an early age.

From her earliest days, their younger sister, little

Theresa, was also deeply religious. She had an extraordinary ability, unusual in one so young, to totally immerse herself in prayer.

When she was fourteen, she told her father that she wanted to join her two older sisters at the Carmelite convent at Lisieux. Her father resisted at first because he thought she was too young to make such a lifelong commitment. Moreover, he felt it a bit much to have three members of his family in a convent that supported a mere twenty members.

Although she won her father's support in the end, and the support of the prioress of the convent, other religious bodies were reluctant to agree to let one so young join the Carmelites.

When her father took her on a pilgrimage to Rome to help celebrate the pope's anniversary jubilee, Theresa took advantage of an audience with Pope Leo XIII to win his support.

Although warned by Vatican officials not to address the pope during the audience. Theresa spoke up. "Holy Father, in honor of your jubilee, let me enter the Carmel at fifteen."

After a few minutes of thought, the pope agreed, "If it is God's will."

On April 9, 1888, she entered the convent, where she would spend the rest of her short life. She took the name Theresa of the Child Jesus.

A victim of tuberculosis, she suffered terribly but bore her suffering with courage and resignation. In her final days, she writhed in pain, but welcomed suffering because she recognized it as a means that brought her even closer to Christ by sharing in his suffering on the Cross.

Before she died, she told her fellow nuns that she planned to spend her life in heaven praying for sinners.

Prayer for the Intercession of St. Theresa:
God our Father, you destined your kingdom for your children who are humble. Help us to imitate the way of

St. Theresa so that, by her intercession, we may attain the eternal glory that you promised, and grant us that favor for which we ask in her name. Amen.

# St. Francis of Assisi,
# Patron Saint of Ecologists, Merchants,
# Animal Lovers, and Catholic Action

A brave warrior turned man of peace, the great Francis of Assisi, in his later years, also became a stigmatic—bearing the painful wounds of Jesus on his own body.

Few people have not heard the famous prayer of St. Francis of Assisi, which begins: "Lord, make me an instrument of your peace. Where there is hatred, let me sow love. . . ."

It may well be the best-known prayer of the turbulent, war-torn century in which he lived. St. Francis may be the best known of all saints in this age because of the sensitive words of the prayer that bears his name.

Francis Bernadone was born in 1182, the son of a wealthy cloth merchant. As a youth, he was known as a man who loved life and lived it to the fullest.

He wore the best and most fashionable clothes, was popular with everybody, partied like a twentieth-century playboy, and reveled in being around people.

He had a sunny disposition that helped soften his martial side. For Francis was also a warrior—a knight known for his chivalrous ways, his courage and courtesy, and his mercy to his vanquished enemies.

He lost much of his zest for combat, however, during the interminable wars between his native Assisi and neighboring Perugia. The two cities treated each other much as Croats, Muslims, and Serbs treat each other today in war-ravaged Bosnia. The glamor of knighthood faded during one particularly vicious combat between the two cities.

"His brief career in the military, which included a period of defeat and imprisonment, disillusioned him," according to Father McBride in his book *Saints Are People.* "The viciousness of mortal combat, the curses, the naked hatred, the numbing humiliations of jail, brought him to a moment of truth and an experience of radical self-evaluation."

The experience transformed him, and he surrendered himself to Jesus, giving himself up to a life of service and poverty.

This gentle man, who had been courageous in the vicious hand-to-hand combat of the wars, found the courage to abandon everything—wealth and prestige as a member of a powerful family—in favor of a life of service to the poor.

His decision angered his proud family, who tried everything to get him to give up his new vocation. They became so embittered when he persisted that they were never reconciled.

His father disinherited him and Francis went off into the world penniless—determined, as he put it, "to wed Lady Poverty." He was determined to live poorer than the poor he would serve. His selfless example soon inspired others to join him.

Three years later, in 1210, he got permission from the pope to establish what became known as the Friars Minor, a religious order that would later become known as the Franciscan Order of Priests.

But Francis never became a priest himself—he didn't believe himself worthy!

His Franciscans' work among the poor, however, and their example of humility, poverty, and love so inspired others that within a period of nine short years the order had grown to a membership of five thousand.

In 1224, Francis became a stigmatic—he bore the

wounds of Christ and suffered terribly from them. He also went blind from an eye disease.

Worn out by the rigorous, spartan life he had led, Francis died at sunset, October 3, 1226. At the moment of his death, he was singing Psalm 142: "Lead me forth from prison that I may give thanks to your name."

"Francis of Assisi has captured the heart and imagination of men of all religious persuasions by his love for God and man, as well as all God's creatures, by his simplicity, directness, and single-mindedness, and by the lyrical aspects of his multifaceted life," according to the book *Lives of the Saints*.

"However, he was far more than an inspired individualist. He was a man possessed of vast spiritual insight and power; a man whose all-consuming love for Christ and redeemed creation burst forth in everything he said and did."

Prayer for St. Francis's intercession:

God, you enabled St. Francis to imitate Christ by his poverty and humility. May we walk in his footsteps, follow your son, and be bound to you in joyful love. Through his intercession, grant this favor we ask. Amen.

# St. Elizabeth Ann Seton, the First American Saint, Patron Saint of Mothers, Widows, and Working Women

Elizabeth Ann Bayley was born in New York City in 1774. Her family was socially prominent and wealthy, with roots deep in colonial New York society.

Except for her father, they were devout Episcopalians, the faith in which Mother Seton was raised.

Her father was a surgeon for the British Army—a position that caused him and his family much anguish when the American Revolution broke out. Emotionally a royalist, Dr. Bayley reluctantly cast his lot with the rebels who rose up against British colonial rule, thus sparing him from the exile that befell many loyalists after the war.

When Elizabeth was sixteen, she fell head over heels in love with William Magee Seton, a member of another old and wealthy New York family. Their marriage at Trinity Church was a major social event presided over by the pastor of that prestigious church, the Reverend Dr. Henry Hobart.

Deeply religious, despite her father's hostility to religion and his constant attempts to enlist her in his crusade for atheistic humanism, she was further inspired by Dr. Hobart, who took it upon himself to become her spiritual adviser.

Her marriage was a happy one. She had five children, three boys and two girls, in rapid succession. But after nine years, life began to deliver a series of vicious blows to Elizabeth Ann and her family.

It began when her husband's business went sour, plunging him into a financial crisis that seriously affected his health.

Some friends, the Fillichis of Leghorn, Italy, an aristocratic and wealthy Catholic family, invited Elizabeth, her husband, and her oldest daughter to come live with them in Italy in the hopes that, with their help, her husband might be able to recoup both his wealth and his health.

Her other four children were left behind in the care of various Seton and Bayley family members.

Tragically, within six weeks of arriving in Italy, William Seton died. Over the next six months, the Fillichis surrounded his widow and her daughter with warmth and compassion.

Elizabeth was so impressed by their deep attachment to their church that, by the time she left for America, she was well on the way to becoming a Catholic herself.

Back home, her growing attachment to the Catholic Church was met with outright hostility by her family and friends—especially the Reverend Dr. Hobart, who was horrified that this granddaughter of the former pastor of his church would have anything to do with Roman Catholicism.

Elizabeth persisted in converting and, after a year, was received into the Roman Catholic Church on March 4, 1805.

Her conversion immediately closed all doors behind her. She became an outcast, spurned by her family and friends in predominantly Protestant, anti-Catholic old New York.

Broke, friendless except for her former Italian host and ally, Antonio Fillichi—who had come back to America on a business trip—and desperately in need of a means to support herself and her children, she went looking for a teaching job, armed with letters of support from the loyal Antonio.

Her first attempt—a partnership in a plan to establish a private school—failed and things looked grim indeed.

At that point, however, a Baltimore priest, Father William Du Bourg, the head of that city's Sulpician Order, asked her to come to Maryland to put together a girls' school.

She didn't know it at the time, but that offer would lead to the very foundation of the Catholic school system in the United States.

She opened the school, dedicated to providing education for even the poorest girls unable to pay tuition.

Two years later, with the help of Bishop Carroll,

she founded a religious order, the Sisters of Charity of St. Joseph. They, in the years to come, would pound a highly disciplined elementary school education into the heads of generations of Americans, including this writer's.

She founded two orphanages and two schools over the next fourteen years and still managed to keep a careful eye on her own children.

One of her sons left school and the chance to become a banker with Antonio's help and went off to sea as a merchant sailor. His disappointed mother never ceased to urge him to live a pious life devoted to his church and his fellow man.

It must have sunk in—he eventually married, settled down, had children (one of whom became a priest), and went on to become an archbishop!

Elizabeth died at the age of forty-five and was canonized in 1976.

Prayer for the intercession of St. Elizabeth Ann Seton:

Dear Lord, you drew St. Elizabeth Ann Seton into a life of service and prayer and inspired her to lay the foundations of America's parochial school system, which educated generations of your children. Through her intercession, grant us the favor we seek in her name.

## Church Begins Inquiry into Sainthood for Mother Drexel

Born the daughter of a millionaire philanthropist, young Katherine Drexel could have enjoyed a pampered life as a privileged socialite. But this pious and humane young woman renounced the opportunity of riches and comfort to dedicate her life to the needs of underprivileged blacks and Native Americans.

Before her death in 1955 at age ninety-six, her achievements in this area were quite miraculous. Although she died just as the civil rights movement was swinging into action, Katherine Drexel's work on behalf of those less fortunate is testimony that she was a woman way ahead of her time—as founder of the nation's only black Catholic university, Xavier of Louisiana, plus missions and schools from Indian territory to Harlem to Haiti.

Today supporters of Blessed Mother Katherine Drexel are claiming that she is still performing miracles—healing miracles, that is—and, with the support of the Archdiocese of Philadelphia, they are advocating her sainthood.

The Vatican has already validated one miracle in the name of Mother Drexel—and her supporters are working in secret to have one other miracle validated by the Vatican.

Miracle number one was first published in 1988 when Vatican doctors decided that they could find no medical reason why a young boy called Robert J. Gutherman regained his hearing.

In 1974, the boy, then fourteen, lost hearing in his right ear after a severe infection. Doctors said it could not be cured, but after family and friends prayed to Mother Drexel to intercede, his hearing returned.

Now campaigners for Mother Drexel's sainthood are claiming a second miracle—that of an infant born deaf whose newfound ability to hear has at least a dozen doctors stumped.

So far witnesses have included the parents, relatives, and friends who prayed for the child's healing, plus records from three hospitals, six doctors, and medical dossiers.

Family and friends must convince authorities that they prayed strictly for Drexel's intercession, not to any other saint or holy figure. Vatican theologians must decide on the purity of their prayers.

"At this stage, we are not saying it is a cure, we are not saying it is a miracle," said a spokesman for the archdiocese. "It is simply a healing with the intercession of Mother Drexel. What makes a miracle is when there is no possible medical explanation for the healing whatsoever."

If the Vatican decides to accept it as the second miracle, it will then be up to the pope to decide whether Mother Drexel should be canonized.

Rules for canonization have changed in the Roman Catholic Church. It no longer takes three or four miracles, only two. But one must occur after a candidate is beatified, a papal declaration based on a candidate's holiness and suitability for sainthood.

Mother Drexel was beatified in 1988.

To many believers, Mother Drexel is already a saint. Since her death, hundreds have turned up to pray for her intercession on their behalf at her crypt in the Sisters of Blessed Sacrament mother house in Bensalem, Pennsylvania.

Meantime, in Philadelphia, Cardinal Anthony Bevilacqua has ordered hearings. And the Reverend Alexander Palmieri, chancellor of the archdiocese and vice postulator for the Drexel cause, is preparing a strong case for consideration by the Vatican's Congregation for the Causes of Saints.

The Reverend Palmieri says the local hearing is a fact-finding proceeding that makes no recommendations. That's up to the Vatican's Consulta Medica, drawn from a pool of about sixty Rome physicians, which rejects more than half the alleged miracles they review.

But the case for Mother Drexel stands a strong chance if it is referred to the pope for his last call. To date, Pope John Paul II has set a record. Through 1995, he has made thirty-eight canonizations—several of them mass declarations involving 875 individuals, plus 208 beatifications.

Born in 1858 into the wealthy Drexel banking family, Katie Drexel was a teenager when she made her decision to turn her back on a society lifestyle.

After her father's death in 1885, she traveled to Europe with her mother and two sisters, and was both surprised and delighted when Pope Leo XIII—recognizing her piety and devotion—urged her to become a missionary to the Indians.

In 1888, she founded a school for black children, which later became St. Peter Claver, Philadelphia's first black parish. She went on to found Indian missions before entering a convent in 1889, amid scandalous headlines about the socialite nun.

At age thirty-three she founded the Blessed Sacrament order, the same day she took her vows—February 12, 1891.

When she founded Xavier in New Orleans—still the nation's only predominantly black Catholic university, although no longer run wholly by her order—she sat in the balcony at its dedication, unrecognized. She forbade the mention of her name.

Although she poured millions from her Drexel inheritance—$20 million in interest alone from her father's trust fund—into her causes, Mother Drexel didn't hold back one cent for her own earthly comforts. In fact, she was renowned for her spartan lifestyle.

This is apparent from a glass case on display at the Sisters of the Blessed Sacrament in Bucks County, Pennsylvania, outside Philadelphia, which displays the thread she used to mend her clothes. This symbolizes the extreme in which the onetime heiress carried her vow of poverty.

Mother Drexel used to wear her clothes out until sisters replaced them without her permission. At meals, she always chose the smallest, least palatable portions. She cut unused paper from edges of letters and wrote notes on the scraps. She fasted so rigorously at times her colleagues were alarmed.

Mother Drexel suffered a stroke in 1935 and lived as a near-recluse the last two decades of her life.

# Patron Saints and Their Causes

Abandoned children—St. Jerome Emiliani
Accountants—St. Matthew
Actors—St. Genesius, St. Vitus
Advertising—St. Bernadine of Siena
Air travelers—St. Joseph of Cupertino
Altar servers—St. John Berchmans
Anesthetists—St. Rene Goupil
Angina sufferers—St. Swithbert
Animal lovers—St. Francis of Assisi
Amputees—St. Anthony of Padua
Architects—St. Barbara, St. Thomas the Apostle
Art—St. Catherine of Bologna
Art dealers—St. John the Evangelist
Arthritics—St. James the Apostle
Artists—St. Luke
Astonomers—St. Dominic
Athletes—St. Sebastian
Authors—St. Francis de Sales
Aviators—St. Joseph Cupertino, St. Mary, St. Theresa
  of Lisieux

Bakers—St. Nicholas, St. Honoratus
Bankers—St. Matthew
Barbers—St. Cosmas, St. Damian
Barren women—St. Anthony of Padua, St. Felicity
Battle—St. Michael
Beggars—St. Alexius, St. Giles

Birds—St. Francis of Assisi
Blacksmiths—St. James, St. Dunstan
Blindness—St. Lucy, St. Odilia, St. Raphael
Blood banks—St. Januarius
Boatmen—St. Julian the Hospitaler
Bookbinders—St. Peter Celestine
Bookkeepers—St. Matthew
Booksellers—St. John the Evagelist
Boy Scouts—St. George
Breast cancer—St. Agatha
Breast disorders—St. Agatha
Brewers—St. Augustine, St. Luke, St. Nicholas of
 Myra
Bricklayers—St. Stephen
Brides—St. Nicholas of Myra
Brushmakers—St. Anthony
Builders—St. Barbara, St. Vincent Ferrer
Businessmen—St. Frances Cabrini
Butchers—St. Peter, St. Anthony, St. Hadrian, St.
 Luke

Cab drivers—St. Fiacre
Cabinetmakers—St. Anne
Cancer victims—St. Peregrine Laziosi
Candlemakers—St. Ambrose, St. Bernard of Clairvaux
Canonists—St. Raymond of Penafort
Carpenters—St. Joseph
Catechists—St. Robert Bellarmine, St. Charles Boor-
 romeo, St. Viator
Catholic action—St. Francis of Assisi
Catholic Church—St. Joseph
Catholic press—St. Francis de Sales
Charitable organizations—St. Vincent de Paul
Childbirth—St. Gerard Majella
Childless women—St. Anthony of Padua
Children—St. Frances Cabrini
Chivalry—St. George
Choirboys—St. Dominic Savio

Civil servants—St. Thomas More
Clergy—St. Charles Borromeo, St. Gabriel
Clockmakers—St. Peter
Comedians—St. Genesius, St. Phillip Neri, St. Vitus
Communications workers—St. Bernardine
Composers—St. Cecile
Compositors—St. John the Evangelist
Confectioners—St. Joseph
Confessors—St. John Vianney, St. Alphonsus Liguori.
   St. John Nepomucine
Convulsive children—St. Scholastica
Cooks—St. Lawrence, St. Martha
Coppersmiths—St. Maura
Courage—St. Isaac Jogues
Court workers—St. Thomas More
Cranky children—St. Sebastian
Cripples—St. Giles

Dancers—St. Genesius, St. Vitus
Deafness—St. Francis de Sales
Dedication to duty—St. Isaac Jogues
Dentists—St. Apollonia
Desperate situations—St. Jude, St. Gregory of Neo-
   caesaria, St. Rita of Cascia
Dietitians in hospitals—St. Martha
Doctors—St. Luke, Father Damien
Dog owners—St. Roque
Domestic animals—St. Anthony
Doubt—St. Joseph
Druggists—St. Cosmas, St. Damian, St. Raphael, St.
   James the Less
Dyers—St. Maurice, St. Lydia
Dying people—St. Barbara, St. Joseph
Dysentery victims—St. Matrona

Earthquakes—St. Emygdius
Ecologists—St. Francis of Assisi
Editors—St. John Bosco

Emigrants—St. Francis Xavier Cabrini
Enemies of religion—St. Sebastian
Engineers—St. Joseph, St. Ferdinand III
Enlightenment—St. Mary, Mother of God
Epileptics—St. Dymphna, St. Vitus, St. Genesius
Estrangement—Blessed Kateri Tekakwitha
Expectant mothers—St. Gerard Majella
Eye problems—St. Raphael, St. Lucy, St. Herve

Faith—St. Anthony
Falsely accused—St. Raymond Nonnatus, Father Damien
Families—St. Joseph
Family harmony—St. Dymphna
Farmers—St. Isidore the Farmer, St. George
Fathers—St. Joseph, St. Maximilian Mary Kolbe
Fever—St. Peter
Fire—St. Lawrence
Firemen—St. Florian
Fire prevention—St. Barbara, St. Catherine of Siena
First communicants—St. Tarcisus
Fishermen—St. Andrew
Florists—St. Theresa of Lisieux
Foot problems—St. Peter
Foresters—St. John Gualbert
Founders—St. Barbara
Foundlings—The Holy Innocents Slaughtered by Herod
Funeral directors—St. Joseph of Arimathea, St. Dismas

Gardeners—St. Theresa of Lisieux, St. Sebastian, St. Adelard, St. Dorothy, St. Fiacre, St. Phocas, St. Gertrude of Nivelles, St. Tryplon
Girls—St. Agnes
Glassworkers—St. Luke, St. Mark
Goldsmiths—St. Luke, St. Dunstan, St. Anastasius
Grandmothers—St. Anne
Gravediggers—St. Anthony
Greetings—St. Valentine
Grocers—St. Michael

Hairdressers—St. Martin de Porres
Hatters—St. James the Less
Haymakers—St. Gervase, St. Protase
Headache victims—St. Terese of Avila
Healing wounds—St. Rita
Heart patients—St. John of God
Home builders—St. Mary, Mother of God
Horsemen—St. Anne
Hospital administrators—St. Basil the Great, St. Vincent de Paul, St. Francis Xavier Cabrini
Hospitals—St. Camillus de Lellis, St. Vincent de Paul, St. John of God, St. Jude Thaddeus
Hospital patients—St. Frances Cabrini, St. Vincent de Paul
Hotelkeepers—St. Armand, St. Julian the Hospitaler
Housekeepers—St. Anne
Housewives—St. Anne
Humor—St. Phillip Neri
Humility—St. Phillip Neri
Hunters—St. Eustachius, St. Hubert
Husbands—St. Maximilian Mary Kolbe

Illness—Father Damien
Impossible situations—St. Jude Thaddeus
Infantrymen—St. Maurice
Interracial justice—St. Martin de Porres
Invalids—St. Roque

Jewelers—St. Luke, St. Eligius
Journalists—St. Francis de Sales
Judges—St. Ives
Jurists—St. John Capistran

Laborers—St. Isidore, St. James the Apostle, St. John Bosco, St. Joseph
Lace makers—St. Francis of Assisi
Lawyers—St. Genesius, St. Ives, St. Thomas More
Learning—St. Ambrose

Leather workers—St. Crispin, St. Crispinian, St. Catherine
Lepers—Father Damien, St. Vincent de Paul
Librarians—St. Jerome
Lighthouse keepers—St. Dunstan
Lightning—St. Barbara
Loneliness—St. Rita
Long life—St. Peter
Lost articles—St. Anthony of Padua
Lovers—St. Raphael, St. Valentine

Maidens—St. Catherine of Alexandria
Mariners—St. Michael, St. Nicholas of Tolentine
Machinists—St. Hubert
Married women—St. Monica
Married couples—St. Joseph
Masons—St. Peter
Mathematicians—St. Hubert
Medical technicians—St. Albertus Magnus (Albert the Great)
Mentally ill—St. Dymphna
Merchants—St. Francis of Assisi, St. Nicholas of Myra
Messengers—St. Gabriel
Metalworkers—St. Eligius
Midwives—St. Raymond Nonnatus
Millers—St. Arnulph, St. Victor
Miners—St. Barbara
Ministers—St. Theresa of Lisieux
Missions—St. Francis Xavier, St. Theresa of Lisieux, St. Leonard of Port Maurice
Monks—St. Benedict
Mothers—St. Monica, St. Elizabeth Ann Seton
Motorists—St. Francis of Rome
Mountaineers—St. Bernard of Montjoux
Musicians—St. Cecilia, St. Dunstan, St. Gregory the Great

Nerves—St. Dymphna
Notaries—St. Ives, St. Mark, St. Luke

Nurses—St. Agatha, St. Camillus de Lellis, St. John of God, St. Raphael, Father Damien

Nursing services—St. Catherine in Siena, St. Elizabeth of Hungary

Orators—St. John Chrysostum

Orphans—St. Jerome Emiliani, St. Frances Cabrini

Outcasts—Blessed Kateri Tekakwitha

Painters—St. Luke

Papermakers—St. John the Evangelist

Paratroopers—St. Michael

Parish priests—St. John Vianney

Pawnbrokers—St. Nicholas of Myra

Peace—St. Mary, Mother of God

Peasants—St. Lucy

Peddlers—St. Lucy

Peril at sea—St. Michael

Pharmacists—St. Cosmas, St. Damian, St. James the Greater

Pharmacists in hospitals—St. Gemma Galgani

Philosophers—St. Catherine of Alexandra, St. Justin

Physically disabled—St. Giles

Physicians—St. Luke, St. Cosmas, St. Damian, St. Pantaleon, Father Damien, St. Raphael

Pilgrims—St. James

Pilots—St. Mary, Mother of God; St. Joseph of Cupertino

Pioneers—St. Joseph

Plagues—St. Roque

Plasterers—St. Bartholomew

Poets—St. Cecile, St. David

Poison victims—St. Benedict

Policemen—St. Michael

Poor—St. Anthony of Padua, St. Lawrence

Porters—St. Christopher, Father Solanus Casey*

*Candidate for Beatification

Postal workers—St. Gabriel
Potters—St. Sebastian
Preachers—St. Catherine of Alexandria
Pregnant women—St. Gerard Majella, St. Margaret, St. Raymond Nonnatus
Priests—St. John Vianney, St. Theresa of Lisieux
Printers—St. Augustine, St. John the Evangelist, St. Genesius
Prisoners—St. Barbara, St. Dismas, St. Vincent de Paul
POWs—St. Leonard
Prisons—St. Joseph Cafasso
Public relations—St. Bernadine of Siena
Publishers—St. John the Evangelist

Radiologists—St. Michael
Radio workers—St. Gabriel
Retreats—St. Ignatius of Loyola
Rheumatism—St. James the Apostle

Saddlers—St. Crispin, St. Crispinian
Safe journeys—St. Raphael
Sailors—St. Michael, St. Brendan, St. Cuthbert, St. Elmo, St. Erasmus, St. Eulalia, St. Peter Gonzales, St. Nicholas
Salesmen—St. Lucy
Scholars—St. Brigid, St. Thomas Aquinas
Schools—St. Thomas Aquinas
Scientists—St. Albertus Magnus (Albert the Great)
Sculptors—St. Luke, St. Claude
Secretaries—St. Catherine, St. Genesius
Secular priests—St. John Vianney
Seminarians—St. Charles Borromeo
Servants—St. Martha, St. Zita
Servicewomen—St. Joan of Arc
Shepherds—St. Raphael, St. Drago
Shipbuilders—St. Peter
Shoemakers—St. Crispin, St. Crispinian
Sick people—St. John of God, St. Camillus de Lellis, St. Michael

Sick and poor—St. Martin de Porres
Silversmiths—St. Andronicus, St. Dunstan
Singers—St. Cecile, St. Gregory
Sinners—St. Theresa of Lisieux
Skaters—St. Lidwina
Skiers—St. Bernard
Skin diseases—St. Peregrine, St. Marculf
Social justice—St. Joseph
Social workers—St. Louise de Marillac
Soldiers—St. George, St. Hadrian, St. Ignatius Loyola,
    St. Joan of Arc, St. Martin of Tours, St. Sebastian
Speleologists (cave experts)—St. Benedict
Spinsters—St. Catherine
Stationers—St. Peter
Stenographers—St. Cassian, St. Genesius
Stockbrokers—St. Matthew
Stomach problems—St. Charles Borromeo
Stonecutters—St. Clement
Stonemasons—St. Sebastian, St. Barbara, St. Rhein-
    hold, St. Stephen
Storms—St. Barbara
Students—St. Catherine of Alexandria, St. Thomas
    Aquinas
Surgeons—St. Cosmas, St. Damian, St. Luke
Swordsmiths—St. Maurice

Tailors—St. Homobonus
Tanners—St. James, St. Crispin, St. Crispinian, St.
    Simon
Tax collectors—St. Matthew
Teachers—St. Francis de Sales, St. Gregory the Great,
    St. John Baptiste de la Salle
Telecommunications workers—St. Gabriel
Television—St. Clare of Assisi
Temptation—St. Michael
Theologians—St. Alphonsus Liguori, St. Augustine,
    St. Thomas Aquinas
Throat—St. Cecile, St. Blase

Tongue—St. Catherine

Toothache—St. Patrick

Travelers—St. Christopher, St. Anthony of Padua, St. Nicholas of Myra, St. Raphael, the Three Wise Men (Magi)

Tuberculosis—St. Theresa of Lisieux

Tumor—St. Rita

Ulcers—St. Charles Borromeo

Undertakers—St. Sebastian

Universities—Blessed Contardo Ferrini

Unjustly accused—Father Damien, St. Raymond Nonnatus

Vanity—St. Rose of Lima

Veterinarians—St. Francis of Assisi, St. James

Vocalists—St. Cecile

Vocations—St. Alphonsus

Watchmen—St. Peter of Alcantara

Weavers—St. Anastasia, St. Anastasius, St. Paul the Hermit

Widows—St. Paula, St. Elizabeth Ann Seton

Winegrowers—St. Morand, St. Vincent, St. Francis Xavier

Wine merchants—St. Armond

Women—St. Frances Cabrini

Women in labor—St. Anne

Working men—St. Joseph

Working women—St. Elizabeth Ann Seton

Writers—St. John the Evangelist, St. Francis de Sales, St. Lucy

Yachtsmen—St. Adjutor

Youth—St. Aloysius Gonzaga, St. Gabriel Possenti, St. John Berchmans

# Chapter Eleven

❧

# Angelic Miracles

If you ever find yourself up to your eyeballs in trouble, there's no need to panic or despair—there's a whole legion of caring guardian angels just waiting for your call for help.

Take time to learn how to make contact with them and you will have made the best group of friends you're ever likely to meet.

Every one of us has a guardian angel that we can call on. They have been assigned by God to intervene in times of trouble. They are there to look out for us, particularly when we are in life-threatening danger.

It's a pity that few people are open to the idea of the existence of angels. Sadly, many individuals go through life blissfully unaware that this tremendous support system even exists.

Some angel experts—"angelologists," as they're often called—believe we each have only one guardian angel who watches over us all through our lives. But other experts are convinced every one of us has at least two guardian angels—usually one male and one female—who are there to take care of us when the going gets tough. And there are other angel scholars who are equally convinced we can have as many angels as we want.

"There are angels for every occasion and God has made it possible for us to call on any one of them," one diehard angel expert told me. "I talk to many angels all the time—dozens of them. I consult angels for traveling, for career plans, for affairs of the heart. And I follow their advice with confidence. They haven't let me down yet."

Here's a simple five-step technique you can follow to get in touch with your own guardian angel:

- After a quiet moment of prayer, listen carefully for the soft voice of your angel. Your angel may even make its presence known with a gentle, almost imperceptible caress, or a gentle gust of wind.
- Find a place where you can be alone without being disturbed and meditate on angelic thoughts. Find yourself a dimly lit room where you can get away from noisy children or barking dogs.
- Visualize angels in your mind's eye. Remember, your angel can take on any pleasing form you care to imagine.
- Write a letter to your angel—as you write you may sense your angel's presence. You must remember not to make unreasonable demands on your angel—requests for material possessions out of greed or vanity will *not* be acknowledged.
- Clear your mind of stressful thoughts as you lie in bed at night. Angels often make themselves known to people in that twilight state just before you drop off. Remember, you need never be scared.

If you clear your mind of worry and concentrate on contacting your angels, you'll begin to feel their calming influence. All it takes is an open, loving heart.

Now, from my ever-growing dossier on real-life angel experiences, here is a selection to warm your heart.

## Inspiring Musical Angel Saves Holocaust Victim

A musical angel delivered a musical miracle to Shony Alex Braun and saved him from being beaten to death in a concentration camp during World War II.

Today, in his eighties and living in Los Angeles, Shony Braun never forgets the day the angel guided his fingers on the strings of a violin and helped him play a song that saved his life—a song he didn't even know!

He remembers vividly the evening an SS officer came into his barracks with a violin. He announced that anyone who was able to play the instrument for the commandant would be given food.

Although it had been years since he last played the instrument, the desperately hungry young Braun put his hand in the air. Along with two other older male volunteers, he was marched right away to the commandant's office.

They were nervous as they faced the commandant—a steely-eyed man in jackboots with an attack dog by his side.

The oldest man in the group was first to hold the violin. He tuned it, then played a sonata quite beautifully.

"Awful!" screamed the commandant, shocking the nervous prisoners. They gasped in horror as the sadistic commandant ordered the guards to smash the man with iron pipes, killing him in front of their eyes.

The second prisoner was so nervous that he couldn't play a single note. The guards beat him to death too.

"I tried to run away, but a guard caught me and shoved the violin into my hands. I'd never even held an adult-size violin because I had only played a little one as a child," remembers Shony Braun more than half a century later.

His mind went blank and his fingers could barely press the strings. Then, suddenly, he felt a powerful force seize control of his hands.

"I could actually fell an angel guiding my fingers and the violin bow. To my surprise, beautiful music began pouring out. I recognized it as the "Blue Danube" waltz by Strauss—a tune I'd never, ever played before. I knew immediately that God had sent the angel to guide my hands," the elderly Holocaust survivor told the *National Enquirer*.

When his bow played its last sweet note, the cruel commandant, now visibly mellowed, growled, "Give him the food!"

Shony Braun's life was saved! He went on to become a father and grandfather—all because of a miracle angel who knew how to play the violin!


## Caring Angel Keeps Dad From Losing a Leg

Thanks to an angel who gave her miraculous instructions, Helen Hasapes saved her father's leg from amputation.

Helen, of Tarzana, California, thought her father was going to lose his limb after he fell from a tree and his leg swelled to twice its normal size.

Although her dad, Theo, was seventy-two at the time, he was in good shape for his age and, in fact, still lifted weights with his buddies.

After the fall, doctors diagnosed the swelling as stemming from damage to his lymphatic fluid system.

As the days passed, his leg became increasingly discolored. The family feared amputation might be the only solution.

With this grim diagnosis heavy on her mind, Helen was worried and teary-eyed when she went to open the family flower shop in Encino one morning a week after the accident.

As she opened the front door for business, she suddenly felt a rush of cool air. Before her, she saw a woman surrounded by a blur of bright light, dressed in a long white skirt and a blue blouse trimmed with white lace. Long brown hair flowed to her shoulders.

In a soft voice, the woman asked Helen why she was crying and suggested that she might be able to help in some way.

Overcome with grief and emotion, Helen poured out her heart. She told of the accident and how now her fit and active father was in danger of losing a leg.

Calmly, in her even-toned soft voice, the woman stranger explained to Helen, step by step, how her father's leg could be saved—using olive oil and rope!

Then, just as suddenly as she had appeared, the stranger disappeared from the store.

Although her father was skeptical, he agreed to let Helen try the olive oil and rope treatment on him. She proceeded to wrap the rope around his leg, tying one end to a beam above the couch to support his leg. Next, she rubbed olive oil on his calf and above his knee.

By morning, all the stagnant fluid miraculously drained out of her dad's leg! Six days later, he was back at the gym, working out with his pals.

Says Helen today, "Although I tried to find the woman, I never did. But Dad and I firmly believe she was a living, breathing angel sent by God."

# A Little Boy Angel
# Perched in a Tree

He was just a little boy perched in a tree beside a lake—but to Freda Morris-Walter and three other teenage girls he will always be the angel who saved their lives.

The four girls were paddling around in a borrowed aluminum canoe on a deep Ohio lake one balmy summer day in 1967.

Freda, of Westerville, Ohio, remembers today how her group had foolishly neglected to take life jackets with them on their outing. And she, for one, did not know how to swim.

They paddled toward the shadow of a massive oak tree that hung over the water's edge. Suddenly, a young boy appeared out of nowhere at the base of the tree. He began calling out, "The tree is falling! The tree is falling!"

Mysteriously, he vanished from sight. The girls screamed as the tree began toppling down at them!

Freda remembered thinking, "Oh, God, if we get caught in the branches, we're all going to drown!"

Miraculously, the falling tree suddenly froze in midair as if a giant hand were holding it up. Freda remembered thinking, "That little boy—he must be an angel. He's making sure we're not going to be pinned beneath the falling tree and drown!"

As if the little boy were reading her thoughts, the heavy tree suddenly swung to one side, as if being pushed by a powerful invisible hand. It crashed into the water well away from the canoe and its vulnerable crew. Only its outermost branches landed on the canoe.

"After that I felt the angel give me the strength to shove our canoe out from under the giant branches," recalled Freda. "When we got back to shore, we looked everyone for that little boy. No one had seen him, but we all knew he was an angel sent by God."

## "Wings of an Ice Angel Kept Truck From Crushing Me"

Linda Maurer was driving down a snowy highway outside her hometown of Detroit one Christmas when an ice crystal angel saved her life.

A treacherous snowstorm had turned the roads into a slippery sheet of ice. Visibility was virtually zero, and the highway had high concrete walls on both sides.

Suddenly a huge tractor trailer began trying to pass her, recalled Linda, a public relations manager. Obviously there wasn't enough room for both vehicles.

She tried hugging the right-hand side of the lane and was right up against the concrete wall, her car door practically rubbing against it. To Linda's horror, the truck began swerving into her lane. She couldn't hit the brakes or she'd spin out of control. There was nothing she could do but keep on driving—and start praying.

"I was reciting the Lord's Prayer when suddenly a beautiful angel made out of snow and ice crystals appeared," Linda told the *National Enquirer*. "He was about ten feet tall with huge wings that glittered above him. As I watched, the angel floated down between my car and the truck. He placed one massive hand against the truck and the other against my fender. Then he cloaked my entire car with his left wing.

"He pried the two vehicles apart and guided the truck safely away from me. It was a miracle!

"As quickly as he'd taken shape, the angel dissolved back into tiny flakes of swirling ice and snow. I thought, 'Thank you, God, for sending the angel to save my life.' "

# Barefoot Angel Saved
# Son From Rattlesnake

Chariss Cyr, her husband, and their five children were living in a trailer in the desert when a giant angel with bare feet saved her six-year-old son from a rattlesnake.

The Cyr family had moved into the trailer after the family business failed. Chariss, who now lives in Alpine, California, never felt comfortable living in desert surroundings. She was always worried about the kids playing outside where there were poisonous snakes. And her worst fears came true when her daughter Kathryn, who was four at the time, ran into the kitchen one day screaming, "Mommy, a rattlesnake got Phillip!"

Chariss ran outside where Phillip had been watering the tiny family vegetable garden. He appeared to be in a kind of trance. Nearby, Chariss saw the reason— the hypnotic, twitching rattle of a snake as it slithered away.

She yelled to her son to show her where the snake bit him. "Quick, show Mommy where the snake bit you!"

To her surprise, Phillip responded, "The snake missed, Mommy. The snake tried to bite me but he fell down and crawled away. I got no bites."

Chariss checked her son up and down. To her amazement, she found he was right.

That night Phillip asked her, "Mommy, why don't angels wear shoes?" He continued, "My angel had bare foots. When that snake came to get me, I tried to squirt it with the hose. But he jumped at me—and that's when my angel saved me.

" 'My angel has really big bare foots and he put his big foot between the snake and me so the mean old snake couldn't bite me. My angel's big bare foots saved me from that snake!' "

That was the one and only time in his life Phillip

cared to discuss the rattlesnake incident. Says mom Chariss, "Phillip has never mentioned another angel story. But I thank God every day for sending the angel with 'big bare foots' to save him from that deadly snake."

## Angel Lifted Him to Safety

Seventy-six-year-old Gene Jakiela is convinced he was lifted to safety by his guardian angel and escaped being crushed by a heavy tractor.

Mr. Jakiela, of Crystal Lake, Illinois, writes me about his miracle: "About three years ago, I was mowing my grass on a severe slope. My big eighteen-horsepower tractor hit a rut and flipped over on its left side. That's when I feel that my guardian angel helped me.

"All of a sudden, I felt like someone lifted me over and dropped me on the soft grass about twelve feet away from the tractor, which turned over upside down. The steering wheel was completely buried in the ground.

"If I had still been sitting on the tractor as it fell on me, my chest would have been crushed by the steering wheel.

"Thanks to my guardian angel, I came out of this accident without a scratch."

## Angel Alerts Motorist to Danger

On two separate occasions, a guardian angel alerted a motorist to danger ahead.

Writes Mrs. Bernice De Ridder of Norway, Michigan: "As I write this I am wearing my guardian angel necklace my son Jerome sent me on Mother's Day this year. My son is a true believer of angels watching over us.

"While he was attending college at Marquette, Michigan, he used to drive back and forth to our family home in Norway. One dark, foggy night he was unusually tired and sleepy as he made the trip.

"For some mysterious reason, his foot slipped off the gas pedal and saved him from crashing into a string of cars that had come to a halt just ahead of him at a railroad crossing.

"To this day he's convinced an unseen presence removed his foot from the accelerator so he could stop in time. Otherwise he would have been killed or crippled.

"Another time he was attending college in Lincoln, Nebraska, but residing with his wife in Missouri. He would come home weekends.

"On his way home one weekend—just before he came to this dangerous intersection—his car kept stalling and rolling to a halt every few minutes. This happened several times.

"There was nothing apparently wrong with his car. But he found out why it was happening when, a few more minutes into his journey, he arrived at a four-way intersection and the scene of a very bad accident in which several people were killed.

"He is convinced that if some power had not been causing his car to act up he would have been involved in that fatal pileup.

"He told me, 'That's the second time in my life I felt someone watching and caring for me.'

"Since I live alone, he sent me my guardian angel necklace and said, 'Wear it always, Mom, so someone will always be watching over you, keeping you safe.'

"I am eighty-six years old and have glaucoma and

am hard of hearing, but I know my angel is near me. I am also a true believer."

## A Three-Time Winner!

Three times in his life James H. Kelley felt guardian angels were watching over him in times of crisis.

Mr. Kelley, of Cooper City, Florida, writes: "Regarding guardian angels, there have been at least three times that I know an angel has come to my aid in times of serious problems.

"The first time was in Manila in the Philippines during the summer of 1945. I was going from my U.S. Army camp to meet my girlfriend. It was just after dark when I was suddenly accosted by twelve to fifteen drunken sailors.

"They were out to 'get them a soldier' because a soldier had beat up one of their buddies a couple of days before. One of them put on a set of brass knuckles and came at me. If they didn't kill me, they certainly would have given me severe injuries, maybe crippling me for life.

"As the first two of them lunged at me, all of a sudden out of nowhere came another group of fifteen to twenty sailors who were sober. Without saying a word, they ran the first group off.

"I don't know where this group of angel sailors came from, but I feel they saved my life.

"The second time I was convinced a guardian angel was looking out for me was during the spring of 1946 when I was attending a concert. As I left the show, I was approached by two tough guys in a parking lot. They were obviously spoiling for a fight. One of them grabbed me while the other prepared to slash at me with a seven-inch knife. Again, out of nowhere, an angel appeared, this time in the form of a big, burly stranger built like a linebacker.

"Without saying a word, he kicked the knife out of the guy's hand and floored him with one punch.

"By this time I had wrestled free of the one who was holding me, so the big guy floored him too. Then he picked him up and threw him on top of the other. Then he disappeared just as quickly as he had appeared.

"My third angelic experience was the morning in 1996 when I passed a very large kidney stone.

"I was going to forget about it, but a voice kept telling me to get myself checked out.

"I did so, and the doctor sent me immediately to the hospital for a CAT scan. When the results came back, my doctor's face was like a ghost.

"It turned out there was nothing wrong with my kidneys, but the examination had discovered a large, life-threatening abdominal aneurysm. My doctor told me if it burst, I would only have had three or four minutes to live.

"As it was, I had to have immediate major surgery. Thankfully, they got it just as it was about to burst. And I am alive and well.

"My angels had come through for me again!"

## Angel Urges Doctor, Seventy-seven, to Leap from Runaway Car

Unable to drive and panicking in the backseat of a runaway car, a lady doctor-preacher is visited by a gentle-spoken guardian angel who gives her the confidence and courage to save her own life.

The Reverend Dr. Mary Leason writes from Federal Way, Washington:

"A few weeks ago my husband left me in the car, saying he needed to get something at the store. I was quietly reading when, all of a sudden, to my surprise and amazement, I felt the car moving.

" 'Oh, my God, this can't be! Is this the way I'm going to die—alone in a car without brakes?' I thought. Would I kill a pedestrian? Or smash into other cars?

"It was in the parking area. I'm originally from Staten Island, New York, and I never learned how to drive. My husband had the car keys with him in the store. And here I was alone in the backseat of a moving car.

"In the midst of my panic, I suddenly heard a strong but gentle voice—it had to be my guardian angel—urging me to open the car door and jump out.

"I started to argue with the voice that I wasn't some kind of movie stuntman trained to jump out of a moving car. I was sure I'd fall under the car or something and be badly hurt.

"But the strong voice insisted, 'Now! Jump out!' So I did. To my amazement, I wasn't hurt in the least.

"The car was still moving. There was only one man walking in the parking lot. I shouted out to him for assistance. 'Help, my car is moving.' But he didn't hear me.

"That's when my angel took control of my voice. I heard myself screaming out in an extraordinarily loud voice.

"The man finally heard my cries and raced to stop the moving car. Then he came to help me. I was still in a panic. My blood pressure had risen to a high level and my cheeks were so hot you could have fried an egg on them. The man helped calm me down.

"By this time my husband had come out of the store. I began to thank the man who had come to my aid profusely. But he just quietly walked away without saying a word. Could he have been another angel?

"Well, when I got home, the first thing I did was to kneel down and thank God for saving my life. I know I could have been seriously injured, hospitalized, or even killed when I jumped from that moving car.

"Every time I think of this I feel very, very strongly that angels do exist. I know now that I have one. I can hear God telling me, 'You are protected, you are loved. You are my child and you do have a guardian angel to protect you.'

"I am eternally grateful for my angels, as I'm seventy-seven years old and still have a lot of work to do on this earth, taking care of my patients."

## Angel Protects Mom in Fear of Killers

Betty Jo Johnson writes from Texas:

"In 1987, one of my sons was murdered near Weatherford, Texas. Shortly thereafter I sold my property and moved out of that area, because I was always fearful that the ones that committed this murder would get drugged up and come to murder me. For they knew that I knew who they were.

"Since then I've made several moves. Everywhere I've lived I've never gone to bed without asking the angels to watch over me while I slept.

"One morning at four a.m., I awakened suddenly. I could hear my angels. Although I didn't see them, I could hear the flapping of their wings.

"I am sure that they had been with me while I slept, and it was time for them to ascend back to heaven. I felt very safe and loved.

"I'd love this published, but don't give my address. Not while these murderers are still free."

# Hit by a Train—Yet
# Hitchhiker Survives

Donald Hopkins has no doubt his guardian angel was beside him the day he was struck by a train—but lived to tell the tale.

From Denning, New Mexico, Mr. Hopkins writes: "I was hitchhiking on Highway 5, north of San Diego, California, in May 1991, when I realized that I'd traveled too far.

"Because there was no hitchhiking allowed on that stretch of highway, I decided to retrace my footsteps south along some railroad tracks.

"With my golden retriever, King, at my side, I was on a bridge over a creek when I saw a train up ahead, about a mile away. I turned to get off of the tracks to walk on a pedestrian path at the side of the bridge. I paused for a second to instruct King to get on the path.

"That's when I was hit from behind by an electric train—the kind of train that makes little or no noise.

"The train hit my backpack and hurled me against a metal guardrail at the side of the bridge.

"In that split second, as I was falling, I had a miraculous experience. I saw my spirit depart from my body. Then, as if in slow motion, I saw my spirit move my right foot off the train tracks before the wheels could run over my foot.

"Realizing I was about to topple off the bridge, I was able to grasp the guardrail before it was too late.

"All of this happened in the space of a second. Luckily, King also survived. He was lying on top of me and I could feel him lick the bald spot at the top of my head.

"As the train passed dangerously close to us, I thanked God I was still alive.

"The train that had been approaching stopped at

the scene. The conductor got out and was amazed to see that I was alive. He was sure the other train had killed me.

" 'Thank God. I'm still alive!' I told him, and continued on my journey."


## Angels at Her Side—
## All Through Her Life!

In the darkest moments, an angel has always been on hand to help and comfort Donna Kauffmann.

He has even called out to her—saving her and her three children from what could have been a horrible car accident.

Mrs. Kauffmann, of Cinnaminson, New Jersey, writes me this touching letter:

"There have been four instances over a period of some approximately thirty-seven years where I feel, after much reflection, very, very strongly that I have experienced the help and blessed interference of a guardian angel—be it my guardian angel or the guardian angel of those persons with me at the time of each of these experiences.

"As I have reflected very deeply about each of these and the impact and mark that they have made on my memory, I will try to explain each of these in the following remembrances as best I can.

"I can attest to the words I thus put down here on the written word of my God, the Bible. I retell these experiences exactly how they happened to me.

"In approximately 1960, I had taken my mother to a late show at a movie theater on a Sunday night. We came out of the movie theater, I'd say somewhere around 12:30 A.M.

"I had parked my car on a street about one block from the theater on one of the side streets, as all the parking spaces on the busy main thoroughfare were occupied.

"When we returned to my car, I found I had left my car keys in the car and locked myself out. I knew I had to get my mother and myself home safely. So I was quite concerned.

"We walked back to the busier main street where the movie theater was located. Because it was a well-traveled thoroughfare, I thought I would find help quite easily.

"However, it was late Sunday night and everything was closed, no gas stations anywhere in sight, no telephones, no traffic to speak of at all.

"There wasn't a soul around. When I turned to my mother, we both had a sinking feeling about the situation. I didn't know quite what to do. We kept looking around for help and could find no one in sight.

"Then, as if out of nowhere, there appeared this young man, approximately twenty-five to thirty years of age. Suddenly, he was standing in front of us.

"You must remember, we had been looking back and forth in every direction for someone to help us. We could see no one.

"Now here was a young, blondish man who all of a sudden seemed to have materialized from nowhere and was standing there in front of us.

"We were both startled, to say the least, because we hadn't heard a sound or seen one thing moving, even though we kept looking both ways.

"He said to us, 'Is there something I can help you with?'—without even knowing why we were there or what our problem was.

"I proceeded to tell him how I had mistakenly locked myself out of my car. He then said, 'Maybe I can help you.'

"He walked with us back to my car and he said, 'I can help you get in, but I'll have to break the small vent window.'

"I said I didn't care. He then raised his hand and, with his fist, broke the side window—with the most gentle of blows.

"It was a soft blow, like a feather striking the window. We could hardly hear the glass breaking!

"Then he put his hand through the broken side window and unlocked my car.

"In gratitude, I said, 'I want to give you something for helping us,' and I started to take some dollars out of my wallet.

"He put his hand up in an emphatic 'No!' gesture and proceeded to walk away, calling softly over his shoulder as he left, saying, 'No, thanks, that's what we're here for—to help each other.'

"Those words are words that are etched in my memory to this day.

"When I got into my car to drive off, my mother said to me, 'Where in the world did that young man come from? He wasn't there one second and the next he was standing right in front of us.'

"She took the words right out of my mouth. I was about to ask her the same thing.

"The second incident, which occurred in approximately 1968 or so, my three children were in the car with me. They were in the backseat of my car—my oldest girl, age twelve, and my son, age four, and my daughter, age two—the two youngest ones in their baby car seats.

"At the time, I had a small Rambler and I had been having trouble with the emergency brake, even when the car was in the parked position. I had thought it was taken care of once and for all after I took it to a garage for repairs.

"I had gone into a nearby convenience store to buy milk and bread. I put the car in park and put on the emergency brake because it was parked on a hill that led down to a major, heavily traveled highway.

"While standing at the store counter, which couldn't

have been more than three minutes after I left the car, a young man came into the store. (Upon reflection, he resembled the young man my mother and I had seen years earlier when I couldn't get back into my car.)

"He looked at me and said, 'Is that your red Rambler out there?' When I said yes, the young man proceeded to tell me that as he pulled up he saw my car beginning to roll down the hill backward toward the highway.

"He told me, 'Seeing that no one was at the wheel, I got out of my car and jumped into your car and put it in park with the emergency brake on.'

"I thanked him for doing this. Curiously, instead of staying in the convenience store and purchasing something, the young man just turned around and left.

"Again, he just seemed to disappear into thin air. I asked the cashier if she knew him, and she said she had never seen him before. I asked myself, 'If he went into the store to purchase something, why did he abruptly turn and leave after stopping my moving car and saving my children from possible harm?'

"The third incident happened to me at about the same time in 1968. Once again, I had my three children with me in the car.

"I had just come out of the supermarket with my children. I put my two youngest in their car seats in the backseat of my car and my oldest, almost thirteen at the time, in the front passenger seat with her safety belt on.

"I drove out of the supermarket parking lot and turned toward a main road intersection where I stopped at a red light.

"As the light turned green, I was preparing to cross the intersection when I heard a clear, very audible voice say to me, 'Don't go! Don't go!'

"The voice was so clear and real that I turned to my daughter at that moment and said, 'Why not? Why shouldn't I go?' She replied, 'I didn't say anything, Mommy!'

"I found myself staring at the traffic light. It was still green. But the voice was telling me, urgently, 'Look both ways!'

"I did, looking to my right and then to the left. To my utter amazement, I saw a car speeding about ninety miles an hour—totally ignoring his or her red light, while my traffic light was still green.

"If I had proceeded through that green light I would have been involved in a horrendous collision. We owe our lives to that mysterious voice that told me not to go ahead.

"That voice, I believe to this day, had to be a voice sent by God to protect all four of us from harm's way.

"My fourth unforgettable experience was in 1995. I had to go to Philadelphia to take my stepfather to the doctor, as my mother had passed away earlier that year. He was seriously ill with a brain tumor (which neither of us knew at that time) and he had lost the use of one leg.

"When I got to his apartment to take him to the doctor, he said that he didn't think he could make it to the car. I told him I would help him and he and I could do it together with God's help. I helped him to the top of a long staircase (he lived on the second floor). He used his one good leg while I carried and supported him on the other side.

"He made it—or rather we made it—down the long staircase one step at a time, with him sitting down and sliding down one step while I lifted both his feet down to the next step (he had also lost almost all feeling in both feet).

"We finally made it down to the last step and I found the strength to pick him up from the bottom step and get him out a double door exit.

"I saw a neighbor and asked if he could help get

him in my car, which was parked just around the side of the building a few feet away.

"He kindly obliged. He took one side and I took the other and we got him into the passenger seat of my car. Then the neighbor disappeared into his apartment building next door.

"My troubles weren't over. There had been a pretty heavy snowstorm earlier that day and the spot where I had parked was covered with eight to ten inches of snow.

"I thought to myself, 'I hope I can back this car out of here and get him to the doctor.' As I have explained, my stepfather was in pretty bad shape. As I started the engine, my stepfather even said, 'I don't think you'll be able to get out of this spot with all of this snow around and under you.'

"I said a silent prayer to God, 'Dear God, help me to get Sam to the doctor's so that he can get the help he needs.' I put the car in reverse and my foot on the gas full force several times. Then I tried moving forward, with no luck. The car was snowbound.

"I was about ready to give up when I saw a young man in my rearview mirror approaching the car. I rolled down the window, and he said, 'Can I help you?'

"I told him the trouble I was having. The young man again said, 'Maybe I can help you.' Uncannily these words rang familiar to me, and his looks, too, were similar to the young man whom I and my mother had encountered some thirty-five years or so earlier.

"He instructed me, 'When I raise my hand, it means that you put your car in reverse and put your foot full force on the gas pedal.'

"After saying this, he walked toward the front of my car. My stepfather thought it was a lost cause, saying, 'He's wasting his time, he can't get this car out of here. You're stuck here. Only a tow truck can pull you out.'

"Nevertheless, I was going to follow the young man's instructions. When he signaled, I put the car in reverse and my foot on the gas pedal. I don't think my foot was all the way down on the pedal.

"At the same time, the young man put one hand on the front of my car and pushed it backward as easily as if he were pushing a feather. Immediately my car shot backward.

"It seemed like I wasn't even doing anything to make it go backward. It just moved when he put his hand on the front of the car. It was if he breathed on the car—and it moved!

"I was clear of the snow in a matter of seconds. I couldn't believe that it had happened. I was almost dumbstruck. My stepfather spoke first, 'I don't believe he did that!'

"Thinking he was another neighbor, I asked my stepfather who he was and which apartment he lived in. My stepfather replied, 'I never saw him before. I don't know where he came from.'

"I opened my driver's side window again—it was a bitterly cold night—and thanked the young gentleman for helping us. He answered simply, 'That's what we're here for—to help each other.'

"And with those words, he seemed to vanish from our sight.

"It was later, in the doctor's waiting room, that I reflected on the young man's parting words, 'That's what we're here for—to help each other.'

"Those words kept going through my mind, over and over and over through the coming days. Then it finally and clearly dawned on me—those were the exact words that the young man had said to me some thirty-five years earlier when I had locked myself and my mother out of my car!

"And what was particularly unsettling was the fact that he looked just like the young blondish man that helped me and my mother that night.

"These are my four miracle stories. I have zillions more I could tell, but these stand out because of the strong similarities of the angel involved.

"Yes, I sincerely believe that the young man or men who interceded to help me and those in my care in our hour of need and danger were angels sent by my Lord and God to help me and protect me and those I loved.

"I thank God from the bottom of my heart to this day and evermore for His help to me in my times of great need.

"I cannot, I will not, and I must never forget these miraculous moments in my life. It is written on my heart that God is always there to help us when we ask him—even when we don't ask him and even when we don't expect it or least expect it.

"God does indeed work in mysterious ways. He catches us off guard at times, with his protective sense of humor, too, and loving heart.

"He is always there for us, whether we realize it or not. He does hear us. He does see us. He does know us. He sees what we need and He does know what we need and what is truly best for each of us.

"Whether we perceive this with our way of thinking, let us accept whatever God sends us, whether we think it good or bad, because only He really knows what is good or bad for each of us."

# Bibliography

*Akron Beacon Journal:* May 23, 1992; Jan. 9, 1993; Jan. 1, 1994; Nov. 13, 1994; Jan. 25, 1995; April 6, 1995; June 12, 1995; June 25, 1995; July 4, 1995; July 13, 1995; Dec. 4, 1995; May 12, 1996; June 5, 1996; Oct. 17, 1996

*Country Weekly:* Sept. 20, 1994; March 4, 1997

*Baltimore Sun:* June 25, 1995; Dec. 8, 1996; March 11, 1997

*Daily Mail:* June 12, 1997

*Enchanted Spirits:* Sept. 1996

*National Enquirer:* May 8, 1984; Jan. 8, 1985; Oct. 29, 1985; Feb. 25, 1986; Dec. 29, 1987; April 19, 1988; July 5, 1988; Aug. 8, 1988; Oct. 18, 1988; Jan. 17, 1989; Oct. 31, 1989; April 3, 1990; Nov. 27, 1990; Dec. 4, 1990; Dec. 18, 1990; March 26, 1991; April 23, 1991; May 7, 1991; May 14, 1991; July 9, 1991; Oct. 22, 1991; Nov. 12, 1991, Feb. 25, 1992; June 16, 1992; June 30, 1992; Aug. 4, 1992; Aug. 11, 1992; Sept. 22, 1992; Oct. 6, 1992; Nov. 10, 1992; Dec. 12, 1992; Dec. 29, 1992; March 9, 1993; April 6, 1993; May 25, 1993; June 8, 1993; June 22, 1993; July 27, 1993; Aug. 17, 1993; Aug. 24, 1993; Aug. 31, 1993; Oct. 12, 1993; Nov. 9, 1993; Nov. 16, 1993; Dec. 14,

1993; Jan. 4, 1994; Feb. 1, 1994; Feb. 8, 1994; Feb.
15, 1994; Feb. 22, 1994; March 1, 1994; March 15,
1994; March 22, 1994; April 19, 1994; April 24, 1994;
May 10, 1994; May 17, 1994; May 24, 1994; June 14,
1994; July 19, 1994; Sept. 6, 1994; Oct. 18, 1994; Oct.
17, 1995; Dec. 26, 1995; Feb. 13, 1996; March 5,
1996; May 7, 1996; June 25, 1996; July 30, 1996;
Aug. 6, 1996; Aug. 13, 1996; Oct. 8, 1996; Nov. 26,
1996; Dec. 31, 1996; Jan. 14, 1997; Jan. 21, 1997;
Jan. 28, 1997; Feb. 4, 1997; Feb. 18, 1997; Feb. 25,
1997; March 11, 1997; May 6, 1997; May 27, 1997;
June 6, 1997

*National Examiner:* Jan. 31, 1984; Feb. 7, 1984; April
3, 1984; Feb. 5, 1985; Feb. 12, 1985; April 4, 1985;
April 16, 1985; May 7, 1985; Aug. 20, 1985; Sept.
17, 1985; Oct. 29, 1985; Dec. 3, 1985; Feb. 25, 1986;
May 6, 1986; June 17, 1986; July 22, 1986; Sept. 16,
1986; Oct. 14, 1986; Dec. 23, 1986; Jan. 20, 1987;
Feb. 3, 1987; March 3, 1987; March 24, 1987; June
2, 1987; June 16, 1987; Oct. 20, 1987; Nov. 10, 1987;
Dec. 8, 1987; Jan. 29, 1988; April 5, 1988; April 19,
1988; June 14, 1988; June 28, 1988; July 12, 1988,
July 19, 1988; Aug. 2, 1988; Aug. 23, 1988; Aug. 30,
1988; Sept. 6, 1988; Sept. 20, 1988; Sept. 27, 1988;
Oct. 4, 1988; Jan. 31, 1989; Feb. 18, 1989

*Fort Lauderdale Sun-Sentinel:* Oct. 9, 1994; Jan. 21,
1995; Feb. 26, 1995; July 16, 1995; Aug. 14, 1995;
Jan. 20, 1996; June 3, 1997

*Globe:* Aug. 10, 1982; April 3, 1984; Dec. 25, 1984;
Dec. 17, 1985; Sept. 20, 1988; Oct. 25, 1988; March
7, 1989

*Ladies' Home Journal:* May, 1995

*Mail on Sunday:* Dec. 29, 1996

*Miami Herald:* June 13, 1994; April 16, 1995

*New York Daily News:* March 1, 1995; May 20, 1995;
Aug. 11, 1995; Aug. 25, 1995; Dec. 15, 1995

*New York Post:* March 3, 1994; March 2, 1995; July
24, 1995; Dec. 15, 1995

*Palm Beach Post:* March 30, 1994; Aug. 28, 1994; Oct. 8, 1995; Oct. 25, 1996; Dec. 20, 1996; Dec. 25, 1996; Dec. 27, 1996; Jan. 17, 1997; Feb. 10, 1997; April 30, 1997; May 23, 1997

*People:* June 29, 1987

*Philadelphia Inquirer:* Jan. 12, 1997

*Redbook:* Dec. 1993

*Self:* Dec. 1994

*Star:* April 19, 1994; Feb. 25, 1997; May 20, 1997

*Time:* Dec. 23, 1996

*USA Today:* Dec. 10, 1996; Dec. 23, 1996; Jan. 8, 1997; May 23, 1997; Aug. 11, 1997

*US News & World Report:* March 29, 1993

*Washington Post:* Oct. 14, 1994

*Weekly World News:* Feb. 14, 1984; Feb. 26, 1985; Sept. 10, 1985; Dec. 24, 1985; May 21, 1985; July 15, 1985; Aug. 27, 1985; Nov. 26, 1985; March 4, 1986; May 20, 1986; Aug. 12, 1986; Aug. 19, 1986; Aug. 26, 1986; Sept. 16, 1986; Sept. 30, 1986; Dec. 16, 1986; Dec. 30, 1986; Aug. 3, 1993; Feb. 4, 1997; Feb. 25, 1997; March 11, 1997; March 28, 1997